TARIQ RAMADAN

Islam:
The Essentials

A PELICAN BOOK
Translated by Fred A. Reed

PELICAN
an imprint of
PENGUIN BOOKS

PELICAN BOOKS

UK | USA | Canada | Ireland | Australia
India | New Zealand | South Africa

Penguin Books is part of the Penguin Random House
group of companies whose addresses can be found at
global.penguinrandomhouse.com.

Penguin
Random House
UK

First published 2017
004

Text copyright © Tariq Ramadan, 2017
Translator copyright © Fred A. Reed, 2017

The moral right of the author has been asserted

Book design by Matthew Young
Set in 10/14.664 pt FreightText Pro
Typeset by Jouve (UK), Milton Keynes
Printed in Great Britain by Clays Ltd, St Ives plc

A CIP catalogue record for this book is
available from the British Library

ISBN: 978-0-141-98050-8

MIX
Paper from
responsible sources
FSC® C018179

Penguin Random House is committed to a
sustainable future for our business, our readers
and our planet. This book is made from Forest
Stewardship Council® certified paper.

www.greenpenguin.co.uk

For Caroline,
with all my gratitude and
boundless respect

Contents

ACKNOWLEDGMENTS

Achieving simplicity proved to be anything but simple. This book – an initiation into Islam – was intended to be accessible and concise. Little did I realize the effort involved in making it so! In finished form at last, it represents the synthesis of lectures, studies and essays too numerous to mention, and of actual experience gained over the years as a student, as a teacher, a Muslim scholar and thinker deeply involved both in public debate and at the grass-roots. These are the major factors, combined with the contributions of so many women and men encountered along the way – Muslims, believers of other confessions or without any particular confession – that have given me the impetus and the strength to write. My debt to them constitutes the guiding spirit of this short introductory volume.

First and foremost, I would like to thank Penguin Books, and particularly Helen Conford, for her confidence, her trust, her kindness and her friendship. Her commitment has proven immeasurable. My warmest and most fraternal thoughts go to Cynthia Read, who has accompanied me for so long with heart, attention and professional discipline. Deepest thanks, as well, go to my friend and translator Fred A. Reed for his contribution and his devotion despite the years of tight deadlines and an often-trying work schedule. Finally, a word of thanks to Drew Anderla, Shoaib Rokadiya and Annabel Huxley: each has contributed, in their respective fields, to the conception and distribution of this book. To all: the work of writing would be for naught without your clear-eyed and fine-tuned professional collaboration.

This book, in its present form, would never have seen the light of day without the contribution of Caroline Davis, my assistant and Program Manager at Oxford University: a woman of heart and of principle, and a model of great professionalism and deep humanity. To her I respectfully dedicate this work. Jennifer Reghoui, who managed my European office for five years, was unfailing in her support. My dear and supportive colleagues at the Middle East Centre at St Anthony's College, University of Oxford: Eugene Rogan, Walter Armbrust, Michael Willis, Laurent Mignon, Toby Matthiesen, Philip Robins and Avi Shlaim. Walaa Quisay, one of my doctorate students, for her conscientious research assistance. The entire team of the Research Center for Islamic Legislation and Ethics that has stood by me for four years will find in these pages ample reminders of our animated discussions. My profound gratitude goes to each and every one of you.

For Iman, always and intensely. For Maryam, Sami, Moussa and Najma with a father's heart. For Shaima and Ali, with love. And, multiplying that same love today, for Kylian, Noor, Amin...and the others soon to come, God willing. How much I owe you all! Nor can I ever forget my mother, to whom my debt is so great, may God protect her; my father, may God's grace be upon him; and Aymen, Bilal, Yasser,

Arwa, Hani, my sister and my brothers. May their children and our children explore the high road and the byways of the great journey with hope and conviction. And may that journey always be one of beauty.

My thanks, my true and deepest thanks.

Oxford, November 2016

INTRODUCTION

Hardly a day goes by without some mention of Islam. And yet many people, if pressed, will admit that they know very little about the religion of one quarter of the human race. We hear much talk of violence, terrorism, the status of women and slavery. Muslims are frequently pressured to provide answers and to justify what Islam is *not*. Yet there is very little space in society or in the media for an exploration and an explanation of what Islam genuinely *is*.

Hence the objective of this short book: to introduce readers in the simplest, most direct and the most thorough manner to Islam – to its principles, its rituals, its history, its diversity and its evolution, not forgetting the numerous challenges facing Muslims today.

Tackling an entire religion and civilization requires some mental preparation. The Islamic universe is no less complex than that of Hinduism, of Buddhism, of Judaism or Christianity. The basic texts can be abstruse and their interpretation widely divergent and often contradictory; Islam's schools of thought and its cultures do not always facilitate access to its essence as a world religion.

Before venturing into a belief system that possesses its own well-established principles, an inner coherence, and a distinct conception of humanity, life and death, readers may wish to put aside their preconceived notions and open their minds to something that may strike them as both familiar and strange. Islam comes complete with its own sacred texts, a system of references, eternal principles and applications to daily life; as such, religious, historical and legal knowledge is needed to understand its nature, its historical development and the challenges confronting it today.

For many readers, this journey of discovery will require both curiosity and effort. But it will also require intellectual humility as the path unfolds before us; a willingness to reconsider opinions often presented as established fact, to overcome stubborn prejudices and to suspend judgement for the duration of our voyage together. As we progress, these considerations will take on prime importance, for they will enable us to join the debate over key issues and to begin a process of critical reflection that is so sorely needed today, free of knee-jerk reactions, fears or attempts to justify the unjustifiable.

Written to be as accessible as possible, this brief introduction to the essence of Islam assumes no specialized knowledge on the reader's part. It is designed to guide readers into the complexity of the multifaceted world of Islam as a religion and a civilization. The first chapter presents an introduction to the history of Islam, beginning with the Prophet Muhammad and the Revelation of the Qur'an, the prophetic mission and the basic elements of the Islamic Message, followed by a rapid survey of the evolution of the religion after the death of the Prophet Muhammad, the great schism between Sunni and Shi'a and the creation of the great empires. Chapter 2 describes Islam's fundamental tenets, its texts, the meaning of the word 'Islam', the search for God, and Islam's relationship with the other monotheistic faiths. The third chapter deals with the pillars of faith and with ritual practice, with its obligations and prohibitions. Chapter 4 introduces the concept of sharia – 'the Way' – with its multitude of definitions and priorities, with the forms of jihad and the primacy of social action. The final chapter takes up the multitude of challenges facing today's Muslims, both in societies where they form the majority and those in which they are in the minority.

Each chapter is divided into short sections, making it easy for the reader to locate a specific subject or theme and to find there a concise and easily understandable explanation. The presentation is never strictly theoretical: each section first takes up the governing principle, then examines the diversity of interpretation and even the contradictions between declared principles and their application by Muslims down through history to the present day.

Most of the topics seen as hypersensitive today – sharia, jihad, the status of women, polygamy, slavery and violence – are dealt with in these pages. My approach is not apologetic, but is designed to offer readers a general yet thorough consideration of Islamic teachings. These questions are then integrated into a broader analysis and placed in perspective, for to deal with them in isolation would inevitably be misleading.

In fact, this introduction should be seen as a voyage of initiation and exploration – into the terminology, principles, practices and aspirations of Muslims. As you read through this book, you will find the answers to a number of questions that, despite their topicality, cannot alone exhaust the richness of the voyage into the heart of Islam and its teachings.

Following the Conclusion, there is a short exercise entitled 'Ten Things You Thought You Knew about Islam', which will give you an opportunity to confront several currently received ideas and stereotypes and get to grips with certain notions that are insufficiently understood by many people (including more than a few Muslims): sharia, jihad, fatalism, dress codes, sexual equality, ritual slaughter, 'Who is a Muslim?' to name but a few. You can use this section to evaluate what you have learned and perceived and thus to broaden and deepen your understanding.

NOTE ON THE TEXT

All Qur'anic references are indicated by *sūrah*, pl. *suwar* (chapter) and *āyah*, pl. *āyāt* (verse) in brackets after the quotation. Arabic terms that are now commonplace in English, such as sharia, jihad, halal, Hajj, Ramadan, hadith and others, have not been italicized. Other, more specialized terms appear in italics with diacritical marks. They appear once or several times in the text along with their translation and/or explanation, and are defined in the Glossary. All the translations are my own.

You will also find a detailed glossary of all the Arabic terms that appear in this book, along with short translations. Also appended is a short bibliography for those who wish to pursue their self-education and acquire a broader knowledge of Islam and its diversity.

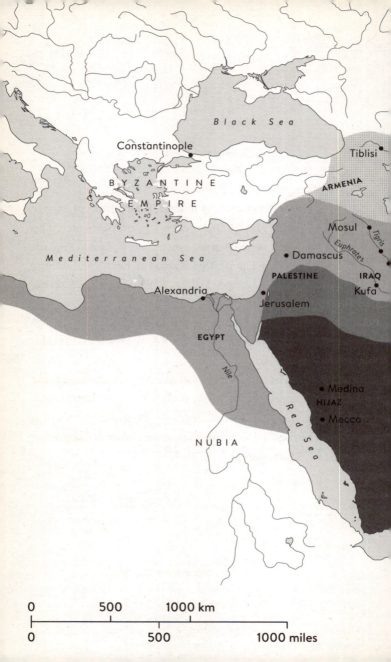

Black Sea

Constantinople

Tiblisi

BYZANTINE

ARMENIA

EMPIRE

Mosul

Tigris

Euphrates

Mediterranean Sea

Damascus

PALESTINE

IRAQ

Alexandria

Kufa

Jerusalem

EGYPT

Nile

Medina

HIJAZ

Mecca

Red Sea

NUBIA

| 0 | | 500 | | 1000 km |
| 0 | | 500 | | 1000 miles |

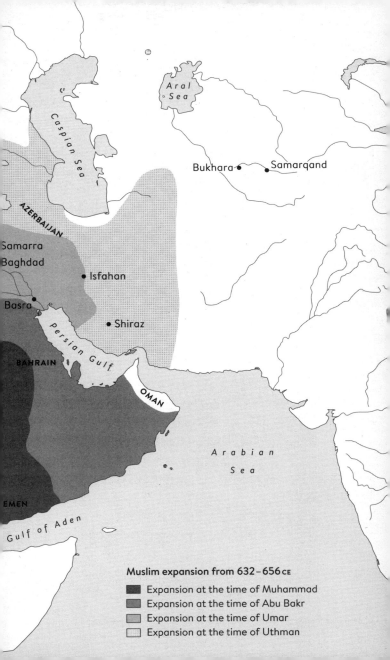

Bukhara • • Samarqand

Samarra
Baghdad
Basra •
• Isfahan
• Shiraz

Aral Sea

Caspian Sea

AZERBAIJAN

BAHRAIN

Persian Gulf

OMAN

Arabian Sea

EMEN

Gulf of Aden

Muslim expansion from 632–656 CE

■ Expansion at the time of Muhammad
■ Expansion at the time of Abu Bakr
■ Expansion at the time of Umar
□ Expansion at the time of Uthman

History

Islam emerged in Mecca, in the Arabian Peninsula, in the early seventh century. The Arabs of the day were primarily polytheists, worshipping idols, but among them were Jews and Christians, many of whom lived in the region of Yathrib, which was later to become known as Medina. Small groups of individuals who were neither Jews nor Christians also professed the monotheism of the Abrahamic tradition; they called themselves *ḥunafā'* and rejected idol worship. The two great empires of the day, Byzantium and Sassanid Persia, were locked in conflict for control of the peninsula. The rapid expansion of Islam would come as a surprise to both and shake them to their foundations.

Muhammad: a Religion Is Born

This section will introduce you to the highlights of the life of the Prophet Muhammad, as reported by the Muslim tradition. The Prophet's life forms the bedrock of the beliefs held by the immense majority of the world's Muslims, over and above sectarian differences, such as those that divide Sunni and Shi'a, and different schools of thought, from literalist to mystical via reformist.

Muslim scholars and historians have relied on three sources of information for the life of Muhammad, which have given form, over the course of centuries, to the core of the Muslim tradition. The primary source is, of course, the Qur'an, containing Revelations from God, followed by the prophetic traditions – known as hadith – which are the sayings of Muhammad, and thirdly the various biographies of the Prophet. The fundamental historical reference works, such as the Persian scholar Tabari's celebrated history of the beginnings of Islam, draw on these three sources and occasionally upon the accounts of Jewish or Christian chroniclers. Most of the earliest accounts were transmitted orally, meaning that dates and places cannot be established with any certainty. Over time, historians and chroniclers cross-checked and verified their information: certain suppositions would be called into question, certain dates readjusted and, as in the case of more than a few prophetic traditions, some were simply rejected outright. The task of criticism continues to this day; many questions remain to be elucidated, such as the authenticity of some prophetic traditions and the chronology of specific events.

BIRTH

According to Ibn Ishaq, one of his first biographers, Muhammad 'was born on a Monday, during the night of the twelfth of the month of *Rabi' al-awwal*, in the year of the elephant',[1] which corresponds to the year 570 CE. While doubts have been expressed about the exact date, given the Islamic calendar (explained on p. 271), it is a date widely accepted by most Muslims and marks the celebration of his birth in many countries. His mother was two months pregnant when his father Abdullah died. As a fatherless boy, his social standing suffered, even though he was a descendant of the noble Meccan clan of Banu Hashim. Caught between her obligation to respect the nobility of the clan by remaining dignified and her inability to support her family, his mother Aminah's situation was precarious. The Meccan custom of the day was to consign infants to wet nurses from the nomadic Bedouin tribes of the surrounding desert. But because his father was dead, one wet nurse after another refused to accept him, fearing they would gain no benefit. Ultimately a woman called Halimah, who alone remained after all the town's other infants had been placed with wet nurses, agreed to accept him for fear of returning empty-handed to her village in the desert.

AS AN ORPHAN

Muhammad was to live with Halimah in the desert for four years, in extremely difficult conditions. The experience had a powerful impact on his entire life. One day the wet nurse took fright; she had noticed strange things going on around the baby and, fearing that he might be stricken with illness, promptly returned him to his mother. Muhammad would remain with his mother Aminah for two years until, one day, on the road to Medina, she too died. He found himself, at the age of six, orphaned, poor and alone. The Qur'an, later, was to remind him of his childhood poverty.

The little boy was brought back to Mecca, where his grandfather cared for him. But before long, he too died, and Muhammad's uncle Abu Talib took him in and raised him like a son. Muhammad became a shepherd and grew accustomed to travelling with his uncle, whose business was encountering serious difficulties. At the age of twelve he travelled to Syria with Abu Talib, accompanying a caravan of traders. During that journey a Christian monk noticed the young man and brought the uncle's attention to his exceptional character. It was not the first time that his singular nature had been noted: from his earliest days his mother, his wet nurse and those around him had observed things that were difficult to explain (light around him, abundance of milk, etc.). Moreover, from an early age he had displayed signs of moral virtue that no one could miss: honesty, helpfulness and gentleness.

As a twelve-year-old he took part in a council of the tribal chiefs. The meeting had a strong influence on him. The chiefs concluded that membership of a clan, whether powerful or not, would no longer protect a man in Mecca, whether a resident or a visitor; instead, the principle of justice should prevail, irrespective of the person's status. They went on to sign the agreement known as the Pact of the Virtuous (*Ḥilf al-fuḍūl*); years later, after the Revelation of the Qur'an had begun, the Prophet would remember the pact and confirm that its principles were in accordance with those of Islam.

MARRIAGE

Muhammad was building a career in trade: his reputation for honesty was already bringing him success in business. A wealthy independent businesswoman, Khadijah, heard of the young man's qualities and offered him employment. He proved worthy of her confidence and was a particularly effective businessman. Khadijah was drawn to him and sent him a marriage proposal, which he accepted. He was then twenty-five years old, while she, according to tradition, was forty. However, several other sources give her age as twenty-eight. They had several children: the first-born, Qasim, died at the age of two, followed by Zaynab, Ruqayyah, Um Kalthum, Fatimah and finally 'Abd Allah, who also died before his second birthday (Muhammad's only surviving children were his daughters). He continued to work as trader, and his reputation grew apace. At Mecca he was known as 'al-Ṣādiq al-Amīn' – he who is trustworthy and true to his word. But in his thirty-fifth year he felt himself possessed by a powerful sense of spiritual longing. He had never believed in the Meccan idols and sought answers more in tune with his temperament. He began to spend close to a month meditating alone in a cave on the outskirts of Mecca, in the hope of a response, something he continued to do each year.

REVELATION

Muhammad was forty years old when the Archangel Gabriel appeared to him and announced that God had chosen him. He was to be God's Messenger – *Rasūl Allah* – the last one to be sent to humanity. Terrified, he returned home to his wife Khadijah, who comforted him, reassuring him that he was so virtuous that what he was experiencing could not be the work of the devil. She led him to her cousin Waraqah ibn Nawfal, a Christian, who confirmed that indeed Muhammad bore the seal of prophecy and predicted that his own people would deny him.

'Read in the name of your Sustainer, who has created!'

(Qur'an 96:1) were the first words Muhammad heard from God. They would be followed by a flow of Revelations that would continue, often at irregular intervals, for the next twenty-three years. It is these Revelations that form the Qur'an, the Holy Book of Islam. He transmitted the Message to those around him, who, like his wife Khadijah and his cousin Ali, accepted the new Message. But others, such as his uncle Abu Talib, who had taken him in and loved him dearly, did not respond to the call. Soon he began to preach in public and was persecuted by the Meccan aristocracy, who understood that Muhammad was calling into question their beliefs, their society and their hold on power. They promised him money, influence and women; he refused, declaring that even if they were to offer him 'the sun in his right hand and the moon in his left' to stop preaching his message, he would not; he had a mission and he intended to complete it.

The Message turned on four cardinal points: faith in the uniqueness of God – *Tawḥīd* – the Qur'an as the word of God, the imperative of prayer and good deeds, and, ultimately, the return to God on the Day of Judgment. For thirteen years he preached this Message, passing on the Revelations that were sent down to him. Openly, then secretly, more and more of the inhabitants of Mecca joined the new faith, women as well as men, and a majority of the poor or slaves, who saw liberation in his preaching.

PERSECUTION AND MIGRATION

After thirteen years of Muhammad's preaching, persecution had reached such intensity that it was no longer possible for believers in the new faith to live in Mecca. Several of the first

the city. This ran contrary to the prevailing custom which was to execute the male members of the conquered clan and deliver their wives and children into captivity.

Muhammad was again to encounter some of those whose lives he had spared, this time members of the Banu Nadir tribe, who once more betrayed and attacked him. Yet again he refrained from applying the rule of execution and instead sent them off into exile. When he learned that the Banu Qurayzah, in league with the exiled members of the other two clans, had betrayed him a third time, he dispatched an army that promptly defeated them. This time he called for them to be judged according to their own Jewish tradition – by a judge they had previously accepted. The sentence was carried out without mercy – and the men were executed. The punishment, which was only applied after three acts of treachery had been committed, had the desired effect: the neighbouring clans stopped betraying the pacts they had entered into.

It was not long before the Muslim community of Medina had achieved a degree of stability in the region and over time they concluded alliances that gradually came to assure their security.

LEADERSHIP

Meanwhile, Muhammad had remarried, to the daughter of his friend Abu Bakr, Aishah. Tradition recounts that she was six years old at the time of marriage and nine when it was consummated, as was often the custom. But a substantial body of research has raised doubts about her age and, when cross-checked with the historical events that form a part of Muhammad's biography, most of the evidence indicates that

Aishah would have been between sixteen and eighteen years old. The Prophet had remained monogamous for twenty-five years. But he married eleven women after taking up residence in Medina. Most of these marriages consolidated alliances with the clans, in keeping with the custom of the day. He continued to nurture regional relationships that helped neighbouring tribes and nations understand that the Muslims were not the 'mindless madmen' that the rulers of Mecca, the Quraysh, suggested they were. For example, Muhammad received a Christian delegation from Najran and allowed them to pray in his mosque in full respect of their rites. It was also at this time that a key change occurred within the practice of the faith. Up until Muhammad's arrival in Medina, the Muslims had prayed facing Jerusalem, considered the holy city of the three monotheistic faiths. But in Medina the Prophet received a Revelation that commanded him to turn towards Mecca, the site of the Kaaba, an empty cube which in Muslim tradition had been built by Abraham, but was then defiled by idols and representations. Abraham cleansed it, but after his death it once again became home to idols, until they were finally cast out by Muhammad. It was to become the holy mosque, the symbolic 'house of God', the centre towards which Muslims turned their faces in prayer, as they turned their hearts and lives towards God: 'Turn, then, your face towards the [Inviolable] Sacred Mosque; and wherever you all may be, turn your faces towards it [in prayer]' (2:144). So it is that all mosques face Mecca, while Jerusalem, which had been the first direction of prayer remains a holy place in Muslim tradition.

THE TRUCE OF AL-HUDAYBIYYAH

These victories, diplomatic and military, strengthened Muhammad's reputation as the 'king of the Arabs', as he was called by the great neighbouring powers. But following the Revelation to turn towards Mecca, in the sixth year of the Hegira (628), during the month of Ramadan, the Prophet dreamt that he would accomplish a pilgrimage to Mecca. He ordered his Companions to prepare to march, and to go unarmed to show the Meccan leadership that the expedition had no hostile intentions. The Quraysh would not agree to this and, after protracted negotiations (to the disadvantage of the Muslims), 'the truce of al-Hudaybiyyah' was signed. Under its terms the Muslims agreed to turn back to Medina and to perform the pilgrimage the following year.

Although the pilgrimage failed, this truce brought peace to the remaining front around Medina, and the Prophet sent a message to the rulers of the neighbouring empires: to the Negus of Abyssinia, to Khosrow II, the Shah of Persia, to Heraclius, the Emperor of Byzantium, to Muqawqis, the ruler of Egypt, and to several other regional sovereigns. In the message, he sought recognition as 'Him who is sent by God' and invited them to accept Islam. In the event of refusal, he would hold them responsible before God for having misled their peoples. Responses varied: the Negus accepted Islam, but the others reacted angrily, humiliating or killing the emissaries.

THE CONQUEST OF MECCA

The following year the Prophet and his community performed what is now known as the minor pilgrimage – the *'umrah* – under the terms of the truce of al-Hudaybiyyah.

One year after this, the allies of the Quraysh, who were unhappy with the terms of the truce, broke the pact by attacking clans who lived under Muhammad's protection. Muhammad judged that by breaking the pact they had broken the whole truce and he resolved to raise an army to march on Mecca. After a short siege, the Muslims forced Mecca to capitulate during Ramadan, in 630 (year eight of the Hegira). The Prophet entered the city on horseback, leaning forward in prostration, personally destroyed the idols stored in the Kaaba, and henceforth dedicated this sacred space to the adoration of the one and only God. He then assembled the inhabitants of Mecca who had fought him for twenty years. He told them: 'Go in peace, you are free', granting them pardons, and he once again took up residence in his native city. He was to reside there for a time before returning to Medina, where he continued to administer the affairs of the fast-growing community.

Delegations from the surrounding clans and tribes came to swear allegiance to his now-solid and recognized authority. Muhammad would only return once more to Mecca to carry out what is now known as the major pilgrimage – the Hajj. This came to be known as the 'farewell pilgrimage'. There in Mecca he delivered his celebrated sermon recalling the faithful to the fundamental tenets of Islam. It was then that he received the following Revelation, one of many of similar meaning: 'Today have I perfected your religion for you, and have bestowed upon you the full measure of My blessings, and willed that Islam shall be your religion' (5:3). Muhammad knew now that his mission was drawing to a close.

DEATH

On his return to Medina, Muhammad continued to oversee the community before falling ill. He insisted that all his material, emotional and spiritual debts be settled and prepared to depart this world. The final cycle of prophecy in the Abrahamic tradition had come to an end; it was now time for Muhammad to return to God. In 632, the eleventh year of the Hegira, Muhammad died in the arms of his wife Aishah. 'Umar, his close Companion, in a state of near-collapse, announced that Muhammad would soon be resurrected and that he would personally kill anyone who dared to affirm that the Prophet was dead. Abu Bakr, the Prophet's friend and a man usually known for his emotional disposition, pushed 'Umar aside, displaying a sense of calmness and self-control. He stated: 'If any amongst you used to worship Muhammad, then Muhammad has passed away. But if anyone of you used to worship God, then God is alive and shall never die.'[2] And then he recited this verse or *āyah*, from the Qur'an:

> Muhammad is no more than a Messenger: many were the Messengers that passed away before him. If he died or were slain, will you then turn back on your heels? If any did turn back on his heels, not the least harm will he do to God; and God will swiftly reward the grateful. (3:144)

After the Death of the Prophet

THE SUCCESSION: SUNNI AND SHI'A

Who would succeed Muhammad? There was no unanimously recognized prophetic tradition that gave a clear answer to this question. Tensions arose rapidly, as two opposing factions began to form. The first, supported by a majority (which would ultimately prevail), held that the Prophet had left no indication as to his successor's identity, that by God's will he had no son (daughters were not considered possible successors), and that a successor – a Caliph – must be selected by his community. The Caliph should be chosen for his moral pre-eminence, his integrity and his competence. The choice turned almost naturally to the Prophet's faithful long-time friend Abu Bakr al-Siddiq, who had been appointed by the Prophet to lead the ritual prayers during his final illness. Those who had previously held this position were Sunni, who affirmed that they were following the Prophet's path and tradition – known as the Sunnah – by holding strictly to what he had said, done or approved.

The other camp held that the succession should devolve upon one of the members of Muhammad's family, and that his cousin and son-in-law, Ali, one of the first converts to Islam, should naturally become the first successor to Muhammad, as well as the Imam – the guide and religious leader – of the Muslims. They pointed to a saying of the Prophet that confirmed their choice: 'I am the city of knowledge, Ali is its gate; so whoever desires knowledge, let him enter the gate.' The Sunni consider this saying inauthentic, but it forms a part of the corpus of texts invoked by the 'partisans of Ali', as they were first known, to confirm Ali as the legitimate successor. Soon to become known as 'Shi'a' – the partisans – they rallied to the cause of Ali, and to his sons Hassan and Hussein.

The differences between Sunni and Shi'a were at first political, turning on the question of prophetic succession, but they rapidly mutated into a theological and philosophical dispute. The Caliph, whether elected or approved by the community of believers, received his legitimacy from below, while the Imam, as the leader among the Shi'a was known, was a religious figure, receiving authority from above, by virtue of his family ties, through the twin considerations of blood and knowledge. Their beliefs about succession were to lead to the absence of a clergy or formal hierarchy among the Sunni, while the Shi'a were to develop a defined structure of authority centred on the lineage of the first imams. This dispute was to mark indelibly the early history of Islam.[3] The imams, descendants of Ali, are infallible in the eyes of the Shi'a and enjoy access to the hidden and secret meaning of the Qur'an; their role was that of teachers and guides, standing midway between mankind on the one hand and the Prophet and the Qur'an on the other. Two religious traditions thus took shape, with numerous differences concerning the classification and interpretation of the scriptural sources, religious authority, the role of reason, freedom and latitude in producing legislation, to name but a few.

What followed was a period of struggle between these two main groups over the spiritual direction of Islam. First to lead was Muhammad's close friend Abu Bakr, who served as Caliph for two years (632–4) and before his death nominated 'Umar ibn al-Khattab as his successor. 'Umar's reign lasted ten years before he was assassinated, and he was followed by Uthman ibn Affan (644–56), who was also killed. Ali, the first choice of the Shi'a and cousin of the Prophet, then assumed the mantle of Caliph, but his was a troubled reign that saw certain Muslim leaders, including the Prophet's widow Aishah, demand that he punish Uthmân's murderers, which Ali did not do.

Various splinter groups formed, one headed by a former scribe of Muhammad, Mu'awiyyah, that also called Ali's legitimacy into question and rose against Ali in battle at Siffin in 658. They were defeated, and Mu'awiyyah called for arbitration, which Ali accepted. A group known as the Kharijites had supported Ali up until then, but they thought that he should have acted forcefully to crush the secession, and rebelled. Another group, the Ibadi, distanced themselves from Ali's rule and, rejecting violence, settled in Oman, where even today they are in the majority, as well as in Zanzibar, which was an Omani colony.

After Ali's murder at the hands of the Kharijites in 661, tensions were running high. Ali's son Hassan succeeded him, but gave conditional recognition to the authority of Mu'awiyyah, who went on to found the Omayyad Empire in present-day Syria. Hassan died in 670 and his younger brother Hussein was killed at the battle of Karbala (in modern-day Iraq) in 680, in another battle waged over issues of succession. This tragic event – the end of the direct lineage from Muhammad – marked the historic beginning of the Shi'a tradition of Ashura (the Day of Remembrance) which invokes the death of Muhammad's grandson Hussein as a quasi-foundational act.

This period is now known as the first major *fitnah* (the Arabic term for disorder, crisis, division and internecine strife) and includes the death of Muhammad's last surviving male relative. Today, Sunnis represent approximately 85 per cent of the world's Muslims, while the Shi'as account for 14 per cent – they form the majority in Iran, Iraq, Azerbaijan, Lebanon and Bahrain; the Ibadi make up 1 per cent, and are mainly to be found in Oman and Zanzibar.

EXPANSION

By 632, the year of Muhammad's death, the entire Arabian Peninsula had come under Muslim control, and even during the ensuing internal unrest, territorial expansion continued apace. Within twenty-four years (632–656), under the first three Caliphs, territory under Muslim rule had expanded to Arabia, Palestine, Syria, Egypt, Libya, Mesopotamia and parts of Armenia and Persia. Even after the assassination of the third Caliph, Uthman, and despite the schism between Sunni and Shi'a, rapid expansion continued. It was driven by several factors: tension and divisions between the older, neighbouring empires, with their corruption and frequently authoritarian and intolerant rule often causing the conquering Muslims to be welcomed as liberators, though the southern Arabian tribes did attempt to rebel soon after Muhammad's death.

The vigour of the Muslim armies and the simplicity of the legal structures they imposed on the freshly conquered lands – payment of taxes in return for military protection without having to change religion – quickly overcame the great but fragile empires that lay on their periphery. When Mu'awiyyah consolidated his authority and founded the Omayyad dynasty in 661, with Damascus as its capital, expansion accelerated; less than sixty years after the death of Muhammad, the territory of the new Muslim Empire stretched from the Indus River to the Iberian Peninsula, with

Frankish leader Charles Martel halting the advance of the Muslim forces at the Battle of Tours.

The earliest Muslim conquests were by land, but by the early eighth century the Muslims had constructed a fleet and rapidly became a naval power that could control territory and access by sea, from southern Europe to India, while simultaneously monitoring every movement across broad expanses of Africa, the Mediterranean basin and Central Asia.

The explosive expansion of the first hundred years of Islam was halted by the resistance of the Franks in the west, and of the Byzantine Empire in the east, which repelled two major sieges of Constantinople, in 678 and 718. The speed of expansion was inversely proportional to the integrity of the new territories. The forces of conquest displayed religious and cultural flexibility, but were dependent on local administrators and institutions that they neither fully controlled nor understood and that were often hostile to them. Internecine strife between peoples, cultures and national groups, the privileges enjoyed by some and grave deficiencies in the protection of equality and social justice weakened the new empire from within.

OMAYYADS, ABBASIDS, OTTOMANS

The Omayyad dynasty was founded in 661 and was to endure for a century, undergoing the rapid expansion described earlier, as well as the civil wars that would ultimately undermine its authority and lead to its fall. The second *fitnah* followed on the heels of the death of Mu'âwiyyah, who had chosen his son

Yazid as the next Caliph, thus inaugurating the principle of hereditary succession in the Sunni tradition. This new form of political organization did not at all correspond to the original position of the Sunni, who had opposed the principle of prophetic succession. It would have a profound impact on the course of legal and political thought in both the Sunni and Shi'a traditions.

But for all the inner turmoil that racked it, the Omayyed dynasty was powerful and flourished – commercially, intellectually and culturally – as it integrated a diversity of traditions while recognizing their right to exist and to develop. In the end it was a new coalition, known as the Abbasids and formed in direct challenge to the Omayyed Caliphate, which brought about the end of the dynasty in 750. When they seized power, the Abbasids massacred almost the entire Omayyed leadership. Only a few escaped with their lives. Among them was Abd al-Rahman, who refused to recognize Abbasid authority and, fleeing westward, established the Emirate of Cordoba in Spain in 756. There, in an isolated, truncated form, the Omayyed dynasty survived until 1009.

The Abbasid dynasty, which chose Baghdad as its capital, lasted for over five centuries. During its first two centuries, despite internal conflict, Islamic thought developed in virtually every field: the religious sciences, law, theology-philosophy, Greek-influenced philosophy and the experimental sciences, architecture and the arts. The reign of the celebrated Caliph Harun al-Rashid (786–809) was distinguished by an intellectual efflorescence that stretched over several decades. Despite internal political unrest and foreign threats, the dynasty was able to conserve its intellectual, cultural and scientific vigour until the end of his reign.

This period is now known as the 'Golden Age of Islam' for the contribution of its thinkers, scholars and artists to the flowering of knowledge and culture. But political unrest gradually undermined the creative energies that had been given free rein. The Seljuks, a Turkic tribe that had converted to Sunni Islam in the ninth century, captured Baghdad in 1050 and reconfirmed the founding Sunni character of the Abbasid Caliphate, following a period of domination by the Shi'a. The Mongol invasions were finally to bring the dynasty to an end in 1258; most of the Abbasid rulers were executed, imprisoned or enslaved. But the military created by the Abbasids, made up primarily of foreign-born soldiers known as Mamluks, escaped the Mongol repression and fled to Egypt, where they seized power and continued to rule as local representatives of Abbasid power.

The year 1299 marked the founding of what would become the Ottoman Empire at Bursa, in western Anatolia in modern-day Turkey, from whence it would expand into Eastern Europe. In 1453, the Ottomans – a Turkic tribe – captured Constantinople, sounding the death knell of the Christian Byzantine Empire. The Ottoman state gradually extended its authority over most of the Muslim-majority societies of the Middle East, reaching a climax with the conquest of Egypt in 1517 by Sultan Selim I, bringing Abbasid Mamluk rule to an end. Henceforth the Ottoman Sultans were to use the title of Caliph to assert their authority over the entire Muslim world. The reign of Suleiman the Magnificent (1520–66) was remarkable for its foreign conquests and, internally, for its far-reaching social, administrative and institutional reforms, accompanied by a proliferation of intellectual, literary, poetic and artistic activity. Ottoman supremacy was not unchallenged, though. From the seventeenth century on, the empire would come under attack on several fronts, which increased in the eighteenth century as Russians, Persians and entire regions of Eastern Europe resisted Ottoman authority or openly rebelled against it. As internal conflicts multiplied, entire regions were lost.

By the nineteenth century the empire, described by Russian Tsar Nicholas I as 'the sick man of Europe', had begun to decompose, racked by internal strife and military defeats. The decline was a lengthy one and finally terminated with the fall and the dismantlement of the empire in the early twentieth century. While it had thrown in its lot with Germany and the Central Powers and lost the 1914–18 War, the empire also faced the British-inspired Arab Revolt in 1916–18. The Ottoman political Caliphate was abolished by the secularist revolutionary Mustafa Kemal in 1922, and its spiritual authority came to an end two years later when the Turkish National Assembly endorsed Kemal's decision. Turkey became a Republic and the nation-state would from this point on become the political reference for the world's Muslims, even for those – like the modern-day pan-Islamists (see p. 232) – who call for the renewed unity of the Muslims against colonialism, for the re-establishment of the Caliphate, or for both at the same time.

Religion, Philosophy and Civilization

Islam is, first and foremost, a religion possessing a creed (*'aqīdah*), fundamental principles (*uṣūl*), rituals (*'ibādāt*), obligations (*wājibāt*), prohibitions (*muḥarramāt*) and a moral code (*akhlāq*). The first Muslims, by professing their faith, accepted a structure based on a direct personal relationship with God and the Message of the last Prophet. This is the very meaning of the testimony of faith (*al-shahādah*): 'I attest that there is no god but God and that Muhammad is the Messenger of God.'

But from these fundamental considerations there also emerges a general philosophy with its own conception of life, of death and of humankind. Sharia – best understood as the Way to the Source, the Way of Fidelity – as we will see, calls believers to adopt a holistic approach to their religion that, drawn from the relationship of humanity to God, determines a philosophy of life. This religion, and the philosophy that flows from it, has always demonstrated a high regard for culture, enshrining it in terms of law and jurisprudence as a secondary source of law (*uṣūl al-fiqh*). Whatever, in a given culture, did not contradict a tenet of Islam was integrated into the religious substrate of that culture, so much so that it has always been extremely difficult to distinguish between religion and culture.

Throughout history, all religions have been integrated into cultures, and in turn have always influenced and modified them: there can be no religion without culture, or culture without religion. But religion is not culture. Islam, as a religion, has had an enormous influence and even shaped Arab, African and Asian cultures down through history. The influence of Islam is palpable. Many Jews, Christians or even atheists in Arab, African or Asian cultures define themselves by 'Muslim culture' without sharing the Muslim faith. Islam is not 'a culture', but its impact upon the cultures with which it has mingled has transformed it into a cultural marker of the greatest significance.

Over the course of history Islam stood as a cardinal point for great empires whose political and military power, social and economic organization and, above all, artistic and cultural production it so powerfully influenced. There is no single definition of 'civilization',[4] but we can agree that all civilizations contain common characteristics of an intellectual, artistic, social, institutional and even economic nature. From this perspective, Islam is indeed a civilization whose references and distinguishing features cut across eras and cultures: the social, intellectual and artistic life that flourished under the Omayyeds found an echo in the golden age of the Abbasids, which in turn would resonate not only among the Ottomans, but also in the particular genius of African, Persian and Asian cultures, extending into Europe through Andalusia and even beyond.

Islamic civilization was rich, multifaceted and diversified thanks to its many schools of thought and above all to the innumerable cultures in which the Muslims established themselves and that nourished their way of thinking. What held true from the earliest days of Islam remains true today, with the presence of Muslims in the West: they have put down roots and have become Western Muslims, nourished as much by the corpus of Islamic principles as by Western culture. In so doing they have given birth to Western Islam, which fully respects the religious principles of Islam – for in this sense, there is only one Islam – but draws inspiration from Western civilization and from its cultural diversity, to express itself and shape the way Muslims live. Standing at the point where the two civilizations converge, Western Muslims enrich both the West and Islam and promise to create the linkages that will lead to fertile encounters and to dialogue. Similar processes have been and are at work in China and India, and even more broadly in Africa and Asia.

Fundamental Tenets

Before examining the meaning of faith in Islam and the ritual practices of its believers, we must look more closely at several central concepts, the better to gain a clearer idea of Islam's fundamental tenets. The Islamic Message and its value system are based upon a body of scriptural sources, and it is here that we must start our discussion.

The very notion of 'Islam' may be understood in several ways, and on multiple levels. Islam is part of the ancient tradition of monotheistic faiths, and Islam's relationship with Judaism and Christianity needs to be elucidated and understood. In this brief overview we will outline a particular conception of humanity, which will help us gain understanding of the meaning of the Islamic creed and ritual. But first we must begin with the Message, the Revelations that were given to Muhammad by God.

The Message

The Revelations that began in 610 with the words 'Read in the name of your Sustainer' would be received by Muhammad over the next twenty-three years until his death in 632. He received them irregularly, depending on his personal circumstances and those of the community he founded. The final verse revealed, according to most scholars, is verse 281, of chapter 2: 'And be conscious of the Day on which you shall be brought back unto God, whereupon every human being shall be repaid in full for what he has earned, and none shall be wronged.'

GOD, CREATION

The initial Revelations were designed to convert the hearts and minds of both the Prophet and his first Companions. They deal above all with the nature of God, with His oneness and His presence, which is made manifest through various signs that the believers are invited to observe and to meditate upon. The earliest verses are gathered, for the most part, at the end of the Qur'an as it exists in its final compilation. They invoke Nature – the skies, the dawn, the sun and the moon, trees, mountains, the desert, water – and all are presented as signs pointing to the existence of the Creator. They are no longer to be seen as merely natural elements with no particular significance, but as signs that recall His presence and the ultimate meaning of life: 'We shall show them Our signs in the horizons [of the universe] and within themselves, so that it will become clear unto them that this [Revelation] is indeed the Truth' (41:53).

The intimate connection with Nature described in the Qur'an mirrors a new and intimate relationship between the individual and the entirety of the universe. This is something found in much of Asian spirituality, a summoning of the human being to seek inner peace. To utter God's name – to *find* God – is to reconcile ourselves with our innermost nature, with our *fiṭrah* (see p. 68): 'for, verily, in the remembrance of God [human] hearts do find solace' (13:28). The sense of deep satisfaction, of inner peace, is a sign of the way God speaks to our hearts when they are converted, literally, by a faith that offers a new way of seeing both the world and oneself. It is a question of seeing more clearly that which surrounds us and lies within us, which before we had seen without seeing, without discerning meaning. 'Verily, in the creation of the heavens and the earth, and in the succession of night and day, there are indeed signs for those who are endowed with insight' (3:190). The presence of the divine is like a light that transforms our perceptions, an experience in opposition to which the Qur'an describes the 'deniers of truth with veiled hearts' (*kuffār*): 'Have they, then, never journeyed about the earth, letting their hearts gain wisdom, and causing their ears to hear? Yet, verily, it is not their eyes that have become blind – but blind have become the hearts that are in their breasts' (22:46).

THE POOR

Just as we are summoned to observe the Creation that surrounds us, and to invest it with meaning, we must also consider the poor among us, who are invisible in our daily lives, and to value and cherish them. The earliest revealed chapters (*sūrah*) of the Qur'an repeatedly call upon the believers to attend to the poor who are neglected, ignored and so little respected. The Qur'an describes sincere believers as those 'who give food, out of love for Him, unto the needy, and the orphan, and the captive [saying], "We feed you for the sake of God alone: we desire no reward from you, nor thanks"' (76:8–9).

Conversion by way of faith entails a change in the heart's disposition towards the poor.

Muhammad would customarily invoke God by saying: 'O God, we ask of you [to bestow upon us] the love of the poor.'[1] Faith transforms our vision by bestowing a new value upon beings and things: the poor, perceived as useless and wholly invisible and negligible in daily life, suddenly become the centre of spiritual attention. Nature, which constitutes our environment and is neglected by the very fact of its normality, becomes a book of signs upon which we must meditate. The first Revelations evoke God as unique, invisible and unlike any other, and at the same time they make visible to the heart, by conversion, that which the eyes could not see in the beauty of Nature and the humanity of the poor and the orphan.

PRAYER AND THE LAST JUDGMENT

During the early years of Muhammad's prophethood, the Revelation speaks of itself as the revealed word of God, in a clear Arabic tongue, that contains the Truth – *al-Ḥaq*. Its task is to recall to humankind the core of all preceding prophetic messages. The Qur'an itself has multiple names that indicate its function: it is 'the Book', 'the Light', 'the Remembrance', and 'the Discernment', to name only a few. The revealed Text's primary function, however, is to restate the presence of God, the Creator, His Majesty and Mercy. It goes on to confirm that humankind depends on God, a situation that flows from our inability to know and to respond to questions of truth, of the meaning of life, and to the realities of the unseen, on our own.

The Revelations given to Muhammad lay bare a relationship with God in the light of which humanity is expected to elevate itself through prayer. This establishes a dialogue, a correspondence between God and humankind mediated through the Qur'an, which lends direction and purpose to prayer and confirms humankind in its conscious choice of acceptance of God. Muslims were first asked to pray twice a day, and during the night, before the five daily prayers were prescribed.

One recurrent theme emerges from the first Revelations delivered to Muhammad: that of the intellectual and spiritual education to which humankind must commit itself, the better to draw closer to God. This education is helped by a reminder of the Day of Judgment, when human beings will return to their Creator, and must – alone – account for what they have done: 'the Day on which neither wealth will be of any use; nor children, [and when] only he [will be happy] who comes before God with a sound heart [in its original state]' (26:88–9).

We, as individuals, are accountable for our actions; Paradise will be bestowed upon those who have chosen piety and goodness, while hell will be the destination of those who have denied God, worked evil and spread corruption on earth. The Revelation contains a clear warning to this effect: God is the Supremely Merciful, who receives those who come to Him, and proclaims punishment for those who deny Him, or act unethically. Later in the sequence of Revelations, love of and for God will be presented as the source and motivation for the quest for Him: 'Say [O Prophet]: "If you love God, follow me, [and] God will love you and forgive you your sins"' (3:31). And the Prophet will affirm that ultimate salvation is not in the paradise of reward, but in the joy of being in God's presence.

THE MECCAN AND MEDINAN PERIODS

As we have seen, the Revelation began with the great themes whose function was to convert, in the most literal sense, the heart, the mind and the understanding of the believer. As a result, the Qur'an is filled with the stories of the ancient Messengers and Prophets; each of these stories brings to mind a meaning and evokes moral principles, and helps the believer to gain access to the fundamentals: a God to be adored, a Book to be understood, a Call to be heard and a Destination to prepare for. The same histories recur in cyclical fashion to widen the believer's vision in the course of her or his spiritual evolution. Reason alone might see little more than repetition, but a spiritual reading with the heart sees instead a confirmation, a deepening and a revealing of new secrets embedded in the Text.

Over time, the Revelations received by Muhammad came to correspond with the realities of the first Muslim community, and to respond to its needs. In them, we can distinguish two major periods in the historical sequence of twenty-three years.

The Meccan period (610–622), dating from the beginning of the Revelation up until the Hegira, is characterized by the exposition of the great themes and overarching principles that we have already outlined. The Medinan period (622–632) coincides with the establishment of the Muslims in Medina, and encompassed numerous points of detail relating to law and jurisprudence (known as *fiqh*), to interpersonal and social relations and to trade and business transactions (*mu'āmalāt*) henceforth addressed increasingly to the community of believers. The first chapter – and the longest – revealed at Medina is the second in the Qur'an, *The Cow*, which abounds with references to the specific context of Medina, to the conflicts that took place there, to the hypocrites, and to the prescriptions that regulate behaviour and devotional practices.

It is as if, from Mecca to Medina, the Revelation has shifted away from an exposition of guiding principles to a practical application in response to the constantly evolving circumstances of the Muslim community. Moreover, the Medinan Revelations touch upon both social and cultural situations; rules emerge progressively and do not set out to reform, oblige or forbid in a singular and definitive manner. Clearly, the reforms did take into consideration the times, the collective psychology of the community, and the culture; the Qur'an, through a kind of divine pedagogy, lays down broad guidelines to be followed, applied and extended, but it neither formulates nor provides all the practical details.

UNDERSTANDING THE MESSAGE

Understanding the Qur'anic Message demanded a substantial effort on the part of the *'ulamā'* – the scholars, scriptural interpreters (or exegetes) and jurists of the growing Muslim community. For this eternal Text is grounded in a specific history. Its principles, although timeless and universal, can only be grasped by situating them in the historical context in which they were revealed. The task of human intelligence is to grasp the meaning of the Texts in the light of their specific context, and from it to derive norms and lay down general directions. This was the undertaking of the earliest legal scholars. The first commentaries on the Qur'an – known as *tafsīr* – by Tabari, Ibn Kathir and Qurtubi, to name the most eminent, systematically established that the Text and its principles could not be understood without detailed knowledge of the society that received the Revelation.

That alone was not enough, however. It was equally essential to link the fundamentals and the theoretical framework revealed in Mecca with their real-life application in Medina. The exercise, which proceeded both by deduction (from theory to practice), and by induction (from practice to theory), made it possible not only to formulate practical rules of law and jurisprudence, but also to lend them coherence. In the light of this theoretical framework, it was possible to establish a system or, better, a veritable philosophy of law. This philosophy would provide a theoretical structure, establish meaningful connections between rules (*ahkām*) and, above all, make it possible to identify the objectives (*maqāṣid*) that constitute the *raison d'être* of the entire Message.

Finally, scholars had to determine, in light of the diversity of Revelations on a given subject and the order in which they were revealed, the direction that the Revelation suggested and therefore which humankind must then attempt to follow. The Qur'an does not go into much detail. God, as a prophetic tradition puts it, 'has remained silent about many things, out of Mercy and not forgetfulness':[2] but this silence is a blessing, as nothing is set in stone. Human beings are called upon to make a constant effort of analysis and application that is rigorous, realistic, progressive, wise and balanced.

WAR

In grappling with the role and significance of war in Islam, Western orientalist authors have claimed that the Prophet began as a pacifist in Mecca and became mainly a military leader in Medina. This analysis fails to take into account the relationship between the Revelations covering the two periods. During the Meccan period the Prophet received the founding principles, which were to form the structure and the objectives of the Revelation: war and conflict were to be avoided, and conciliation and the preservation of peace were to be sought by all possible means. The earliest believers did not respond to the attacks of the Quraysh in Mecca, and remained passive in the face of stigmatization, persecution, torture and even murder. When two of his followers were being tortured, the Prophet counselled them: 'Be perseverant, O family of Yasser, for your final home will be in Paradise.' When these men were eventually killed, the Muslims did not retaliate. Passive resistance would continue for more than a dozen years until the persecution became too much to bear. In this light, the Hegira can be seen as a pacifist response to repression. If they were to survive without resorting to retaliation, the Muslims had no alternative but to seek shelter in Medina.

After the earliest Muslims arrived in Medina, the hostile Quraysh continued to pursue and attack them. They persecuted and tormented those who had remained in Mecca, seizing the assets and property of those who had fled and concluding alliances in order to attack those who had migrated. These were the circumstances in which a verse (*āyah*) that allows self-defence was revealed: 'Permission [to fight] is given to those against whom war is being wrongfully waged – and, verily, God has indeed the power to succour them' (22:39). The Muslims had tried everything: from passive resistance to exile. The newly founded community of faith now faced the choice between survival or extermination. Only self-defence remained.

The preservation of peace still remained a fundamental principle, but in practice this could now include legitimate self-defence against persecution and oppression. This rule remained in place throughout the entire Medinan period. Muhammad never initiated hostilities, but responded to the aggressive actions of the Quraysh and their allies, or of those who betrayed their pacts and sought to attack the Muslims. Far from being the aggressive military leader that certain critics have labelled him, he made peace, conciliation and truce his priorities. What he did apply during that decade was the principle of legitimate defence against the attacks of those who, despite the Muslims' choice of voluntary exile, continued to do all in their power to pursue and destroy them.

The Revelation laid down the basic principle: peace is primordial, and non-violence the first choice. But if the oppressor does not cease, resistance is legitimate until the aggression ends; then peace must be re-established, as confirmed by numerous Medinan Revelations. Methods of resistance are determined according to those used by the oppressor:

Hence, if you have to respond to an attack, respond only to the extent of the attack levelled against you; but to bear yourselves with patience is indeed far better for those who are patient in adversity [those who know how to control themselves]. (16:126)

When the oppressor ultimately chooses peace, all violence must cease: 'But if they incline to peace, incline you to it as well, and place your trust in God: verily, He alone is all-hearing, all-knowing!' (8:61). The Prophet's practice in Medina thus evolved within the broader conceptual framework laid down in Mecca.

ALCOHOL, INTEREST AND SLAVERY

The obligations and prohibitions that became an integral part of Islam were not revealed all at once during the Medinan period. As the chapters and verses of the Qur'an are not arranged in chronological order, their sequence must be reconstructed in order to identify specific prescriptions and their meanings. This is crucial for grasping the ultimate objectives of the divine Revelations. The example of alcohol is especially revealing: the first verse revealed does not prohibit alcohol but only draws attention to its harmful effects. 'They will ask you about intoxicants and games of chance. Say: "In both there is great evil as well as some benefit for man; but the evil which they cause is greater than the benefit which they bring"' (2:219). A second Revelation, adding restrictions, stipulates: 'O you who have attained to faith! Do not attempt to pray while you are in a state of drunkenness' (4:43). Complete prohibition only comes afterwards: 'O you who have attained to faith! Intoxicants, and games of chance, and idolatrous practices, and the divining of the future are but a loathsome evil of Satan's doing: shun it, then, so that you might attain to a happy state!' (5:90).

According to traditionalist scholars, the three Revelations were transmitted over a period of seven to nine years. As alcohol was part of pre-Islamic Arab culture, it was necessary to alert the earliest Muslims to the reason for the prohibition and slowly bring them to the point of ceasing their consumption altogether. We find the same principle of gradualism in the four Revelations that deal with money, whose ultimate prescription was to ban interest and usury. Though the Revelations are timeless and divine, the Qur'an itself is inscribed *in* time and in a particular context, as it guides followers of the faith to reform their conduct. It is not just the literal meaning of the verses that needs to be taken into account, but also their place in a historical sequence that lends significance to each and points the way towards a certain objective. The task of legal scholars is thus also to highlight this sequence of successive Revelations; the non-chronological order of the Qur'an (in the way it has been compiled) prevents the average Muslim from reaching quick conclusions from a too literal reading. A deeper study of the overall message is required, so that the rules can be understood in the context of their Revelation. The need for this human agency in apprehending the Texts and structuring its legal framework is intended to avoid arrogant literalism and invite intellectual humility as regards the scholars' opinions.

The same logic can be found in the Qur'anic treatment of slavery, a practice that preceded Islam and was the norm in seventh-century Arab society. The first Revelations, and those that were to follow, take the social reality of slavery as their point of departure and direct the Muslims towards a new obligation: as every Muslim must be free to choose, every human being must likewise be free. First came the general theoretical framework, which was an appeal to free consciences to accept faith or not. This was the logic of the earliest Muslims who systematically emancipated slaves, who then converted. Then came the earliest prescriptions, particularly those related to atonement, which summoned the Muslims to free their slaves.

The general thrust of the Revelation is a clear requirement to bring the practice of slavery to an end and, step by step, to enable the emancipated slaves to find a place in society, rather than ending up free but marginalized and indigent. The entire philosophy of Muslim law lies embedded in this methodology, which takes full account of reality, calls for its transformation over time and with an objective that is clearly spelled out – in the case of slavery, nothing less than its abolition. The timescale for slavery is longer than that for alcohol, for here nothing less than a thoroughgoing transformation of society was required. But the scriptural sources, as explained by many scholars, point towards the imperative of abolishing slavery. The objective was a step-by-step reform, on the reasoning that abolition without preparation could backfire against the very people it intended to liberate. Muhammad declared that he would be, on the Day of Judgment, the adversary of three persons, one of whom is 'a

41

man who has sold a free man (thus enslaving him)'.[3] The words of the second Caliph of Islam, 'Umar, in his criticism of the practices of the Arabs, have the same meaning: 'When did you enslave people even though they are born free?'[4] He was reacting to practices which were contradictory to the Islamic Message. Unfortunately this was not to prevent numerous Muslims from trading slaves for centuries until the present day – with some '*ulamā*' (Muslim scholars) going as far as justifying through a distorted (literal and not contextualized) reading the scriptural sources. The modern slavery we witness today in so many Muslim-majority countries (African and Asian countries, the Gulf States) is in complete contradiction to Islamic teachings.

The Texts: Qur'an and hadith

Islam considers Judaism and Christianity to be revealed religions and thus views their respective practitioners as *ahl al-kitāb*, 'people of the Book'.[5] As part and parcel of the same monotheistic lineage, Islam is likewise a 'religion of the Book', founded upon the Qur'an, which Muslims consider to be the last Message revealed by God to humankind. The Qur'an thus concludes a chain of Revelations reaching back to the first Prophets, and including the Jewish Torah and the Christian Gospel.[6]

THE QUR'AN

For Muslims, the Qur'an is the word of God, revealed directly 'in Arabic speech, clear (in itself) and clearly showing the truth' (16:103) to Muhammad, who is considered the last

Prophet and Messenger of God.[7] The Revelation took place over a span of twenty-three years (from 610 to 632). Its revealed verses relate both to universal moral principles and values and to stories of earlier prophecies; they establish rituals (with their accompanying obligations and prohibitions); and, finally, they describe or evoke the historical circumstances that the first Companions of the Prophet encountered in Mecca and later Medina.

The Qur'an is the eternal word of God. Nevertheless, its interpretation has always been inextricably linked to the historical events surrounding its revelation. There are two reasons for this: in the first place, because it was revealed in a large number of distinct sequences and in a chronological order that is essential to understanding and determining the rituals and obligations it lays down; and secondly, because many verses can only be understood if the circumstances of, or the reasons – known as *asbāb al-nuzūl* – for their revelation are understood. The work of interpreting the Qur'an, grasping its meaning and the sequence of its revelation, gave rise to an independent and fundamental discipline: the sciences of the Qur'an (*'ulūm al-Qur'ān*), which elucidate the morphology, the semantics, the chronology and the relation of the universal Text to the historical circumstances of its revelation.

READING AND COMPILING THE QUR'AN

The Qur'an can be read and understood on various levels.[8] On the spiritual level, the accounts of the Prophets of the past, the metaphors and the moral teachings are immediately accessible to everyone; any believer can delve directly into

43

the Text, meditate on its meaning and gain instant access to the Revelation. When it comes to rules, rituals, obligations and prohibitions, however, matters become considerably more complicated. As we have seen, the Qur'an, as it has come down to us, does not follow a chronological order; instead, its verses were arranged in a unique thematic order over the course of the twenty-three years of the prophetic mission.

Tradition holds that Muhammad received the Revelations through the intermediary of the Archangel Gabriel, a figure known in the preceding monotheistic traditions, and immediately committed them to memory. The Archangel likewise instructed him in the arrangement of the chapters as *suwar* (114 *sūrah*), and verses, (*āyāt*) (6,263 in total),[9] and caused him to recite all of the revealed verses thus far received once each year during the month of Ramadan.[10] *Sūrah* 2, coming after the opening *sūrah* (al-Fātiḥah), was the first to be revealed after the Prophet's migration to Medina, thirteen years after the first chapter revealed in Mecca, many of which are found at the end of the Qur'an. Clearly, then, the Text is not arranged in chronological order, and provides no immediate insight into the order or the nature of its prescriptions. To grasp these nuances the Text must be read from a historical perspective, combined with a linguistic and juridical analysis. The average Muslim is more often than not poorly equipped to do so; instead, specialized scholars and jurists (*fuqahā'*) have over time devised methods of interpretation, categorization and Qur'anic commentary (*tafsīr*). These are based on the global nature of the Message, as well as the distinction between those chapters revealed during the Meccan period (610–22) and those of the Medinan period (622–32), alongside the ebb and flow of Revelation and its historical circumstances. Muslim scholars also developed a corpus of methods and rules that made it possible for believers to grasp the essence of the Message with regard to the rituals, rules and ethics of behaviour.

The Qur'an is the primary scriptural source for all Muslims. The Text to which all refer is identical to that compiled and disseminated by the third Caliph, Uthman ibn 'Affan (d. 656), less than twenty years after the death of the Prophet.[11] From the very first, the Qur'an had been memorized, befitting the oral tradition widespread among the Arabs of the time. Many of the Prophet's numerous Companions memorized the Text, and today hundreds of thousands, and perhaps even millions, of women and men are able to recite it from memory.

HADITH (PROPHETIC TRADITIONS)

The second of Islam's scriptural sources is the compilation of prophetic traditions known as ḥadīth (pl. aḥādīth), also called the Sunnah, which comprises everything the Prophet is recorded as having said, done or approved. At the inception of the Revelation, the Prophet insisted that a clear distinction be made between divine and human speech. Consequently, his Companions avoided transcribing his words throughout his years of prophethood. Later, the prophetic traditions were handed down orally. Transmitted and compiled to create the second source of reference, they have become indispensable for understanding and interpreting certain passages of the Qur'an. From reading the Qur'an we know that ritual prayer is a daily obligation, for example, but the manner of prayer (its movements and cycles) has only come down to us through the traditions of the Prophet, who instructed his companions to 'pray as you see me pray'.[12] The prophetic traditions concerning prayer form the basis upon which the ritual has been codified.

In the course of elaborating, classifying and refining the prophetic traditions, three major challenges emerged. Over time, many of these traditions were either invented outright or falsified for personal, collective or political ends, a development that has given rise to a painstaking process of authentication that became the basis of the 'sciences of hadith', called *'ulūm al-ḥadīth*. The task was to verify the validity of the chain of transmission – known as *isnād* – of every single prophetic tradition and then to assign each one to a category of authenticity. From those certified authentic to those roundly rejected, there exist more than forty recognized categories of authenticity.

Hadith specialists (*al-muḥaddithūn*) likewise turned their attention to the contents of each tradition, analysed them and studied their relation to the Qur'an and their actual use. This two-pronged approach – verifying the chain of transmission and content analysis – led to significant differences in the compilations, classifications and even the acceptance or rejection of certain traditions. Among Sunni Muslims, six compilations are held to include the most authentic traditions, while the Shi'a claim four. But even with regard to these compilations there are sharp differences of opinion, multiple interpretations and even contradictions over certain specific and secondary questions.

THE RELATIONSHIP BETWEEN THE QUR'AN AND HADITH

The second challenge to the science of hadith interpretation arises from their relation to the Qur'anic Text. As the prescriptions found in the revealed Text are more often than not general, prophetic traditions are commonly used to fill in the details or to complete them. But the literalist interpretation of these prophetic traditions, coupled with ignorance of their historical context and, in certain cases, their human dimension, has led to an extremely reductive and even deficient reading of the Qur'an.

This means that the general principles of the Qur'an are often understood in the distorting light of a limited number of traditions whose authenticity and whose figurative or literal meanings are, to say the least, debatable. The result has been to restrict interpretative leeway and limit the broader meanings inherent in the Qur'anic verses themselves. For instance, while the Qur'an is referring to the principle of modesty, some scholars, relying on a literal reading of the prophetic traditions, will determine that the only model of modesty for Muslims is in the way the Prophet and the Arabs dressed. This is one of the key points of debate between the literalist and reformist schools of thought (and law and jurisprudence): the status of the prophetic traditions and their relationship to the Qur'an.

There exists a third major challenge, that of the very substance of the prophetic traditions. Certain hadiths – called *qudsī* – are described as being inspired directly by God but expressed in the words of Muhammad. The key issue, then, becomes to ascertain the human component – the role of opinion – in these utterances, and the position taken by

Muhammad himself. What portion of a hadith can be attributed to religious prescription and thus lay claim to divine origin, and what portion to the human condition? Such reflection upon the status of the hadiths reveals one of the principal points of divergence between literalist, traditionalist and reformist trends (see p. 127). The same difficulty also underlies the diversity of opinions and approaches that is one of the hallmarks of Islam's rich history of religious, philosophical and legal thought. The dominant status of the Qur'an and hadith has provided a framework for Islam, but that status has not meant the end of interpretation, nor has it allowed any particular trend of thought to codify the scriptural references once and for all. Unity may never have truly existed in Islam, but certainly uniformity has never been imposed.

Over time, and in this highly specialized field of law, the compilation of prophetic traditions ended up being named 'al-Sunnah', whose original meaning was much more inclusive (taking into account the cultural and social context). As a result, today it is commonly asserted that the two scriptural sources of Islam – irrespective of whether one is Sunni, Shi'a or so on – are the Qur'an and the Sunnah, and that these two define the terms and concepts of what constitutes and defines Islam as a religion, and as a body of values and rituals with its conception of God, of humanity and of the universe.

IJTIHĀD

As we have now learned, on certain practical matters the Texts are silent. They may enunciate general principles, but the Qur'an can sometimes be lacking in detail. A prophetic tradition reports that the Prophet, on dispatching one of his Companions, Mu'adh Ibn Jabal, to Yemen, asked him: 'How will you judge?' Mu'adh answered: 'According to what is in the Book of God.' 'What if it is not in the Book of God?' 'Then with the tradition of God's Messenger.' 'And what if not in the tradition of the Messenger?' Then the Prophet's envoy exclaimed confidently: 'Then I will strive [*ajtahidu*] to form an opinion.' Satisfied with his answer, the Prophet concluded: 'All praise is due to God who has made suitable the messenger of the Messenger of God.'[13] So it was that even during the Prophet's lifetime, and even in Arabia, people would encounter situations for which the Qur'an provided no direct guidance: between the silence of the scripture and the specificity of the context, a judge would then have to form an opinion and find an appropriate answer.

This intellectual discipline is known in Islamic legal tradition as *ijtihād*, which is based on principles identical to those discussed above relating to alcohol, interest or slavery in terms of understanding the Texts, their broader meaning and objectives. But in cases of *ijtihād*, where there is no clear or specific textual reference to the subject in question, the scholar or jurist turns to the scriptural sources and seeks out, by analogical reasoning, a similar case cited in the Qur'an or derived from the broader teachings. Bearing in mind the ethical and legal framework surrounding that case, the jurist (*faqīh*) uses this process to produce a 'fatwa' – a detailed legal opinion. It must be noted that such an opinion is never restrictive, unlike the rules (*ahkām*) directly drawn from the sources. In legal terms, *ijtihād* is best defined as the individual or collective effort of scholars and jurists to pro-duce a specific, new and creative legal opinion that respects the meaning of the Message. It demands the rigorous use of reason to apply requirements laid down by Revelation to new social, scientific, technological and other questions. The timelessness of the Qur'an depends on the temporal exercise of *ijtihād*: there can be no Revelation without reason.

Ijtihād, far from simply a mere Islamic legal instrument, lies at the very heart of human history. The double objective is to remain true to the principles laid down by the Qur'an and to change the world for the better. It requires an under-standing of human societies and knowledge, and the neces-sity of reform, as well as a clear vision (with its priorities) to implement that reform. As an effort to reflect upon reality, and as an exercise in rationality, the work of *ijtihād* is inti-mately linked to the place of humankind in the universe, to human freedom and human knowledge. Revelation has been given to us, and is, in terms of overriding ethical and legal principles, complete; but, using reason, human beings must undertake a two-sided double intellectual effort, a double *ijtihād*: on the one hand, focused on the Texts, when they provide latitude for interpretation, or without the Texts, while respecting the emphasis of the Message; and, on the other hand, focused upon reality, with the objective of trans-forming the world for the better. *Ijtihād*, the exercise of autonomous human ethical reasoning, stands at precisely the critical point between respect for eternal principles and the ethical imperative of making the temporal world a better place.

The Meaning of the Term 'Islam'

A glance at the work of the majority of Muslim scholars and intellectuals, not to mention that of Western scholars, might lead one to conclude that a consensus has been reached on the meaning of the word 'Islam'. That is, the word 'Islam' must be translated as 'submission', and Islam thus means 'submission to God'. It is true that Islam, unlike Judaism or Christianity, is defined not by its connection to a tribe (Judah) or a Prophet (Christ) but by an act of faith, by an attitude towards God. It would be inexact, however, to reduce it in summary fashion to 'submission'. The principal meaning of 'submission' is forfeiture, by the believer, of her or his will, liberty and autonomy. To believe in God, and to be at one with God, would thus involve a diminution, or worse, an amputation of a believer's humanity, and of her or his stature and faculties as a free being.

PEACE

However, the Message of Islam is quite precisely the opposite, and to translate the term in such a superficial way is to misunderstand its origins. The Arabic root of the word 'Islam' is *'sa-la-ma'*, which means 'peace'; one of its variants refers to the notion of 'giving oneself up' (the meaning of surrender in English), or making a 'gift of oneself'. These two definitions provide a more just, more complete and more profound idea of the notion of 'Islam'; the human being's act of faith consists of, consciously and voluntarily, a gift of her- or himself to reach peace (with God and with that self).

A Qur'anic verse expresses the experience: 'O you who have attained to faith! Enter wholly into the peace [of God]' (2:208). More than simply recognizing the existence of a Creator, the goal is to establish a relationship of confidence with God, which in turn allows the believer – who bears the precious trust of faith – to accede to the peace of God.

'Islam' can be best understood as the act of faith by which the human being sets out on a quest for peace; that peace to which God has invited the human being (summoned to respond to His call) by praying to Him and loving Him, by respecting the rituals and by pursuing what is good and what is right. Under no circumstances, then, does the human being abandon her or his will, forfeit her or his liberty or renounce her or his humanity. On the contrary, the objective is to assume fully both that humanity and its limitations, to use liberty with responsibility, and to direct one's will towards the attainment of good. Peace with God and with one's self can only be gained through intellectual and spiritual exertion, which the translation 'submission' in no way conveys.

The notion of *salām* – peace – that lies at the root of the word 'Islam' certainly constitutes Islam's supreme value as a religion. One of the names of God is 'Salām', as is one of the names of Paradise (*dar al-Salām*), while 'peace' is the very essence of the Muslim greeting *al-salām 'alaykum*: peace be upon you. The spiritual quest that gives meaning to the act of faith in God is the aspiration to peace with God, and with Creation and with oneself (*salāmah al-nafs*). Instead of demanding the 'submission' of humanity with all its negative connotations, Islam as a religion offers an invitation to draw closer to the divine, to elevate oneself, which requires of human beings that they use their intelligence and will as autonomous subjects and fully assume their liberty.

ISLAM BEFORE ISLAM

It is this attitude of mind and heart that best defines Islam: an act of faith and a way of being with God that precedes and far exceeds the advent of Islam as the ultimate monotheism that appeared with the mission of the Prophet Muhammad. The Qur'an links Islam with Abraham, the father of monotheism: 'the creed of your forefather Abraham, He named you Muslims before, and in this [Revelation]' (22:78). Muslims (pl. *muslimūn*, from the same root as *islām*) are thus those who believe in God, who give the gift of themselves to God in search of His peace. Such was God's call to Abraham:

> When his Sustainer said to him, 'Be Muslim [surrender yourself unto Me!]' (*aslim*), he answered, 'I have given myself over unto You, the Sustainer of all the worlds.' And this very thing did Abraham bequeath unto his children, and [so did] Jacob: 'O my children! Behold, God has granted you the purest faith; so do not allow death to overtake you ere you are Muslims [you have wholly given yourselves unto Him].' (2:131–2)

Clearly Islam, as an expression of an act of faith – adhering to, giving, or searching for the peace of God – far precedes the time when it was codified and became the last monotheistic religion. The roots of Islam can be found in all religions and traditions that profess belief in a one and singular God.

Many scholars have drawn a distinction between the word 'islam' as an act of faith and 'Islam', the last revealed religion, with its creed and its rituals. In fact, Islam as a religion completes and makes whole the meaning of the act of faith, which traces its beginnings back to the creation of humanity. Two Qur'anic verses specify the singular, elected role of Islam: 'Behold, the only religion in the sight of God is Islam [man's self-surrender unto Him]' (3:19) and 'if one goes in search of a religion other than Islam [self-surrender unto God], it will never be accepted' (3:85). What is recognized is the existence of a single, unique God, the act of faith as a gift of self, and the search for peace, which have been expressed throughout the history of humanity through the missions of all the Messengers and Prophets, from Adam, Noah and Abraham to Moses, Jesus and Muhammad.

All, through their Messages and the rituals of their respective religions and traditions, have extolled 'islam' understood as the giving of oneself to God, and were Muslims in the sense that they had lived in and borne witness to the peace of God. Islam, in the sense of the final revealed religion, merely confirms the basic requirement of monotheism, the essential meaning of giving and the search for peace. Thus does one of the last revealed verses express the completion of the cycle of prophecy with the final Message to humanity: 'Today have I perfected your religion for you, and have bestowed upon you My blessings, and willed that Islam [self-surrender unto Me] shall be your religion' (5:3).

Muslims understand this verse as certifying the marriage between 'islam' as an act of faith in God, and 'Islam' as the final religion, which has come to confirm and establish in its ultimate form the recognition of a single God, the hope for His peace and the reconciliation of all the preceding revealed Messages. Muhammad, with his mission, contributed nothing new to the basic articles of faith – 'Say: "I am not the first of the Messengers [an innovator]; and I do not know what will be done with me or with you" for I am nothing but a plain warner' (46:9) – but reminds us of the truth of God, and of the meaning of faith and life.

A Unique and Singular God

Islam is a strictly monotheistic religion. Its central and unifying principle, upon which the combined elements of its creed and ritual practices are founded, is known as *tawḥīd*, which means the 'uniqueness or singularity of God'. To become a Muslim, one must attest that 'there is no god but God and that Muhammad is the Messenger of God'. The two component parts of the 'attestation of faith' – called *shahādah* – are at once distinct and complementary: the first acknowledges the essential truth of the Message of all previous prophecies (the existence of one sole God), while the second accepts the Message of the last Prophet as laid out in the creed of Islam. God (Allah in Arabic, for Christians and Jews as well as Muslims) has revealed Himself to humankind; He is the Creator with Whom nothing can be associated in His transcendence and His absoluteness. A *sūrah* of the Qur'an sums up this obligation in four succinct verses, which represent symbolically, according to a prophetic tradition, one third of the Qur'anic Message: 'Say: "He is the One God: God is He on Whom all depend [the Uncaused Cause of All Being]. He begets not, and neither is He begotten; and there is nothing that could be compared with Him"' (112:1–4).

TO LIVE WITH GOD

The believer's attestation to the Oneness of God is far from passive or contemplative, for it implies acceptance of a conception of life directly connected to God, He Who is both the source of life and life's ultimate goal. Whether in the face of death, of life or of trial and tribulation, women and men who believe in God repeat: 'Verily, unto God do we belong and, verily, unto Him we shall return' (2:156). Believers are reminded never to forget the source of life that is God, towards Whom their path in life must inevitably lead following death. Life is thus a parenthesis, a pathway towards God that must be lived with full awareness of belonging to Him, and in remembrance of His presence, His grace and His compassion. Yet another *sūrah* reminds the believer: 'And I have not created the Jinns[14] and Men to any end other than that they may worship Me' (51:56). In this verse, believers are called upon to direct their full awareness and their hearts – their entire lives, in fact – to recognizing the presence of God, Whom they may address directly and without any intermediary: 'And if My servants ask you about Me, behold, I am near; I respond to the call of her or him who calls, whenever she/he calls unto Me' (2:186).

The adoration of God entails awareness of His presence but also dialogue that is expressed in prayer, and in the confidence and the assurance that God will answer whoever calls unto Him. The relationship is one of confidence, love and gratitude, those qualities that God inspired in the wise man Luqman in the Qur'an: 'And indeed, We granted wisdom unto Luqman: Thank [be grateful unto] God' (31:12). Here is confirmed the deep meaning of a relationship based on remembrance, gratitude and mutual trust: 'Therefore remember Me, and I shall remember you; and be thankful to Me, and deny Me not' (2:152).

Deep in their hearts and in a reciprocal intimacy, humans nurture and develop, above and beyond remembrance and thankfulness, a deep knowledge of the Creator: 'know that God intervenes [His knowledge] between human being and her/his heart' (8:24). In Islam, the one sole God is both transcendent and near. He reveals and hears, calls and answers, He is above all things, and in the heart of every woman and man.

THE SEARCH FOR GOD

Wisdom, in God's proximity, consists of recognizing Him, loving Him, thanking Him and aspiring to His love by seeking to know Him better, by drawing close to Him. Paradoxically, all begins with a double negation: there is no God but Him, and He is unlike everything else. 'There is nothing like unto Him, and He alone is all-hearing, all-seeing' (42:11). God cannot be defined, described, represented or spoken of beyond what He utters about Himself and His Revelation, and in the inspirations with which He gratified His Messenger. He is God, the Unique, the Merciful (*Raḥmān*); a Being of infinite Compassion (*Raḥīm*), Who possesses ninety-nine names and more, known and unknown, each one of which invites believers to draw near, in mind and heart, to His grandeur and

His grace without ever being able to reduce Him to human rationality, human logic or to our limited conception of causality.

In Islam 'theology', in the strict sense of the term – the study of the nature of God – does not exist. 'Discourse about God' is limited by and to what the scriptural sources reveal. The Divine Names (*al-asmā'*) and attributes (*al-ṣifāt*) have been the subject of learned treatises and debate, as have the absolute knowledge of God and free will, faith and reason, in what is known as *'ilm al-kalām* (literally 'the science of the word'), as discussed in 'Unity and Diversity' (p. 123). The 'science of the word' is often translated as 'theology', but in fact it primarily deals with philosophical reflection (beginning with the Qur'an and the prophetic traditions), less commonly involving strict theological considerations that are generally of secondary importance.

LIBERATION FROM POLYTHEISM

Through the study of the *tawḥīd*, the Oneness of God and through consideration of His names (*tawḥīd al-asmā'*) and Attributes (*tawḥīd al-ṣifāt*), scholars as well as believers have sought a deeper understanding of the nature and the meaning of God's gifts and His requirements in order for them to live faith to the fullest. This life of faith can best be understood as the quest to enter into nearness to Him and His love. Human beings, in this spiritual experience of the One, must free themselves of everything that prevents access to His presence and His absoluteness – there is no god but God (*tawḥīd al-ulūhiyyah*) – and of everything that is not Him (their ego, their desires, their literal or figurative 'idols' such as money and power). They do this to empty themselves and be fully inhabited by the One with Whom nothing may be associated, *tawḥīd al-rubūbiyyah*.

This spiritual experience demands much. It takes place on a personal level and without intermediaries, requiring the most intimate effort – known in Islamic terminology as *jihād al-nafs*. Believers draw closer to God as they turn inwards, liberating themselves through meditation upon His names, His gifts (the self, faith, the Cosmos, Nature, well-being, love) and upon the meaning of that existence, which leads us unfailingly to Him. It is a voyage and a spiritual pilgrimage whose only provision for the long road is the awareness and reverential love of God: *taqwā*. 'And make provision for yourselves – but, verily, the best of all provisions is God-consciousness (*taqwā*): remain, then, conscious of Me, O you who are endowed with insight' (2:197). Thus are believers summoned to Life beyond life: 'O you who have attained to faith! Respond to the call of God and His Messenger whenever they both call you unto that which will give you life' (8:24). With God, this earthly life is already transformed, before the believer enters into the Life to come.

Diversity and the Monotheistic Tradition

Islam belongs to the Abrahamic tradition of monotheism. The long succession of Prophets and Messengers, before and after Abraham, who witnessed the Oneness of God is part of 'islam' in the generic sense, and was often reiterated in Revelations throughout history. A prophetic tradition[15] relates that the total number of Messengers and Prophets exceeds 120,000 (the Qur'an mentions twenty-five), most of whom remain unknown. But all would have been bearers of the Message of divine Oneness, something of which the very first human beings would surely have been aware. Over time, in the wake of each Revelation, two phenomena would repeatedly recur: on the one hand, human beings intervened in the Texts and modified their contents to a certain extent; on the other, these same human beings forgot the teachings of primordial monotheism and slipped back into polytheism. These two historical factors explain why a new Messenger was sent at irregular intervals to remind humankind of the truth of God's presence, His Oneness, and of the meaning of life, as humankind will return to God in the afterlife. According to the Muslim tradition, monotheism came first, followed by polytheism, when the primordial truth was forgotten and corrupted at the hands of humankind.

WHY REVELATION?

The same reasoning helps us to understand Islam's relations with the two great monotheisms that preceded it. In the Islamic view, Judaism arose to remind humankind of the presence of the single God at a time when humanity was torn between polytheism – like that of the Egyptians – and the pretension of certain leaders – such as the Pharaoh – to take on the role of God themselves. But the corruption of the original monotheistic message again led to God being forgotten, which required the sending of Jesus, who would rectify the distortions of the first Message and, once more, remind the people – and not only the Jews, who were still monotheists – of the Oneness of God.

Islam, the last of the three monotheisms, can be understood in the same way, as an integral part of this cycle of prophecy: human intervention had altered the original content of Jesus' Message, and the Arabs, like many of the world's peoples, had slipped back into polytheism and forgotten the existence of a unique God. This uniqueness was precisely what the Qur'an was revealed to reiterate.

The Muslim creed (*al-'aqīdah*) affirms, as one of the six basic articles of faith (see Chapter 3, p. 89), that Muhammad is the last Messenger and Prophet to be sent to humankind. After him, learned reformers would certainly emerge from within the newly revealed religion, but they would not nor could not found an entirely new religion. Thus the historic cycle of prophecy was brought to a close by the Prophet Muhammad. The Qur'an is the last Revelation, and its Text, which is also called 'the Remembrance' – *dhikr* – was revealed without human intervention and modification. One of its verses assures that it will be forever protected from falsification: 'Behold, it is We Ourselves who have bestowed from on high, step by step, this Reminder: and, behold, it is We who shall truly guard it (from all corruption)' (15:9). Muslims understand the last Message to be definitive because of the status of the Qur'an itself: it may be understood in multiple and varying ways, or be misunderstood, but it will never be altered. In the Muslim tradition, the Qur'an is the last word of God, revealed in its entirety, and will remain the ultimate reference for all time.

JUDAISM

What are the most significant differences between Islam, Judaism and Christianity? Why, as Muslims believe, was a new Revelation needed to confirm and rectify the content of the Messages that had come before? Islamic monotheism shares many of the principles of its Judaic antecedent: God is unique and humanity must never attempt either to represent or to describe the Divinity. Majority opinion in Judaism goes further still, refusing even to utter or write the name of God. But three fundamental elements set the two religions apart.

First, Muslim tradition, seen through its scriptural sources and the work of the Muslim scholars, argues that human intervention altered the original Torah and modified significant elements of the original message. The Talmud, which expands and elaborates on the text of the Torah, is considered problematic, having been shaped by religious, political and cultural factors remote from the initial Message. The second and third elements of divergence can be traced directly to the first.

Secondly, the Torah, according to Islam, established a religion based upon an act of faith and not upon ethnic identity. An acceptance of the heart cannot be confused with or reduced to an identity founded on blood. Not all the major currents in Judaism take this position, of course. But in the course of history, most of them came to see the Judaic faith as an ethno-religious one. It was a development that came to be viewed by Muslims as one of the main distortions of humankind's connection with the Divine: a connection that must be, in Muslim eyes, an acceptance by the heart, certified and confirmed in deeds. The Muslim tradition understands Jewishness, in the religious sense, as a choice of conscience and of the heart, and not as a matter of bloodline.

The third element, which is debated in the Jewish tradition itself, is linked to the first two and focuses on understanding the notion of being favoured or 'chosen'. The Qur'an holds that the Jews were indeed favoured: 'O children of Israel! Remember those blessings of Mine with which I graced you, and how I favoured you above all other people' (2:47). This favour, or election, means that the Jews, as believers in a single God, were the bearers of the divine Message and were obliged to transmit it to humankind: by teaching, by example and by service. Here, favour must be understood in a moral sense, entailing additional responsibility in providing service to humanity. There can be no question of favour granted as a function of blood; it is rather granted as religious and moral responsibility in action. Majority interpretations of the Torah and the Talmud have tended to confer an absolute quality on the divine favour granted to bloodline and lineage; still other interpretations do not clearly take one side or another. The interpretation that states a clear position on moral favour remains a minority one that is not always heard.

Such reductive interpretations can be found in the Christian and Muslim traditions as well. The idea of divine favour through 'belief in Jesus' alone, or through the concept of 'outside the Church no salvation' can lead to similar distortions. Many Muslims feel tempted in like manner when they read the frequently repeated Qur'anic verse: 'You are indeed the best community that has ever been brought forth for mankind [insofar as] you enjoin the doing of what is right and forbid the doing of what is wrong, and you believe in God' (3:110). Here, the notion of favour flows from the condition of exemplary morality that is the visible expression of faith. However, the Muslim spiritual community can be favoured only insofar as it stands as a moral example for humanity by transmitting and teaching the Message, but above all by applying and living it. More than a few scholars and schools of thought in Islam have raised this 'favouring' to an absolute status attributable to the sole fact of being Muslim: the same temptation that can be seen in the majority view in Judaism.

CHRISTIANITY

Islam shares with Christianity the idea that faith in God, in the elevation of the human being, must be expressed by love and by nearness to Him. Islam, to slightly oversimplify matters, stands halfway between Jewish legalism and the experience of love that is central to the Christian faith. In these few pages it is not possible to detail all the points of convergence and divergence between Christianity (with its various currents) and Islam, but we can certainly point to three substantial distinctions.

The first, not surprisingly, turns on the conception of God and in particular the codification of the creed by the Trinitarian 'profession of faith' as adopted by the First Council of Nicaea in 325.

We believe in one God, the Father almighty, maker of all things visible and invisible; And in one Lord, Jesus Christ, the Son of God, begotten from the Father, only-begotten, that is, from the substance of the Father, God from God, light from light, true God from true God, begotten not made, of one substance with the Father, through Whom all things came into being, things in heaven and things on earth, Who because of us men and because of our salvation came down, and became incarnate and became man, and suffered, and rose again on the third day, and ascended to the heavens, and will come to judge the living and dead; And in the Holy Spirit.

Muslims view this idea of the Trinity and its mystery as an erroneous conception of the oneness of God, and the status of Jesus is problematic. Islam recognizes him as a Messenger and a Prophet, as was Muhammad, but numerous verses of the Qur'an vehemently reject the idea that Jesus could be the Son of God.

The second distinction centres on the conception of man: Islam rejects the notion of 'original sin', stating that each individual is alone responsible for what she or he has done. Adam and Eve shared responsibility and were pardoned, and thus every individual, woman or man, must account for her or his acts.

The third distinction – that of the status of the Church in the Roman Catholic tradition, combined with the existence of a celibate priesthood – has no equivalent in Islam.

It was in the light of these divergences that the last Revelation came to confirm the essence of faith and rectify, for Muslims, earlier interpretations considered problematic or simply mistaken.

MONOTHEISM, THE COMMON CORE

Despite these divergences, thanks to the central notion of 'the people of the Book', the common core of monotheism remains, and is respected. The teachings of Islam, as the last established monotheistic religion, make clear that the religious traditions that preceded it will continue to exist, and that the original unity of humankind, in its essence, is expressed even in the diversity of religions, civilizations, cultures, languages and nations. Diversity is the will of God, and it is incumbent upon humankind to transform it into a positive factor in its progression towards the good. This the Qur'an makes explicit in several verses:

> O men! Behold, We have created you all out of a male and a female, and have made you into nations and tribes, so that you might come to know one another. Verily, the noblest of you in the sight of God is the one who is most deeply conscious of Him. Behold, God is all-knowing, all-aware. (49:13)

As expressed in the diversity of human life on earth, the original unity of humanity, the primordial drive to monotheism, reaches into the present. There it must be grounded in and experienced as a commitment to 'mutual recognition'.[16] There can be no question of merely 'tolerating' the other, often by ignoring him. Instead, in recognition and acceptance of the divine will, humans must elevate themselves in respect for the other, which in turn implies recognition of his existence through knowledge. All attempts to impose religious belief and all forms of racism stand condemned, as these two Qur'anic verses clearly state:

> Had your Sustainer so willed, all those who live on earth
> would surely have believed, all of them; will you then
> compel people to believe? (10:99–100)

As well as: 'And among his signs is the creation of the heavens and the earth, and the diversity of your tongues and colours!' (30:22).

No form of religious or racial discrimination can be tolerated; Islam by its very nature condemns racism based on skin colour or nationality, as it condemns discrimination founded on religious identity, such as anti-Semitism, anti-Christian prejudice and, by the same token, Islamophobia. Yet another verse confirms this and invites human beings not to reject others on account of their religious identities, but to embrace a positive competition for the common benefit of humanity:

> Unto every one of you [religions, spiritual traditions] have
> We appointed a [different] Way and methodology [praxis].
> And if God had so willed, He could surely have made you
> all one single community: but [He willed it otherwise] in
> order to test you by means of what He has vouchsafed
> unto you. Compete, then, with one another in doing good
> works! Unto God you all must return; and then He will
> make you truly understand all that on which you were
> wont to differ. (5:48)

The verse concludes with an invitation to humility in judgement, for God alone has knowledge of truth and of what hearts hold secret.

The Islamic Conception of the Human Being

The idea of original sin is foreign to Islam. Human beings are born in a state of innocence, which is the determining factor of their humanity. Each human being is made up of a body into which God breathes His spirit (*rūḥ*), after which the human becomes a fully fledged being with a soul.

INNOCENCE AND *FIṬRAH*

Unlike in the Greek tradition and Christianity, which was influenced by it, in Islam neither body nor soul possesses an intrinsic moral quality. As opposed to the Socratic, Aristotelian and Christian traditions, in Islam the soul is neither intrinsically good nor evil. The soul – as the breath of the spirit in the body – and the body in its material presence are at their inception morally neutral. The human being (as body and soul) is inhabited by a multitude of aspirations, many of them contradictory. At birth, the human being is endowed with a natural disposition closely related to an aspiration to elevation, to the search for meaning and for the transcendent, an aspiration that will develop as she or he matures to attain the age of reason and self-awareness. This is the natural disposition called *fiṭrah*, and is described in the Qur'an as 'the natural disposition, which God has instilled into man: there is no changing [altering] in God's creation' (30:30). *Fiṭrah* harks back to the very origins of humanity and forms an integral part of the essential constitution of human beings:

And when your Lord brought forth their offspring from the loins of the children of Adam, He [thus] called upon them to bear witness about themselves: 'Am I not your Lord?' – to which they answered: 'Yea, indeed, we do bear witness thereto. Lest you should say on the day of resurrection: Surely we were heedless of this.' (7:172)

Thus was sealed the original pact between God and humanity, which finds its material expression in this natural disposition, this sense of attraction, this spark in the being of each individual that drives her or him to set out in search of meaning – the question 'why?' – that the Qur'an represents as the natural aspiration for the divine.

A prophetic tradition reaffirms that this disposition is a natural one, adding to it the role that it will fulfil later on, in the development of the individual, their family or society at large: 'Each child is born in a state of *fiṭrah*, then his parents make him a Jew, Christian or a Zoroastrian.'[17] All children below the age of reason are innocent and as such are guaranteed Paradise, according to another hadith that reports a dream: Muhammad saw Abraham in Paradise surrounded by his dead children, who were in a state of primordial *fiṭrah*. Surprised, they questioned him: 'Even the children of polytheists?'[18] to which he responded, 'Even the children of polytheists.' Though the polytheists denied the new religion and oppressed, tortured and killed the Muslims, their children could not be held responsible for the misdeeds of their parents. Born into a state of *fiṭrah* and dead before the age of responsibility, their innocence ensured their salvation.

NATURAL TENSIONS

Born in innocence and possessed of the natural disposition that leads them towards the search for truth and meaning, human beings are likewise torn between two contradictory aspirations: one towards good, the other towards evil. The Qur'an depicts this natural tension in several verses:

> Consider the human self, and how it is formed in accordance with what it is meant to be, and how it is imbued with moral failings as well as with consciousness of God! To a happy state shall indeed attain he who causes this [self] to grow in purity, and truly lost is he who buries it [in darkness]. (91:7–10)

Which is then confirmed by two explicit verses:

> Alluring unto man is the enjoyment of worldly desires through women [sexuality], and children, and heaped-up treasures of gold and silver, and horses of high mark, and cattle, and lands. All this may be enjoyed in the life of this world – but the most beauteous of all goals is with God. (3:14)

But at the same time, and in contradictory fashion: 'God has caused [your] faith to be dear to you, and has given it beauty in your hearts, and has made hateful to you all denial of the truth, and all iniquity, and all rebellion [against what is good]' (49:7).

Such are the two contradictory impulses that struggle within us and that grow and develop in the course of our earthly lives. They coexist in innocence until we attain the age of reason, but a change takes place when consciousness awakens, and humans become aware of the world's realities and thus assume responsibility – *mukallaf* – for the choices they make. The innate aspiration to transcendence (*fiṭrah*) is subverted by the inner tension that thrusts into contradiction two natural loves: the first, which invites human beings to remain faithful to their primary disposition and to reconcile themselves with it by a choice of conscience; and the second, which calls them to submit to their natural instincts, which will ultimately obscure, veil and stifle their original disposition, and thus shackle them to their desires and passions.

RESPONSIBILITY

This Islamic conception of the human being is, ultimately, both positive and serene. Born innocent, humans are torn by contradictory tensions. On reaching the age of reason they become responsible for seeking inner peace by choosing, in full conscience, to reconcile themselves with their original nature, while mastering their attraction to the instinctual, to the desires that pervert and, in the broadest sense, to evil. As man attested, when the original pact was concluded, that God was indeed his Lord, the conscious entrance into Islam is effected with a new attestation, the *shahādah*, which echoes that pact: 'I attest that there is no god but God.' Spoken with heart and mind, this reconciles the individual with her or his *fiṭrah* and, by recognizing God, expresses both their faith and their morale choice of the good action. It also stands for the choice of resistance to evil, resistance to the passions that tempt us through negligence and perversity. Finally, the attestation of faith (*shahādah*) is to the responsible conscience what the *fiṭrah* is to the primordial and innocent nature of every human being: an attestation renewed.

In Islam the soul and body are not evil in and of themselves. Human beings, in full awareness, must choose between good or evil with the faculty of reason, in conscience, through their intentions and in their hearts. When they overcome their naturally degrading impulses, they unchain the surging force of spirituality and of goodness that has always lain within them like a spark, an aspiration. Now, strengthened with faith, it becomes an unveiling, a light and a liberation that draws them nearer to the divine. Qur'anic terminology is here at its most revealing: a person who negates God is 'one who denies, and whose heart is veiled'. The etymological meaning of the Arabic term *kufr* is 'veiled', 'covered', 'sealed off'. The believer, who has turned her or his gaze and footsteps towards the divine, is reconciled with the original essence of her or his being on returning to God with a 'healthy heart' (*qalb salīm*: the state of original health and purity), having consciously and through reason made peace with her- or himself. This is the peace felt by children who experience their inner tensions unconsciously, and are selected to receive it because of their original innocence. The conscious adult's sense of peace will depend thenceforth on the attestation of faith and the decision to pursue the good.

Human Dignity

Human beings enjoy a particular standing within the wider construct of creation in two ways: first, by virtue of their nature and constitution, and secondly, by virtue of the role that they are destined to play on earth, between God, the universe, their fellow human beings and Nature.

KARĀMAH, OR DIGNITY

The outstanding and innate characteristic of human beings is dignity, or nobility, which the Revelation affirms in the most forceful terms: 'And, indeed, We have conferred dignity on the children of Adam' (17:70), thus defining the natural human state. Human beings will be asked to deepen and to surpass this state by virtue of the efforts they expend to educate themselves and improve themselves in the pursuit of spiritual dignity: 'Verily, the noblest of you in the sight of God is the one who is most deeply conscious of Him' (49:13).

Such is the path that the sincere believer is called upon to follow, rising up from the dignity that is her or his natural state to a higher level, where faith, conscience, conduct and self-reform will make her or him, through will and effort, more dignified still. The model to be followed is, understandably, that of the Prophet, of whom the Qur'an declares: 'Verily, in the Messenger you have the best example for everyone who looks forward (with hope and awe) to God and the Last Day, and remembers God unceasingly' (33:21) and adds: 'for, behold, you [the Messenger] keepest indeed to a sublime morality' (68:4). The quest for nobility, for spiritual dignity, can be seen in two ways: as suffused by the reverential love of God; and as reforming the self and moral conduct, striving for the nobility of character that distinguished Muhammad. For it was he who described his mission in ethical terms: 'I have only been sent to perfect good moral character.'[19] Islam,

73

then, is founded as much upon human nature as it is upon the preceding Revelations, which it has been sent to complete and to recall – confirming, as it does, knowledge and education as the noblest of virtues.

FREEDOM

To accomplish this mission through faith and education, human beings require the qualities that spring directly from dignity. The Qur'anic narrative of the origin of humanity is a singular one: God orders the Angels to prostrate themselves before Adam, the first man. How are we to explain the divine command and the superior status granted to human beings when the Angels, who are created from light and whose role is one of perpetual adoration of God, cannot be supposed to lack either dignity or morality? The Angels themselves know it and predict that upon earth humans 'will spread corruption thereon and shed blood' while they 'extol Your limitless glory, and praise You, and hallow Your name' (2:30).

Two qualities set human beings apart from the Angels. The human being is, first and foremost, free: 'Say, "The truth is from your Lord": Let him who will believe, and let him who will, reject [it]' (18:29). The Angels have no choice but to praise God, while humans are free beings who come to God by conscious choice, by a fully willed act of faith and by efforts that honour them not only by virtue of their nature, but also by virtue of the path they have chosen. Freedom is the condition – and one of the causes – of our dignity. We must accept it and make good use of it. Even though the Angels were right in saying that humankind would often make ill use of freedom, that same freedom remains the hallmark of human nobility, and even more so among those who consciously resist evil, corruption and violence.

One short *sūrah* sums up the historical depth of this teaching:

> By time in its flight! Verily, Man is bound to lose himself unless he be of those who believe and do good, and enjoin upon one another the keeping to Truth, and enjoin upon one another patience [in adversity]. (103:1)

Human beings, who are born free, will lose that same freedom if they succumb to the attractions of over-indulgence and hedonism that is also part of their nature, and which can pull them down into corruption, oppression and evil. Conversely, those who make good use of their freedom, complementing their natural dignity with ethical dignity, will distinguish themselves in history and will fully experience ultimate convergence with the divine.

KNOWLEDGE

The second hallmark of the primordial dignity of humankind is knowledge: 'And He imparted unto Adam the names of all things; then He brought them within the ken of the Angels and said: "Declare unto Me the names of these [things], if what you say is true"' (2:31). The Angels recognize their limits, but human beings, through their knowledge, possess the means by which they can manage their freedom. Only knowledge can lead to freedom; only knowledge can truly liberate humanity. Ignorance is nothing but imprisonment. In fact, the Qur'anic Revelation begins with an appeal to learn and to know, as the first chapter received by Muhammad makes plain:

> Read in the name of your Lord-Educator, who has created
> Man out of a germ-cell! Read – for your Lord is the Most
> Bountiful One who has taught (Man) the use of the pen;
> taught man what he did not know! (96:1–5)

Knowledge of names and things is characteristic of the primordial dignity of humans in their quest for truth; God has given them the means to surpass themselves in the two faculties of knowing: the mind and the heart.

As free beings granted the power of knowledge, humans must use this power to the utmost. Theirs is a privileged status, and as a consequence they must assume greater responsibility, standing as they do at the very heart of all Creation: 'Are you not aware that God has made subservient to you all that is in the heavens and all that is on earth, and has lavished upon you His blessings, both outward and inward?' (31:20).

With freedom and the faculties of knowledge that are central to their primordial dignity, humans must seek to learn, to understand themselves and the world, to favour the good and to strive for the lofty stature that best expresses their spiritual dignity. They must constantly recall that they are not the owners of the earth and the universe – 'Unto God belongs all that is in the heavens and all that is on earth' (2:283) – but simply play the role of vice-regent (khalīfah) and are accountable to God for their self-management, and that of all fellow human beings and of Nature.

These are the same principles espoused by the Native Peoples and 'First Nations' of North America and by the spiritual traditions of Asia and Africa: the earth and its lands do not belong to us, and no one can appropriate them. Pierre-Joseph Proudhon, in his critique of private property, asserts that human beings can never exercise possession over the earth, which belongs to all, but only over its enjoyment.[20] The same idea is central in the Islamic conception of humankind and Creation, and of the meaning to be given to the dignity of the former within the latter.

VICE-REGENT AND GUARDIAN

The deposit of faith has been entrusted to humankind. They must use, experience, investigate and explore it, assisted by freedom of conscience and knowledge. It is a trust that grants human beings a privileged status, but it also burdens them with a commensurately weighty responsibility. The Qur'an provides an eloquent image of this demanding and ambivalent position:

> Verily, We did offer the trust [of faith] to the heavens, and the earth, and the mountains: but they refused to bear it because they were afraid of it. Yet Man took it up – for, verily, he has always been prone to be most wicked, most foolish. (33:72)

In tandem with faith given as a trust comes vice-regency over the affairs of the world. We know, as the Angels from the beginning made clear, that humanity is far from capable of managing the world with responsibility, wisdom, humility and morality. Human beings flights of arrogance, which cause them to consider the earth as their property and theirs alone; their violent and warlike instincts, which cause them to oppress those like them and to shed blood; their blind greed, which causes them to destroy Nature and its living species – all these conspire to draw them down into the negative, to brand them with the sign of injustice and ignorance of the very values and virtues entrusted to them.

But there exists another path for those who, in bearing this trust (*amānah*), are aware of their responsibility of vice-regency before God (*khilāfah*) and among humankind. They must recover in themselves the original attraction (*fiṭrah*) of the Transcendent, freely and responsibly choosing virtue and goodness. They must acquire knowledge, educate and reform themselves in spiritual, intellectual, humane and social terms. They must add to the dignity of awareness of the good that of the natural state and thus fully assume both freedom and responsibility. Reconciliation with our most intimate hopes and dreams thus clears the way to peace with oneself. Such is the meaning of Islam as it has been developed in this chapter. In the Islamic tradition, the task cannot be accomplished except through the free and conscious decision to reconcile oneself with God, to enter into His peace, by responding to His call and to always choose the good and the moral.

Vice-regency is a long way from simply being a management of material goods that do not belong to humanity. On a far deeper level, it is a spiritual experience, a symphonic, spiritual harmony in which all the elements sing the praises of the Creator. Thus vice-regency that has fully assumed and accepted its liberty and its responsibility in the recognition of God and in its knowledge of the world is transformed into reconciliation with the universe, the world and humankind.

It ascends to another dimension in its relationship with the environment, which cannot be used without respect and cannot be abused without remorse.

The faith that has converted the heart has also led to a conversion of the intelligence by way of the heart, which sees and understands in different ways.

> The seven heavens extol His limitless glory, and the earth, and all that they contain; and there is not a single thing but extols His limitless glory and praise: but you [O Men] fail to understand the manner of their glorifying Him! (17:44)

When humans finally grasp the secret of the prayer of the natural elements, they stand at the threshold of the greater dignity whose mark is triple reconciliation – a calm and peaceful one – with God, with Self and with Nature. Peace, which lies at the root of the word 'Islam', challenges us to understand, with our hearts and minds, that we cannot protect the inherent dignity of our nature except by resisting its darker side. How? Through a permanent commitment, made in humility and determination, to making moral distinctions.

CHAPTER 3

Faith and Practice

Islam is a religion whose credo (*'aqīdah*) and ritual practices (*'ibādāt*) are particularly clear and strictly codified. A celebrated prophetic tradition considered to be of the highest authenticity reports that the Archangel Gabriel himself came to question Muhammad in order to confirm the fundamentals of Islam: the six pillars of faith (*arkān al-imān*), the five pillars of ritual practice (*arkān al-islām*), as well as sincerity and excellence in faith (*al-iḥsān*). These three central themes, along with social obligations and prohibitions, fully define Islam as a religion.

The Pillars of Faith

The prophetic tradition recounts that Gabriel asked Muhammad to tell him the contents of faith, as if to certify that the Message had been well and truly transmitted and received. Muhammad replied: 'Faith is to believe in God, His Angels, His Books, His Messengers, and in the Last Day [meeting with God], and in fate, both in its good and bad aspects.'[1] Faith, then, consists of belief in all that belongs to the order of the invisible and often the mysterious, which believers must accept in their hearts in the hope of experiencing it spiritually.

The order of presentation in the hadith, which progresses from the visible – the pillars of practice – to the invisible pillars of faith and sincerity, seems designed to make the invisible presence of God 'visible' to the human mind and heart. For the sake of clarity, this chapter begins with the pillars of faith, which in turn give the rituals of Islamic practice meaning and clarity.

GOD

The first pillar of faith is belief in God, Who is unique, Who has no associate, Who neither begets nor was He begotten and Who can neither be seen nor defined. 'There is nothing like unto Him, and He alone is all-hearing, all-seeing' (42:11). Humankind can say about God only what God has revealed of Himself. The believers must make every effort to draw closer to Him through His love and by obeying the revealed laws. The Oneness of God is the founding principle of Islam, and in terms of faith it takes the form of a meditation or an adoration that can be experienced on several levels.

First, by reflecting on God's divine names and attributes – known as *tawḥīd al-asmā' wa al-ṣifāt* – believers can draw nearer to His presence. Then, by recognizing His Being and His grace (as manifested in Creation), a gift overflowing with the signs of His infinite goodness: *tawḥīd al-rubūbiyyah*. And lastly, through a personal effort to combat all that can perturb or confuse faith in God and His oneness by associating Him with other gods or earthly motivations, such as the ego, wealth or power. These are the explicit or implicit forms of polytheism, the supreme sin – called *shirk* – from which human beings must free themselves. Such is the third form of Divine Oneness, *tawḥīd al-ulūhiyyah*.

All the other pillars of faith and ritual practice revolve around this central axis: they are either consequences of a faith in God or the means by which human beings can experience faith as it should ideally be experienced, by attaching themselves to His Being and by gaining access to the refuge of peace and security born of the gift of their selves to God. The Arabic expression *al-imān* thus means not only faith expressed by an act of 'belief in God', but its root, *a-ma-na*, evokes the idea of a place of security, of peace and of fulfilment. To believe in God thus means to enter into His peace.

THE ANGELS

The Qur'an refers frequently, as did the Prophet in his traditions, to worlds of invisible beings. Two types of beings live, act upon and interact with the lives of humans: Angels, created from light, who live in perpetual adoration of God, some of whom have specific missions within the cosmic order; and Jinns, created from flame, who may choose (like humans) to disobey divine commands – they can be beneficial or detrimental and they can assume different forms. On occasion they may even possess a human being. The second pillar of faith recognizes that the cosmos is rife with presence, with life and with energy above and beyond the purely visible elements of Creation. Angels are present in the immediate proximity of each and every human being, in our dwelling places, and in the universe, where – higher than the visible order – they participate in the symphonic chorus that proclaims the glory of God.

From this perspective, Islam is simply and eloquently reiterating what the Jewish and Christian traditions have long held with regard to the existence of Angels, beginning with Gabriel the Archangel, whose historical role has been as a transmitter of Revelations. Believers live with and in the presence of angels, two of which – the Transcribing Angel and the Angel of Death – follow and keep watch over them and exercise their distinct functions.

Believers are invited to greet the visible and invisible beings that populate the entire universe as they do their own dwellings, as in the Muslim salutation *Salām 'alaykum wa raḥmatu l-lāhi wa barakātuhu* (Peace, and God's mercy and blessings, be upon you), a greeting that can be directed towards our fellow human beings and to the Angels and the beneficent Jinns. The Angels protect, see and often inspire. The world of the invisible, either consciously or in dreams, can bring individuals closer to the meaning of life. In the lives of ordinary Muslims, as well as those of the greatest mystics, it functions as a reminder.

Jinns are a popular subject in many Muslim countries. In certain countries, conventional – and often normalized – wisdom about the Jinns reflects an obsession with evil spells and with the practice of sorcery and black magic: this dangerous superstition can lead people to abandon their real responsibilities. Not only are such practices in total opposition to the first principle of faith in a unique God with Whom nothing can be associated, but the spiritual and psychological consequences of such actions betray the aim of faith itself: to liberate humankind from false gods. By perverting the Message, such individuals shackle themselves to superstitions that render them powerless and helpless, perpetual victims of dark forces.

BOOKS

Muslims are not only called upon to believe in the final Revelation, the Qur'an, but also to recognize the Texts that preceded it: the Torah and the Gospel, of course, but also the Psalms of David, and, going back further still, the ancient scrolls (*ṣuḥuf*) of Abraham. There exist known Revelations, and other, unknown ones predating the ultimate Revelation, but the originals of all the others have either vanished or they have been modified or falsified. Faith in the Books provides believers with unique insight into sacred history in particular, and into the meaning of history in general. The Texts demonstrate that God has never abandoned humanity, and at irregular intervals He has sent Messages that remind humankind of the meaning of life, the connection with God and their eventual return to Him. His Books also make it clear that His truth is not exclusive to one religion and that the Truth (God) has been expressed in numerous ways.

The diversity of Messages over time is an invitation to the coexistence of religions in the present through recognition of a common and unique source. In recognizing the Revealed Books, human beings are reminded of their need to be guided and oriented, for reason alone cannot suffice. It can analyse the 'how' of the world but can never formulate with certainty the 'why' of life. Humans thus find themselves in constant need of meaning as conveyed by the Books. At the same time they have never been cut off from and deprived of the meaning that Revelations, throughout history, have conveyed to them. Just as the presence of the Angels deepens the sense of relationship with space, the Revealed Books lend a density of meaning to history. Ultimately, both are inextricably linked with God, Creator of space and time, Who lies infinitely beyond space and time.

MESSENGERS

The belief in Messengers is a vital pillar of the Muslim faith, and recognition of all Messengers and Prophets embraces several major teachings. The first of these is that all the Messengers were human beings who had no divine attributes and were not 'sons of God'. A large number of Prophets among the 120,000 mentioned by tradition are unknown to us, which is a good reason for caution when judging earlier religions. Twenty-five Messengers and Prophets are explicitly mentioned in the Qur'an, including those distinguished – Noah, Abraham, Moses, Jesus and Muhammad – for their patience and their perseverance: *ulū al-'azm*. Faith in their mission implies recognizing a kernel of truth, even though there might be disagreement on a certain number of principles, not to mention ritual practices and the organization of institutions. This last consideration is of capital importance: the Messengers are revered as model human beings, but in no way are they to be given sacred status or blindly venerated. They are beings that God has sent to help humans draw closer to Him. This is what Abū Bakr, the Prophet's close Companion and the first Caliph, declared upon the Prophet's death when he affirmed that those who loved Muhammad must realize that he is dead, and that only God is Living, Eternal and worthy of adoration. We must learn to love the Prophets, and particularly the last one, but without confusing the two orders: the human and the divine, the temporal and the transcendent.

Belief that Muhammad is the last of God's Messengers means that the cycle of prophecy has come to a close. Those who were to come later may well be 'friends of God' (*awliyyā' Allah*) who have risen (or were raised up) to high stature as a result of the sincerity of their spirituality. But under no circumstances can they be considered as Prophets or be sacralized. In like manner, according to a prophetic tradition, scholars will appear in every century to assist the community of believers to renew its religion: 'Verily God will raise up in this nation at the beginning of every century someone [a scholar or a group of scholars] who will renew for them their religion.'[2] Those scholars of renewal, known as *mujadiddūn*, who reshape man's understanding of the Message, carry on the work of the Messengers by breathing new life and vigour into Revelation. In the Shi'a tradition, the Imams act as interpreters and guardians of the Message. Though occasionally excessively venerated in certain social and political currents of thought, their status is never comparable to that of the Prophets.

THE LAST DAY

This life is nothing more than a passage, and death a way station. As in the other monotheistic traditions, one of the fundamentals of the Islamic belief system is the existence of an afterlife which allows human beings to return to God. Life is thus both a gift and a test in which individuals will be judged according to their intentions and actions in their lives: 'no bearer of burdens shall be made to bear another's burden. And, in time, unto your Lord you all must return' (6:164). After death, humans are buried (cremation is forbidden in

Islam) while religious tradition speaks of several stages: those questions asked of the deceased while in the grave, where they will be asked about their God, their religion and their Prophet; those punishments that may take place in the grave; the waiting period in *barzakh*, the residence of souls after death while awaiting the Last Day; and ultimately, the Day of Judgment itself, which will determine whether they enter Paradise or Hell.

For the believers, the return to God implies full awareness that they must account fully to God for the way they lived their earthly lives. The Qur'an repeats, over and over again, that what humans must hope for and know about God is this: His judgement will be at once just – for God is *al-'Adl*, justice – and merciful, for God is *al-Raḥmān*, 'the Merciful and the Compassionate'. The Islamic conception of God and of death directly influences Islam's conception of life: human beings alone are, responsible for their acts in this life, which is not the only life. Salvation depends not only upon God's justice, but also upon His mercy and His love.

Rather than leading to an obsession with the negative consequences of their faults, the Last Day should remind human beings of their limitations, and their need for God in His love and His goodness. The rigorous nature of the Day of Judgment cannot be denied; nor can His welcome, His compassion and His forgiveness be discounted. Thus the tragedy of man alone, confronted by his acts and by God, who keeps accounts (*al-Ḥassīb*), is enveloped in the comfort of hope, of 'the Merciful' and 'the Gentle' (*al-Rafīq*). Beyond the longing for paradise, the recompense of the pious and the just, that which human beings can best aspire to in the afterlife is directly linked to the love for the Divine that they have nurtured throughout their lives: that they may find themselves constantly in His presence, see Him and remain eternally in the shade of His grace.

PREDESTINATION

God is omniscient, above and beyond the past, present and future. His knowledge encompasses all things. It particularly encompasses the fate of every individual. Faith in God's will (*al-qadâ'*) and His decree (*al-qadar*) – the two notions that underlie the concept of predestination – form another pillar of the Islamic creed. This belief has three consequences that touch upon the conception of God and that of humanity. First, God stands forth as the absolute Master of knowledge and time, and His power is beyond human comprehension. Secondly, there is a difference, in absolute terms, between divine order and the rational logic of humans, who can never attain absolute knowledge. Thirdly, God, in His sovereign will and by His decree, is never absent and is always present, and hears our prayers.

For the human being, the consequences of this pillar of faith are fundamental and far-reaching, for it requires recognition of the absolute knowledge of God – and therefore of the relative knowledge of human beings – in order to approach His will and His decree with the appropriate intellectual and spiritual humility. Man must likewise remain within the human order and not attempt to place himself on the same level as God. Predestination has been the focus of much argument, particularly among the theologian-philosophers, as have been freedom, free will and determinism. Many often highly complex treatises on the subject exist among Sunni and Shi'a sources. Within the Muslim tradition can be found staunch partisans of free will, known as *qadariyyāh*, as well as ardent defenders of determinism, called *jabriyyah* or *jahmi-yyah*. Far from these philosophical debates, Sunni and Shi'a legal scholars attempted to craft a strictly religious framework for the understanding of this concept. Divergences over the fine details are numerous, but four basic common principles emerge: 1) God is all-powerful and is fully knowledgeable about human destiny; 2) human beings do not know what God knows and must avoid any attempt to fathom a divine order that lies far beyond their rational capacities; 3) free, and yet ignorant of divine will and decree, human beings must assume their freedom and accept responsibility for their actions; 4) God calls them to Him and answers their prayers, which have the power to change the course of events.

The Pillars of Islam

The same prophetic traditions quoted above contain the five pillars of Islam, the religion, those governing its rituals.

> Islam is that you should testify that there is no god [worthy of worship] except God and that Muhammad is His Messenger; that you should perform *ṣalāt* [ritual prayer], pay *zakāt* [social purifying tax], fast during [the month of] Ramadan and perform Hajj [pilgrimage] to the House [in Mecca] if you can find a way to it [or find the means for making the journey to it].[3]

The 'five pillars of Islam' are often presented in introductory works as an explanation of Islam, but they are little more than the elements of religious practice and ritual that must be examined and understood in the light of what we have already learned in Chapter 2, as well as in the first section of this chapter, concerning the pillars of faith. In the field of law and jurisprudence, they are known as the components of ritual practice, to which is also added ritual purity (*al-ṭahārah*) which is obligatory in the performance of several Islamic rites.

THE ATTESTATION OF FAITH

The attestation of faith is the first pillar and, as such, the first conscious act by which a woman or a man becomes a Muslim. As we saw in the preceding chapter, human beings in the innocence of their infancy and childhood are all – originally – 'Muslims'.[4] Through the double confession of faith (*shahādah*) they consciously become Muslims, adhering in full awareness to the principles of religion as they are called upon to practise its rituals. The first part expresses recognition of the concept fundamental to Islam; namely, the Oneness of God. The attestation of faith is complete when the individual attains full maturity with the age of reason. It requires of the believer a deepening of all the elements that we have described thus far: the six pillars of faith, which provide access to the unseen (that continues to reveal its secrets as faith deepens and grows richer), but also those requirements that touch on the status of humankind with all its dignity, its freedom and its responsibilities. Recognition of the mission of Muhammad and of his status as the last

Messenger – the second part of the *shahādah* – expresses acceptance both of the Qur'an and of the prophetic tradition in its exemplary nature. It implicitly recognizes all preceding Messages and Revelations, and enjoins believers to fully respect other traditions. They also acknowledge before humanity their attestation of the Message.

In this sense, the *shahādah* is the expression of an act of faith in God, and an act of responsibility before God and humankind. God has given life, and life has a meaning. To simply pronounce this attestation, either before two Muslim witnesses or, according to some scholars, before God alone, makes one a Muslim.[5] The formula is powerfully buttressed by the numerous teachings we have thus far described and which must not be neglected. But two dangers lurk: first, a formalism that would reduce acceptance of Islam to the simple fact of its attestation with no regard for its meaning and implications, as in the formal 'conversions' arranged for purposes of marriage. At the other extreme, minority scholars of some schools of law and jurisprudence take it upon themselves to define 'who is a Muslim and who is not' by adding conditions such as ritual practice, thus empowering themselves to excommunicate individuals (a practice known as *takfīr*). Once a person has pronounced the attestation of faith and considers her- or himself a Muslim, no one has the right to challenge that decision or to exclude or remove that person from Islam. A religious institution may rule upon actions or words as not conforming to the creed and principles of Islam, but no authority can rule upon faith and the secrets of the heart.

PRAYER

The ritual prayer (*ṣalāt*) evolved over the course of successive Revelations to Muhammad. It was then codified both in form and frequency. Muslims, irrespective of tradition or school of thought, perform five prayers daily, each one with a set number of cycles. While the Qur'an clearly mentions prayer, it is silent on the form of the rite itself. Our knowledge of the rules of prayer – content, body movement and posture, and cycles – comes to us from prophetic tradition.

The first prayer of the day – known as *fajr* or *ṣubḥ* – must be made within approximately one and a half hours before sunrise; the second, *ḍhuhr*, between the beginning and middle of the afternoon; the third, *'aṣr*, from mid-afternoon until sunset; the fourth, *maghrib*, from sunset until one and a half hours later; and the fifth, *'ishā'*, during the night, from the end of *maghrib* until the beginning of *fajr*. Shi'ites combine the second and third prayers, as well as the fourth and fifth, while the majority of Sunni schools of jurisprudence permit the practice while travelling or in exceptional circumstances.

The prayers must be performed during these set times related to the rotation of the earth on its axis: 'for all believers prayer is indeed a [sacred] duty linked to particular times [of day]' (4:103). Muslims must be disciplined and perform each prayer within the time frame assigned to it. The relationship with time is also an important element of faith: in cosmic terms, Muslims use the sun to calculate their daily prayers, and the moon for the determination of months and years. They thus integrate the two heavenly bodies by whose movement time is calculated: 'And the sun and the moon run their precise appointed courses' (55:5). The *jum'ah*[6] communal prayer is held every Friday at the beginning of the afternoon and is preceded by a sermon either in Arabic or in the vernacular of the respective country. Conversely, the two morning prayers recited on the days of *'īd al-fiṭr* (the religious holiday that marks the end of Ramadan) and *'īd al-aḍḥā* (the main religious holiday commemorating the story of Abraham and Ishmael at the end of the annual pilgrimage)[7] begin with the ritual prayer, followed by a sermon.

Ritual prayers in Islam follow a set pattern. Before beginning, worshippers must perform their ablutions, using a small quantity of clean water, and then, facing Mecca – known as the *qiblah* – carry out the number of *rak'ah* (prayer cycles) required for each of the five daily prayers. They recite passages from the Qur'an that they have memorized, each cycle beginning with the opening chapter of the Qur'an, 'al-Fātiḥah', along with a certain number of invocations. In Muslim-majority countries the call to prayer, the *azān*,[8] inviting the faithful to prepare themselves, is plainly audible to all. A second call to prayer, known as the *iqāmah*, takes place in the mosque and signifies that the prayer is about to begin.

The worshipper begins with the interjection *Allahu Akbar* – God [is] the Greatest – and follows the prescribed prayer cycle, ending with the words *salam 'alaykum wa raḥmatullah* (Peace and God's mercy be upon you) or simply *Allahu Akbar* among the Shi'a. The ritual prayer may be performed individually but congregational prayer (*jamā'ah*) in a mosque is considered twenty-seven times more praiseworthy, according to some prophetic traditions. In the mosque, no distinction by social status, colour or national origin is permitted: when Muslims form lines to pray, nothing must distinguish one from another.[9] Worshippers may also perform additional, supererogatory prayers before or after the prescribed prayer cycles, during the night (*tahajjud*) or during the night in the month of Ramadan, known as *tarawīḥ*.

This highly structured form of prayer is designed to discipline the believer in the use of time, both in relation to God and in this earthly life. Prayer turns on awareness and memory, for the principal aim is remembrance: 'and be constant in prayer, so as to remember Me' (20:14). The aim of the purifying ablutions and facing Mecca, which symbolize life turned to and directed towards God, is to remove human beings from the illusions and the ephemeral quality of life and to focus instead on spiritual elevation, on the direction that their lives should take.

As people are wont to forget, they are summoned five times daily to remind themselves of God's presence, that He is close, very close, and that He hears our prayers and He answers. To pray is to give thanks and to draw closer to God. For this simple reason, no two prayers are ever exactly alike, even though in their form they resemble one another. Sometimes, out of superficial formalism, the body prays more intently than the heart; but sometimes the heart catches a taste of the reverential love of God, investing the prayer with singular fervour. Paradoxically, habit and discipline make it more, and not less, likely that the worshipper will experience one of those instants of loving awe, known as *khushū'*. After the ritual prayer, believers may add freely worded invocations, called *du'ā'*, of their own choosing, in which they speak directly to God, supplicate and give thanks. The Prophet called these invocations 'true adoration'[10] for they concentrate the meaning of ritual prayer and the nature of each person's relationship with God: to remember Him, to thank Him and, in full humility, to recognize our need of Him.

ZAKĀT

The term *zakāt* is often translated as 'obligatory alms', by way of summing up its dual function: a gift given in solidarity as well as a legal prescription. In fact, *zakāt* is the obligatory payment, by every woman and man who is able, designed to spiritually purify the believer's possessions, and to be handed over to the poor who have a 'recognized right' to it, as stated in the Qur'an: 'and in whose possessions there is a due share' (70:24). Bearing in mind this prescription, *zakāt* should be described as a 'social purifying tax', for it is indeed a tax, an obligation that, in addition, possesses a spiritual virtue in that it purifies the property of the believers, just as prayer purifies their hearts, with the goal of social solidarity based on the 'rights of the poor'.

Just as prayer functions on a vertical axis, towards God, but also has a horizontal, social or community dimension expressed in the congregational prayer, so too does *zakāt* link an individual act – handing over a portion of one's worldly goods – to the social imperative of solidarity and justice. Having established the limit of their basic needs – *nissāb* – in accordance with the time and the place, women and men must contribute on an annual basis a certain percentage of their assets (2.5 per cent of their wealth, 5 or 10 per cent of their harvest). They may contribute this to government-run philanthropic institutions or independent charities, or give it directly to the needy.

The underlying principle of this tax is not to maintain people in a state of dependency. It must be paid to the needy (defined according to eight categories set down in the Qur'an) in one's immediate neighbourhood, which means that one must have a thorough knowledge of one's own community in order to identify them. The ultimate objective is to give the needy the means to lift themselves out of their situation, by supporting projects that encourage financial autonomy, and that will ultimately enable them to pay *zakāt* as well. The underlying philosophy of *zakāt* is thus to create a well-regulated social solidarity mechanism that allows the poor to obtain their due in full recognition of their human dignity. In so doing, its recipients should be able to attain self-sufficiency in food supply and financial autonomy.

Proper management of the 'purifying social tax' cannot be restricted to the distribution of charity. It requires a thorough knowledge of the diverse local and national systems of social solidarity, whether state-run or institutional, to organize effective distribution of *zakāt* to complement existing programmes, and above all to free the poor from their status as recipients of social assistance. It must be paid as such, with the intention that it will be used to this end, and the amount of the payment must be pre-determined. Even though other income taxes paid to the state also provide for social solidarity, they can never truly take the place of *zakāt*. *Zakāt*, according to a majority of legal scholars both in the Sunni and Shi'a traditions, must be directed to needy

Muslims, except in exceptional circumstances. Other scholars have maintained that all the poor in a given area are eligible, whether or not they are Muslims (providing the needs of the Muslims have been met). Alongside *zakāt* there also exists another form of donation, *al-ṣadaqah*, which can be paid at any time according to ability and disposition, to any persons, Muslims or not; scholars agree that such donations can be paid to all.

This third pillar of Islam is vitally important and opens up a deeper understanding of the Message of Islam. With God, the believers must nurture their awareness of both the poor on their doorstep and the Cosmos that surrounds them. Faith is an awakening of the senses, of the eyes and of the heart. But it also implies a rigorous sense of justice towards our fellow human beings through a strict and prescribed obligation: justice with regard to Creation, which must be protected, alongside justice towards human beings, who must be respected, be they rich or poor. Just as prayer must be established wherever Muslims settle, the rights of the poor must be immediately recognized wherever a community exists. Faith – in its practical aspect – thus becomes a double responsibility, ecological and humane, out of respect for the natural order created by God, and in a spirit of reform for the human social order that has engendered poverty and slavery. For this order must be transformed, by restoring to each and every one the right to social and financial liberty and independence.

FASTING

The fourth pillar of Islam is fasting during the month of Ramadan, the ninth month of the Muslim lunar calendar. The fast perpetuates and confirms the practice of all religions and spiritual traditions prior to Islam: 'Fasting is ordained for you as it was ordained for those before you, so that you might remain conscious of God' (2:183). Fasting has a threefold function: spiritual, physiological and social. For Muslims, the fast consists of not eating, drinking or engaging in sexual relations during the daylight hours for either twenty-nine or thirty days. It is obligatory from the age of puberty onwards, but pregnant women, the elderly or the sick may be dispensed from the fast, which they can either make up later if they are able, or offer compensation by providing food to the poor. It lasts from approximately one and one and a half hours before sunrise (the beginning of the *fajr* prayer) until sunset (the beginning of the *maghrib* prayer).

The Muslim liturgical year is a lunar one and lasts 355 or 356 days, meaning that for each solar year the fasting month moves forward by ten, eleven or twelve days. Depending on the season and the latitude, a fasting day may last from nine to nineteen or twenty hours. In regions such as the far north, where the sun never truly sets, or in winter, where it never truly rises, legal scholars are unanimous that the fast should correspond to the nearest country in which there is a true sunrise and sunset.

The spiritual virtue of the fast is fundamental. By ceasing to fulfil his or her natural and human needs – food, drink, sexuality – the individual, exercising self-mastery and discipline, turns inwards, towards the heart, and seeks to draw as close as possible to the Divine and to the spiritual breath within. Against all shapes and forms of dependency and the temptation of mass consumption, the fast stands as an experience of liberation from egotism and possessiveness. It signifies a sharp break with life's daily routine, and with the natural rhythms of the body, and invites humankind to introspection, meditation and generosity. For this is the other dimension of the fast, in which the believer draws near to the poor, the disenfranchised and the downtrodden of society. According to one prophetic tradition, the Prophet was a model of constant generosity, but never more than during the month of Ramadan.

The month of Ramadan consists not only of concern for oneself but, in the same spiritual impulse, of giving of what one possesses. To draw closer to God through fasting is to draw closer to the poor by giving. As the days and nights of the month are blessed days and nights, the faithful are called upon to accompany their fast with close attention to their vocabulary, their emotions and their behaviour, and to avoid conflict and contentiousness. Daily reading of the Qur'an and supererogatory prayers and rituals are another hallmark of the fast and qualify as recommended practices. Notable among these are the *tarawīḥ* prayers, which are offered after the five daily prayers and during which the entire Qur'an is frequently recited, in the course of eight-, ten- or twenty-prayer cycles, depending on the school of law and jurisprudence.

On one of the five last odd-numbered nights of the month, the 'Night of Destiny or Power' (*laylah al-Qadr*), Muslims are enjoined to vigilance as they search for spiritual meaning. The spiritual density of that night is incomparable:

it is worth more than 'one thousand months' according to the Qur'an and stands as a moment of intense communion and expiation, of *salām* – 'Peace' – that lasts the entire night. Most mosques celebrate it the twenty-seventh night (that of the twenty-sixth day); but prophetic tradition is indeterminate. Some Muslims make a retreat in the mosques, called *i'tikāf*, during the last ten days to fast, pray, read the Qur'an and, following in the tradition of the Prophet, await the 'Night of Power'. Finally, at the end of the month, Muslims pay the *zakāt al-fiṭr*, the special purifying tax that marks the end of the fast and that is handed over to the poor, extending the action and meaning of the fast. It must be paid before the prayer of *'Īd al-Fiṭr*, one of the two festive days of the Islamic calendar.

Today, heated debate often surrounds the exact timing of the beginning of Ramadan. Some believe that the new moon must be sighted by the naked eye in one's region in order for the fast to begin; others hold that once it has been sighted in one country by the naked eye, all the world's Muslims should follow; still others believe that 'the eye' was the only means available at the time, but that with technical progress and new astronomical knowledge, the beginning of the month can be calculated with a high level of certainty, which would in turn eliminate today's sharp divergences between countries and groups as to the true beginning of Ramadan.

More pernicious still is the emergence of a strictly formalistic approach to fasting, which consists of mastering one's appetites during the day and then gorging during the night, as if all were permitted. The entire month is blessed – both its days and nights – and it is thus incumbent upon believers to exercise self-control and to struggle against impulsive behaviour, but it has now been transformed into a month of hyper-consumption, with night-time behaviour that totally contradicts the original meaning of Ramadan. In Muslim-majority societies, for example in Africa, Asia and the West, the supermarket chains have caught on and now stock their shelves with 'Ramadan products', while the media and the entertainment industry march along in lockstep with their 'Ramadan nights'. For some, the month of self-control and meditation becomes one of conspicuous consumption and entertainment. When Muhammad warned 'Many people who fast get nothing from their fast except hunger and thirst',[11] he was referring to those who respected its form but lost its meaning and spirit.

PILGRIMAGE

The pillars of Islam regulate time: the attestation of faith is pronounced and renewed at every moment; the ritual prayers are held daily; Friday prayer is weekly; the Ramadan fast is annual, as is the compilation and payment of *zakāt*. The pilgrimage (Hajj) must be performed once in a lifetime by everyone who has the means to do so. It takes place each year between the eighth and twelfth day of *Dhū al-ḥijjah*, the twelfth month of the Islamic calendar (see p. 271). Both women and men are summoned to travel to Mecca and there accomplish a certain number of rites. Prior to those rites, pilgrims place themselves in a state of ritual purity. They perform the major ablutions and don a pilgrim's garb: a length of unsewn cloth for men and sewn clothing for women covering the body and the hair, but, imperatively, leaving the face uncovered, according to the consensus of all the schools of law and jurisprudence. In this state, known as *iḥrām*, pilgrims must not cut their hair, their nails, engage in sexual relations or kill any living being.

Upon arrival in Mecca, the pilgrims begin by walking in an anti-clockwise direction seven times around the Kaabah, the great empty cube draped with black fabric that stands at the centre of the sacred precinct. Then they hasten between *al-Ṣafā* and *al-Marwa*, two symbolic hills some 400 metres apart, in remembrance of the desperate efforts of Hajar, the mother of Ishmael, who ran to and fro between them in search of water after being left there by Abraham. They drink the pure water from the spring of Zamzam, which symbolizes the source of water that saved Hajar and her son. Then the pilgrims head for Mina, several kilometres from the city, where they spend the afternoon and night resting. On the morning of the ninth day of *Dhū al-ḥijjah*, they make their way to Mount Arafat, where they spend the day in prayer and invocation until sunset. It was here that the Prophet delivered his farewell sermon at the end of his one and only pilgrimage. After sunset, the pilgrims move to another station, *al-Mudhdalifah*, where they remain until darkness falls. They then return to Mina and after gathering small pebbles, symbolically stone the devil, who had attempted to convince Abraham to disobey God by refusing the command to sacrifice his son Ishmael.

Finally, the pilgrims sacrifice a sheep symbolizing Abraham's acceptance of God's will, or pay the equivalent to specialized services: the meat of the animal must either be eaten or distributed to the poor. They then return to Mecca to circle the Kaabah seven times as a farewell, before leaving their state of ritual purity. At that moment, it is recommended that men shave their heads and that women snip off a lock of hair. Thus ends the major pilgrimage. It is followed by four days of festivities known as *'Īd al-aḍḥā*, the greatest festival of the Islamic calendar.

The pilgrimage is intimately linked to the story and the memory of Abraham, the father of monotheism, from which the Muslim tradition has directly sprung (sacrificing his beloved son for the sake of God's love). Pilgrims are encouraged to offer a special prayer at the place known as the 'station of Abraham' (*maqām Ibrahīm*) where he had invoked his Lord. Seen through its rites, the pilgrimage is rich in teachings. The dress worn by pilgrims is emblematic of their state of poverty, for they are clad in the simplest fashion and in perfect equality before God. Women and men from around the world, of all national origins, colours and social levels, converge upon Mecca to remember the trial of Abraham, 'the friend of God', and to raise themselves up spiritually. Once more, we can see in the rites of pilgrimage the vertical (return to God) and horizontal (a spiritual community of women and men equal before God) axes that remind us of how complementary the two dimensions are. To return, alone, to God through the pilgrimage means implicitly never to detach oneself from the community of destiny that binds humans together in equality, fraternity, solidarity and love.

The pilgrimage is also an implicit departure, a process of cutting oneself loose from earthly bonds to return to the essentials and one's heart. In this way the pilgrimage echoes the voyage towards oneself, for its purpose is to draw nearer to God, Who 'intervenes [and whose knowledge is] between man and his heart' (8:24). Or, as the Revelation reminds us, 'take a provision [with you] for the journey, but the best of provisions is God's consciousness [reverential love for God]' (2:187). At its deepest level, as the mystical traditions so often remind us, the pilgrimage represents the spiritual life that can be satisfied with nothing less than the search for God, through detaching oneself from the world and drawing nearer to God, step by step, through the prescribed rites, through effort and discipline, through His love and for His love.

The second, minor, pilgrimage – the 'Umrah – can be performed at any time during the year and includes the performance, while in a state of ritual purity, of the first two rites of the Hajj – circling the Kaaba and hastening between the symbolic hills of al-Ṣafā and al-Marwa. The 'Umrah is not compulsory, but it is highly recommended.

More than two million Muslims converge on Mecca every year to perform the pilgrimage with unflagging spiritual intensity. However, the facilities for welcoming the pilgrims and the infrastructures built up around the Kaabah have had a negative impact on two of the most important dimensions of the pilgrimage. Equality in deprivation has been undermined by the construction of luxury hotels for the wealthy overlooking the sanctuary of the Kaabah, and by privileged access accorded to the rich and the powerful. Worse, concentrations of luxury shops, American-style malls with their vast areas given over to conspicuous consumption, from jewellery and top-of-the-line clothing to fast-food restaurants, now surround the sacred precinct, where human beings are supposed to be liberated from their possessions and thus freed to experience a spiritual reawakening. The spirit of the

Hajj remains, but it is being increasingly stifled by urban development and by mismanagement on the part of the state authorities.

Social Affairs (*Al-mu'āmalāt*)

Al-mu'āmalāt covers matters of interpersonal relations and of wider social affairs, including behaviour, private and public relations, transactions, politics, finance and economy. In each of these fields, obligations, prohibitions and recommendations can be located in the scriptural sources. Together they constitute the second major domain of Islamic law and jurisprudence, the first being, as we have seen, that of ritual practice. Legal scholars specializing in the principles of law and jurisprudence (*uṣūliyyūn*) and jurisprudence have established five categories for morally and legally classifying the totality of human acts: an act may be obligatory (*wājib*), recommended (*mustaḥab*), detestable (*makrūh*), forbidden (*ḥarām*) or simply permitted (*mubāḥ*), with no particular moral or legal qualification, such as the acts of eating, drinking, etc. In social affairs, the first and unanimously recognized principle is that of permission: to either make obligatory or forbid a given action, an explicit textual reference drawn from the scriptural sources is necessary.

OBLIGATIONS: MODESTY, THE HEADSCARF, HALAL MEAT[12]

Ritual practice aside, there exists in Islam a certain number of obligations and recommendations touching on some of the finer details of life as well as more important situations. In dealing with these questions it is imperative to take into consideration the nature of the Texts being cited – in terms of authenticity, clarity and interpretative leeway – and likewise to classify them. Can a given case be considered as an imperative (*ḍarūriyyāt*), a need (*ḥājiyyāt*), or an embellishment (*taḥsiniyyāt*)? Returning a greeting in Islam is an obligation, but would be classed as an embellishment and not an imperative. It is impossible to extrapolate such classifications, which are based on numerous, specific criteria, from a superficial reading of the sources.

For men and for women, modesty is an essential obligation in Islam. Though it can be categorized as a need (second category), it illuminates all the teachings of religion. The first objective is to guard the body, to protect it from the gaze of others, a stricture that applies to men as well as women. The message conveyed to all is: the worth of my being is to be measured by my heart and not by my body. What is visible by no means reveals the value of my inner life. Moreover, the same message forms a part of an even more fundamental teaching: modesty tells us that there is a value superior to the visible; human beings should not, then, expose themselves thoughtlessly, indecently or arrogantly. Spirituality is intrinsically modest; it summons us to a modesty that is not merely physical, but intellectual and emotional as well.

It is not a matter of revealing nothing, of closing off and stifling ourselves. Instead, the question is to know how, where and to whom we reveal ourselves, share ourselves and offer ourselves. The paradox of immodesty is that we end up smothered and even imprisoned by the gaze of those to whom we show too much. To respect the obligation of intellectual, emotional and physical modesty is to choose freedom in our interactions with others, their gaze and their judgement, for spirituality is itself an exercise in intellectual humility. We must carefully keep our emotions to ourselves and at the same time avoid the excessive exposure of our bodies. The two cannot be separated and should be seen as a unified whole, as a way of being in the world that defines freedom through an intimate relationship with ourselves, one in which our conscience guides us in deciding, with discernment and with humility, what we may offer to others, to ourselves and to our innermost being.

Among the prescriptions most widely discussed today is that of the headscarf (*khimār*), which women above the age of puberty use to cover their hair and breasts. Based on Qur'anic verses, as interpreted by both Sunni and Shi'a legal scholars, the practice is indeed an Islamic prescription.

But three cautionary remarks are in order.

First, according to these same scholars, this prescription is not one of the imperatives or among the most important priorities of practice. Instead, it falls into the second category, as a *need,* or – even more rarely – into the third category of obligations, an *embellishment*. A Muslim woman must, first, attend to the essential elements of faith: ritual practice – prayer, *zakāt*, fasting – good conduct and virtuous action, and not begin with the headscarf while neglecting the fundamentals. As she grows spiritually, she will come to view the headscarf as the fulfilment, and not as the condition, of her faith and practice.

Secondly, the subject has been so hotly debated in a variety of tension-ridden and conflicted cultural, political and social situations – yesterday under colonialism, today under the pressure of globalization, and in several countries in the West – that certain scholars have turned priorities upside down and transformed it into a primary obligation, a marker of identity in reaction to hostile surroundings. But the order of prescriptions, even though it has to be seen in context, cannot be idly reversed. An obligation that belongs to a secondary category cannot be changed arbitrarily into an essential or primary one.

Thirdly, as with every act of faith, to wear the headscarf must be a personal choice made with full and conscious consent. A woman must be free to wear the headscarf, or not. No one – be it the state, the community or the family – can force it upon her. Whatever our interpretation, the most just of positions, both from the Islamic standpoint and that of human rights, is that which is based on principle. No one can oblige a woman to wear a headscarf, and no one can force her to remove it.

As to the *niqāb* (veil covering the face), a tiny minority of scholars consider it an Islamic obligation. The majority thinks it was a specific requirement for the Prophet's wives. Today it is only promoted by the more literalist and traditionalist trends such as the *salafī*, often called *wahhabī*, or the Taliban.

Much has been written and spoken about the obligation to consume only 'halal meat'. In Islamic tradition, animals must be slaughtered in a specific manner after a specific invocation, *Bismillah, Allahu Akbar* – 'In the name of God, God [is] the Greatest' – has been pronounced over them, attesting that only when the divine authority has permitted the killing of the animal can its meat be eaten. The animal must be alive at the moment of its slaughter, which problematizes the slaughterhouse practice of stunning, as in these situations the animal is often dead before its throat can be cut. The ritual is codified, and the conditions governing it, clear-cut.

The obligation to eat halal meat, as with many such obligations, should be properly located in the second category of obligations; for some scholars, and according to the context, it should even belong to the third. Scholars are far from unanimous about whether Muslims can consume the meat of those that follow one of the Abrahamic religions – the 'People of the Book'. Most agree that the meat of the Jews, who follow a very strict ritual, is fit for consumption, but opinions are sharply divided over meat produced by Christians. Is there such a thing as a Christian slaughter ritual? How should we regard industrial slaughterhouses? Do modern-day meat production techniques and technology retain even an iota of religious (Christian) reference? Does the fact that an animal has not been sacrificed for anyone or anything other than God make it halal – lawful – for Muslims? What constitutes halal is clearly a subject of controversy. For some, and paradoxically for a majority of literalists (*salafī*), the meat of the 'People of the Book', in its broadest sense, is halal, while for others only meat slaughtered according to Islamic principles will count.

Around the world, but primarily in the West, a substantial number of Muslim organizations have emerged to administer and perform ritual slaughter. With varying degrees of success, these enterprises track animals from the farm gate to ensure traceability, verifying at every step that the rites have been respected, down to the final product stamped 'halal'. There are, however, problems with this approach, many of which are related to the excesses of consumption described earlier. The almost exclusive focus on the technical aspects of the rite of slaughter has all but obscured its deeper meaning. An animal can only be killed with God's permission. Islamic tradition insists on respect for the living animal whose flesh is to be consumed, which in turn implies paying particular attention to its feeding and grazing conditions, while absolutely avoiding causing it to suffer.

Consideration for the well-being of animals and care to avoid causing them to suffer, which the Islamic tradition teaches and requires through a multitude of textual sources, should lead to a reform of industrial cattle-raising practices. What, today, is more halal – to consume the flesh of an animal bred in spiritual and ethical respect of its life and well-being, and without causing it to suffer, or that of an animal outrageously maltreated but technically slaughtered according to the Islamic rite? Most contemporary legal scholars, demonstrating a lack of ethical coherence, would rapidly – and unfortunately – choose the second option. Halal meat has become, for some Muslims, a priority. Though they may well neglect most of the rituals of their religion and display permissive and sometimes unscrupulous behaviour, the meat they eat is 'halal'.

Once again, this formalism is diametrically at odds with the spiritual essence of Islam, which links the destiny of humanity with the meaning of its rites and with virtuous conduct. Human beings instinctively understand that the lack of respect for Nature and for animals is a direct offence against their own dignity and belief. Ultimately, the authorization to consume meat must be linked with the struggle against excess in one's personal and collective behaviour. Given the current world order and the industrial mode of production, how much better would it be for Muslims to eat less meat and to actively diversify their food sources.

PROHIBITIONS: ALCOHOL, DRUGS, PORK, INTEREST / USURY

As we have seen for the Islamic obligations, there exists a classification of prohibitions that should always be taken into account. At the highest level, we find *al-kabā'ir* (the cardinal sins: idolatry, sorcery, murder, non-respect of parents, theft of an orphan's goods, false witness, calumny, and the like) to be distinguished from all the other sins.

Alcohol, as we have seen (pp. 39–40), was gradually prohibited in the Qur'an, in three stages. The ultimate reason (*ratio legis*) for this prohibition derives clearly from the fact that alcohol can impair one's intellectual and moral faculties and that to permit it makes it difficult to impose a collective sense of restraint. The prohibition of alcohol is clear-cut in all the Sunni and Shi'a schools of law and jurisprudence. If, however, in the event of circumstances beyond one's control (threat to survival, illness, etc.) one must drink alcohol in order to avoid death, to do so would not only be authorized but obligatory, as protection of life is an imperative obligation (*ḍarūriyyāt*). The prohibition of alcohol falls into a category below that of the cardinal sins. In no way can compliance take precedence over the protection of life.

Drawing on the events and situations described in the

Qur'an, legal scholars have sought to deal with new circumstances by using reasoning by analogy, called *qiyās*. Drugs, which are not mentioned in the Qur'an, have been considered as illicit (*ḥarām*) because they produce exactly the same effects as alcohol. In small quantities, they may be useful to health but, taken in excess, they can cause a loss of lucidity, create dependence and have a negative impact on physical and intellectual health. They are thus forbidden, even though some scholars display caution with regard to drugs deeply embedded in local culture, such as the mildly narcotic leaves known as 'qat' in Yemen. Taken with medical prescription, under proper control and to promote healing, drugs may be consumed according to the same principles governing alcohol.

Cigarette smoking has also been the source of lively debate. Despite being injurious to health, smoking does not lead to intoxication; as a result, a large number of legal scholars have ruled it 'detestable' while not forbidding it. Others, evaluating its extremely adverse effect on individual and public health, have deemed it illicit, drawing on the letter, the spirit and the objectives of the Message of Islam.

The prohibition against consumption of pork is clear in the Qur'an and is unanimously recognized by all schools of law. But the principle of necessity to ensure survival applies here as well. Some scholars have attempted to explain the prohibition rationally and scientifically – the nature of the animal, of its meat, of its symbolism – while still others justify it by Qur'anic references alone, which need not be demonstrated rationally. Such are the terms of the long-running debate between the advocates of reason – the *mu'tazilah*, the *matūrīdī* and certain *ash'arī* – and still other *ash'arī* thinkers who reject rational justification in explaining divine injunction as discussed above on p. 125. Modern-day literalists – the Salafī – have adopted a similar outlook to some of the *ash'arī*.

In Islam, the notion of *ribā* covers interest, usury and speculation; that is, whenever money earns money or produces profit without commercial mediation over an object that is either bought or sold. In the latter case, profit is permitted if ethical and contractual rules are respected, while interest, usury and speculation are operations in which money, which can do nothing else than facilitate the transaction, produces money and thus distorts the ultimate goal of commerce. A Qur'anic verse stipulates: 'God has made buying and selling lawful and interest/usury unlawful' (2:275), going on to add that those who gain profit from *ribā* will be 'at war with God and His Messenger' (2:279). A minority of scholars has called into question the definition of *ribā* and its understanding in contemporary economic theory. But for the immense majority of scholars, the prohibition is clear and based upon an economic philosophy that recognizes the right to profit through commerce, all the while emphasizing that economic activity must serve humankind. Furthermore, money can only be produced by actual labour or by an exchange whose terms must be just, equitable and transparent. Such a philosophy is fundamentally opposed to the neoliberal and capitalist economy: economic activity must be reconsidered in the context of its ultimate goals.

In light of this economic philosophy and its directives, numerous organizations, such as 'Islamic banks' and 'Islamic investment funds', have come into being. The stated intention of 'Islamic economy and finance' is to avoid interest and speculation. A host of interesting projects have been launched, with alternative approaches being proposed in certain sectors at the local level, including the use of participatory loans or micro-credit. However, on closer examination of such projects, which are only a first step, it becomes apparent that the concern to avoid *ribā* at all costs has had a perverse impact.

For example, while procedures may be called by different names and interest may be disguised as 'administrative fees', great attention may be paid to the way in which the transaction – now 'Islamized' – is carried out, but no questions are asked about its ultimate goals. Thus the purpose, the efficacy and the success of the 'Islamic economy' as currently imagined would be to be just as profitable as the capitalist system by using other means, which would technically be 'halal'. But as we have seen, in Islam the search for profit is overridden by a philosophy whose primary concerns include respect for human dignity, for the environment, for justice and equality. 'Islamic' economy and finance, whose only purpose is to Islamize the means and the practices of the dominant economic system, which is driven by profit alone with absolutely no ethical regulation, is as dangerous a perversion as the pursuit of interest. Much remains to be accomplished if these contradictions are to be overcome.

APPLYING THE RULES: THE CRIMINAL CODE, APOSTASY, BEARING WITNESS, INHERITANCE

In the Qur'an and the prophetic traditions we find a certain number of Texts whose formulation (*qaṭ'ī*) is clear enough to justify direct and literal application. But we have also seen as

with *ijtihad* (p. 48) that the clarity with which a rule is formulated is not in itself sufficient reason for immediate application. Its *raison d'être* (*ratio legis, 'illah*) and objectives
must first be determined, and the context in which it is applied
must be evaluated. This procedure can be described as a
double *ijtihād* – impinging on both Text and context, even
though the Text itself may seem to offer no margin for interpretation in its apparent explicitness. To apply literally a
clear text with regard to formulating a legal opinion, in
a troubled environment and without taking the state of
society into account, may well be contrary to the very meaning of the rule.

It comes as no surprise that the Texts governing the
Islamic criminal code (*ḥudūd*) require a threefold work of
exegesis, analysis and juridical investigation: what precisely
do the Texts say, taking into consideration their *raison d'être*
and their ultimate goals? What are the conditions (*shurūṭ*)
necessary for their application? In what social and political
context are these rules applicable to begin with? The Qur'an
and the prophetic traditions contain Texts that speak of the
death penalty, of corporal punishments, stoning and the like.
Some are explicit, such as those dealing with thieves: 'As for
the man who steals and the woman who steals, cut off the
hand of either of them in requital for what they have wrought'
(5:38). Not only must this Text be explained and analysed,
beginning with the definition of 'thief', but contextual circumstances should also be considered. For example, it is well
known that 'Umar ibn al-Khattâb, the second Caliph, sus-
pended the penalty in times of drought and famine, for its
literal application would be unjust and in contradiction with

the overall meaning of the Islamic Message (and to the objective of this regulation in particular). Even if certain literalists and traditionalists – joined by political 'religious' extremist groups – reject the idea of contextualization based on the *raison d'être* of a rule, its conditions and objectives, it is clear that the majority of schools of thought in Islam are opposed to the literal application of such texts. Some, even though they hold minority positions, take a clear-cut stance rejecting the death penalty, corporal punishments and stoning.

Prophetic traditions – and not the Qur'an – also speak of apostasy (*al-riddah*) in two Texts. In one, the Prophet is said to have stated: 'Whoever changes his religion, kill him', while the second makes licit the blood of 'one who forsakes his religion and separates from the community'.[13] Over the years, a majority of scholars have held that the sentence for apostasy is death. However, as early as the eighth century, other scholars, as exemplified by the Iraqi jurist Sufyan al-Thawri (d. 778), have expressed a contrasting opinion based on a contextualized analysis of these apparently explicit references. In the first tradition, the chain of transmitters of the Prophet's words (see p. 45) is dubious, as one of them is considered not to be trustworthy. Many have also pointed out contradictions between the two prophetic traditions, especially when they are taken out of context, and the Qur'an and the attitude of the Prophet.

The crux of the issue, in fact, is that these sayings pertain to individuals who, in the midst of hostilities, entered into Islam to glean information and then went over to the enemy, therefore 'separating' themselves from the community. Such individuals were in fact 'traitors' to whom the death sentence could be applied; the second of the two traditions may well refer precisely to such a case. Against majority opinion, several scholars have critically analysed the Texts, placed them in a historical perspective and compared them with the Qur'an, which declares that there can be 'no compulsion in religion' (2:256), and finally with the attitude of the Prophet himself, who never executed a woman or a man for changing religion. They concluded that an individual who changes her or his religion may not be executed, and that she or he must be free to choose.

Extensive commentary has been devoted to certain other rules, such as that governing the legal testimony of men and women. A verse of the Qur'an indicates that two men are required, or if there are not two men, 'a man and two women' (2:282). Exegetes and legal scholars have interpreted this verse (called 'the debt') in several ways, from the most patriarchal to the most sexist: woman, they have concluded, is worth less than man, has less intellectual capacity, is more emotive, is less competent in juridical terms, to name but a few sexist interpretations. A minority of others have succeeded in freeing themselves somewhat from the grip of patriarchal culture, insisting that this particular verse must be understood in light of the Message itself, and of the role that the Qur'an and Muhammad assigned to women. Indeed, women had social and political responsibilities, they pledged allegiance to the Prophet as men did, they followed his teachings as men did and had the right to keep their names, to choose their husbands and to preserve their financial autonomy.

The sexist interpretations we have just described totally

contradict the Message taken as a whole. At issue is the competence and the experience of women who were not actively involved in the economic life and business transactions of their time. In such a case, and only in such a case – where competence and experience are absent – can the requirement of two female witnesses be understood and explained. But as a general rule, the testimony of a woman is equal to that of a man (as is the case in the Qur'an itself (4:6–9), in a situation of mutual accusation between a couple), which must be the rule in daily life, in any professional undertaking or in the courtroom, where a woman can testify and, more specifically, act as a judge or a lawyer.

A full grasp of the context is no less vital in matters of inheritance. The Qur'an has many, very specific $\bar{a}y\bar{a}t$ touching on this subject. Several real-life situations are mentioned, when the heirs are direct daughters and sons, or where other beneficiaries are involved, such as the mother, the father and the family as a whole. Much is made of direct inheritance, in which the daughter receives only one half of the son's share, while there are numerous circumstances in which, when an inheritance is portioned out, the woman receives more than the man.

An inheritance is apportioned according to a very specific conception of the family and the respective role of the man, who must provide for his family's needs and of the woman, who must by rights be provided for. A man who receives twice the inheritance of a woman must spend it for his own well-being and that of his family, while the woman receives her share for herself, and no one, neither her husband nor her family, can oblige her to account for it. These shares are comprehensible and fair in theory, but what happens when, in real life, a woman is not provided for by her family, or when she is divorced and sometimes abandoned with dependent children? Some scholars prefer to avoid these issues and, in the name of textual clarity, apply the rule literally. They declare that it is not the Texts that must be changed, but the conduct of husbands who fail to respect their duties. While scholars agree on this last point, it is also essential to consider the weight of the context – men may occasionally be the victims – and avoid literal applications that would betray the *raison d'être* and the objectives of the rule, namely a proportioned distribution by role, by duties and by rights. Real-life application of the rule (*tanzīl*) requires devising a mode of application that preserves the spirit and the objective but does not create any additional injustice or hardship for women. It might well take the form of a compensation paid to female heirs by the local public authority in cases where the woman has not been provided for, or within the family itself, on a case-by-case basis, depending on the attitude of the brothers to fulfil their responsibility to provide for the needs of their sisters out of the inheritance received. In the event of the men's failure to provide what is due to the women, the apportioned shares must be adjusted on a case-by-case basis to preserve the *raison d'être* and the objective of the inheritance, which is to ensure that women are provided for and their welfare preserved.

Unity and Diversity: Interpretations of Faith

Islam's unity arises from the fact that Muslims, be they Sunni, Shi'a or Ibadi, and of whatever culture – Arab, African, Asiatic or Western – or trend of thought – literalist, traditionalist, reformer, mystic – agree on the fundamental principles of their religion: the oneness of God, its scriptural sources, and the creed. They also agree on its ritual practices and its essential obligations and prohibitions. Yet this unity of principles also produce a multitude of interpretations and affiliations. Divergences as to the meaning of the Message appeared as early as the succession of the Prophet. The issues at stake were not strictly political; already, in the background, loomed differences in the understanding of a certain number of Islamic principles. What role should religion play, who had authority over religious doctrine and over political power, what degree of prominence should be accorded to the community of believers and, finally, how could one or the other position be justified in the scriptural sources? Those who were later to become Sunnis and Shi'as – not to mention the Kharijites and the Ibadi – rapidly came into conflict, and their differences continue. Each of the great traditions – Sunni and Shi'a – would witness a multiplication of its schools of law and jurisprudence (each of which employed different methodologies), its schools of thought (philosophical, theological-philosophical, mystical) and its religious trends.

SCHOOLS OF LAW AND JURISPRUDENCE (*MADHHAB*)

Early on, the Sunni were to develop schools of law and juris-prudence centred on the scholars and jurists (*fuqahā'*) who taught their students specific methods for deriving rules related to rituals or social affairs from the scriptural sources. These jurists were certainly not aware at the time that they were founding a school of law and jurisprudence and may not even have wished to do so. Over time, at least eighteen such schools came into being among the Sunni alone; of these, only four survived: the Mālikī, the Ḥanafī, the Shāfi'ī and the Ḥanbalī. There exists today a new school of law and jurispru-dence that rejects all the preceding ones and seeks, following in the footsteps of the earliest generations – the *salaf* – to return directly to the Qur'an and the Sunna: its followers style themselves *salafī*. Their disagreements lie primarily in the methodology of the rules' extraction from the Texts, the classification of the scriptural sources and, of course, in the interpretation of certain Qur'anic verses relating to ritual practice and prescriptions.

The same phenomenon can be observed among the Shi'as, where two levels may be observed with regard to schools of law and jurisprudence. The first covers the known schools of the Twelvers (who think there were twelve imams to follow after the Messenger), the Seveners (Ismaili), the Zaydi, the Alawi, the Alevi and Khaysani. In certain ways, each can be seen as a school of law and jurisprudence with distinct meth-odologies that often include differing currents. The Zaydi, who nowadays are largely found in Yemen, are closer to the Sunni schools, and certain scholars hold that they should be considered a fifth Sunni school. The Twelvers, who today represent the majority of Shi'as, are not unified, and though Ja'farism (following the teachings of the sixth Shi'ī imam Ja'far al-Sadiq, d. 765) became the official school in Iran following the 1979 revolution, other schools exist and differ in their methodology and interpretation of the Texts. Three currents that differ on the status of the Text and of reason can be identified: the Akhbārī, who give priority to the Text and are considered the most traditionalist; the Uṣūli, who recognize the validity of human reason; and finally the Shaykhī, who seek to return to the scriptural sources and stand for a more literalist approach. The same phenomenon can be observed among the Seveners – Nizari, Druze, Mustali – who use different criteria of interpretation and have developed different understandings of authority: that of the Texts or of the scholars.

SCHOOLS OF THOUGHT

Not only did these divergent traditions witness a multiplication of schools of law and jurisprudence, distinct schools of thought were to emerge among both Sunni and Shi'a, and have a substantial impact on the development of Muslim thought in general. While the jurists insist that the Qur'an and the prophetic traditions are the ultimate sources of law, later thinkers around the eighth century were to focus their attention on questions that preceded these sources: what is the status of the Qur'an, or that of faith, of reason, of freedom and of free will? Intense debate was to develop, derived for the most part from 'the science of the word' (*'ilm al-kalām*, see below), but extending to theology and philosophy as well. The theologian-philosophers were divided on the relative places to be assigned to the Qur'an and to reason in determining what is good and bad, for instance. Three main schools of thought soon appeared: the rationalists (known as *mu'tazilah*), the partisans of the Texts as the ultimate reference (*ash'arī*), and those who held an intermediary position (*matūrīdī*). The debates they kindled then (between the eighth and the thirteenth centuries) remain highly pertinent today.

The theologian-philosophers stood apart from the philosophers (*falāsifah*) who were powerfully influenced by Greek thought and who, from philosophers such as al-Kindi to al-Farabi, and from Avicenna to Averroës, propounded an approach that drew upon neo-Platonic and Aristotelian sources, all the while referring to Islam.

Innumerable mystical circles (*taṣawwuf*) appeared and spread around the world from the ninth century and have persisted down to the present day, each with its own spiritual masters, its specificities, its methods of initiation. Those who followed the mystical path, the Sufis, developed their own schools of thought, but also formed a broad and diffuse movement. Neither specifically Sunni nor Shi'a, these schools cut across religious boundaries, emphasizing one or another of the traits specific to a particular tradition or school of law and jurisprudence. The controversy they created touched on philosophical and theological-philosophical questions such as freedom, autonomy and responsibility. Mysticism, whose dominant concern is the reform, the purification and the liberation of the self, even raised the question of the ultimate goal of the Message of Islam. All the Muslim traditions without exception have experienced and are still fraught with these intense, critical and often sharp debates.

CURRENTS AND TRENDS

Another area of diversity that allows us to gain a better understanding of the attitudes of Sunni and Shi'a to the Texts and to history still remains. Muslims are often classified as 'moderates' and 'fundamentalists'. This is not only simplistic, but also objectively untrue. In fact we can identify, among both Sunni and Shi'a, no fewer than five major trends: 1) the literalists, who read the sources without any historical contextualization and grant little leeway to reason; 2) the traditionalists, who follow a specific school of law and jurisprudence and who hold that all that needs to be said has been said by the scholars of old; 3) the reformists, who refer to the Texts and believe that the Muslims must reshape their understanding by the use of independent reason and science; 4) the rationalists, who affirm that reason must take priority over the authority of the Texts, and whose approach is quite secular; 5) and the mystics who add to the reading of the mind that of the heart and find hidden meaning that will purify and liberate the self.

This cursory list of currents and trends does not span the entire spectrum. But these five currents do cover the main forms of interpretation of both the Texts and of reality itself. They are also strongly influential on different political positions, though we must not be too hasty in identifying connections and affiliations that have no basis in reality. The history of religions in general, and that of Islam in particular, illustrates that religious attitudes towards scripture do not necessarily determine political attitudes towards human beings: a liberal here may very well prove an autocrat there. Political and religious attitudes must not be confused; it is entirely possible to be a liberal or a mystic and support dictatorial or repressive political regimes. Similarly, one may be a literalist or a traditionalist – though this is less frequent – and a defender of democracy. We must never rush to conclusions.

THE FORMATION OF THE 'ISLAMIC SCIENCES'

There are many disciplines called 'Islamic sciences' (*'ulūm islāmiyyah*) because they refer to areas linked to the study of the Islamic scriptural sources or determined religious topics (rules, ethics, mystics, etc.). These sciences have their own areas and specific methodologies, and require a high degree of specialization by the scholars (*'ulamā'*, same roots as *'ulūm*). Their birth, their relationship and the evolution of their respective authority – in determining what is right from an Islamic perspective – are critical when we try to understand Islamic civilization and its internal dynamics with regard to the production, the structure and the hierarchy of knowledge.

The schools of law and jurisprudence emerged from the eighth century onwards and went on to establish the first science to be termed Islamic. Ja'far al-Sadiq (d. 765), recognized as the sixth Imam in the Shi'a tradition, was considered as a great scholar by the Sunnis. He was also the master of the two influential scholars Abu Hanifa (d. 767) and Malik ibn Anas (d. 795), in whose names the first two schools of Sunni law and jurisprudence were established, along with the Shafi'i and Hanbali schools, all of which have also survived down to the present day.

The aim of this science (*fiqh*) was to extract from the

Qur'an and the hadith the body of fundamental principles and rules related to the Muslim creed, ritual practices and, more broadly, to social affairs, transactions and interpersonal relations (in an independent way and far from the influence of the state). Legal opinions (*fatāwā*) were produced that could be applied when the Texts are open to several interpretations as a result of the way they are formulated, the vocabulary employed or the circumstances in which they were enunciated – or, more simply, when the scriptural sources are silent. Over time, yet another science was to arise out of the need to regulate the methods of extracting these rules: the 'science of the fundamentals of law and jurisprudence' – *'ilm uṣūl al-fiqh* – which, as its name indicates, precedes *fiqh*, or law, even though its codification came later. Several scholars had noted that the proliferation of multiple, sometimes contradictory legal opinions had no clear methodological basis; this they sought to correct. The Shi'a believe that the first scholar to establish this science formally was Ja'far al-Sadiq, while the Sunnis attribute its invention to Imam Shafi'i (d. 820). *Fiqh* would go on to become the mother science with which the science of the fundamentals would be naturally associated. It has remained so to this day, and the religious authority of the jurists (*fuqahā'*) stands as the authority of reference (among all the other Islamic sciences) in both Sunni and Shi'a Islam.

Other sciences were to emerge with the passage of time. Two of them – that of the Qur'an (*'ulūm al-Qur'ān*) and of the hadith (*ulūm al-ḥadīth*) – focus on the scriptural sources of Islam. The science of the creed (*'aqīdah*) deals with the six pillars of faith. The theologian-philosophers were likewise concerned with the fundamentals of the creed, but touched on broader philosophical questions, such as faith, reason, liberty and free will. Yet another science would address conduct and, more broadly, ethics (*'ilm al-akhlāq*), even though the subject and recognition of its primacy overlapped the fields of law and jurisprudence and theology-philosophy. A last science, called the 'science of hearts' (*'ilm al-qulūb*) and best known as Sufism, corresponds to Muslim mysticism. Figure 3.1 illustrates the typology and classification of the Islamic sciences.

The Islamic sciences were built up on the basis of unanimously recognized scriptural sources and, with the passage of time, in response to the need for further explanation and to historical circumstances, such as new social, political or scientific challenges. There is a unity and coherence between its respective fields, even if doubts do exist about the legitimacy of some of the sciences,[14] and the whole area of scripture-based knowledge is covered.

Over time, however, this categorization produced several negative effects, as specialization led to fragmentation of knowledge. Specialized scholars did not always possess a global understanding of the questions and the challenges that faced them, a tendency that was amplified by the progressive closing-off of law and jurisprudence from the exact, experimental and life sciences. The science of fundamentals does deal with the knowledge of the world – its cultures, historical periods and sciences – but the specialization of legal scholars and the growing complexity of the information available gradually led to a rift between the sciences that grew progressively wider. The primacy of law

AL-QUR'ĀN ——— **AL-ḤADĪTH**

'ULŪM AL-QUR'ĀN
(Sciences of the Qur'an)
Meccan and Medinan revelations; occasions of revelation; abrogation; etc. One may include among these sciences exegesis (Tafsīr), as well as styles and rules of recitation (tajwīd).

AL-SHARĪ'AH
General concept of the Creation, of existence, of death, and of way of life, derived from normative reading and understanding of the scriptural sources.

'ULŪM AL-ḤADĪTH (Sciences of the Hadith)
Compilation about the transmitters and authentication of the routes of transmission (isnād), together with study and analysis of the content (matn). Degrees of authenticity (ṣaḥīḥ ḍa 'īf etc.) Necessarily dependent on study and analysis of the life of the Prophet (sīrah).

'ILM AL-KALĀM
(Islamic theology-philosophy)
Study of the relationship between Revelation and reason, freedom, morality, the numerous common themes with al-falsafah inspired by the Greek.

'ILM AL 'AQĪDAH
(Science of the creed)
Study of tawhīd (Oneness of God), the names and attributes of God, the Angels, the Prophets, the Books, Destiny, the Day of Judgement.

UṢŪL AL-FIQH
(Principles of law and jurisprudence)
Foundations of Islamic Law. It expounds the principles and methodology by means of which the rules of law and jurisprudence are deduced and extracted from their sources. Study and formulation of the rules of interpretation, of prescription and prohibition, of general principles (ijtihād, ijmā', qiyās), etc.

FIQH (law and jurisprudence)
Study of Islamic Law and jurisprudence presented in two fields.
1. fiqh al-'ibādāt (rites / modes of worship): Study of the rules related to ritual purification, prayer, zakāt, fasting, pilgrimage.
2. fiqh al-mu'āmalāt (other than formal worship): Study of the rules in respect of collective affairs: legislation, commerce, marriage, inheritance, etc.

'ILM AL-AKHLĀQ
(Morals, ethics)
Study of individual behaviour in relationship with God, one's self, the family, neighbours, and society in general.

AL-TAṢAWWUF
(Sufism)
Study of the mystic's path, the respective stages and states of the inward journey towards God.

3.1 Typology and Traditional Classification of the Islamic Sciences and jurisprudence in the hierarchy of the Islamic sciences led to a top-heavy emphasis on rules and norms, increasingly remote from any consideration of meaning and ultimate goals. A kind of formalism set in, and with it came an obsession with protecting oneself from, or adapting to, the dangers of the day, without being able to contribute to the positive transformation of the world.[15] And yet here lies the essence of Revelation: to believe in God is to choose the good, the beneficial and the beautiful; to transform oneself and to transform the world.

Spirituality and Ethics

In the prophetic tradition mentioned at the beginning of this chapter is embedded a third notion, one that Muhammad himself elucidated: that of *al-iḥsān*, generosity, sincerity or excellence in faith. When asked about its meaning, he replied: 'It is that you should serve God as though you could see Him, for though you cannot see Him yet [know that] He sees you.'[16] This definition has in turn generated innumerable commentaries, some of which underline God's presence and watchful gaze (one cannot escape God's gaze) and others His continuous presence (the search for God in all things at every moment). The two approaches are not contradictory, but the second carries the deeper spiritual meaning: through sincerity towards God, in adoration and love, the believer attains the state of the heart that feels and 'sees' His presence intensely, above and beyond time spent in ritual practice.

RULES AND THEIR MEANING

In looking closely at this tradition, we observe a progression from the visible identifying marks of faith – its rituals – to the invisible foundations – the pillars – until we reach an inner state in which the heart attaches itself to God and lives in nearness to Him. Then we can better grasp the meaning of rule and ritual: as a discipline imposed upon human beings in order that they might struggle against forgetfulness and negligence and ultimately develop a new awareness of the divine. Rules and regulations must never be spoken of outside of this perspective lest we fall into the kind of formalism that ignores their significance and ultimate goal.

Such is the literalism of some legal scholars, and their obsession with rules and regulations, that they have reduced Muhammad's response to the question of sincerity and excellence to the idea that God is constantly alert to the believers' faults, and that He monitors every weakness, every transgression, every lapse, warping both the essence and the meaning of rules and ritual. Firstly, according to the literalists, the cardinal virtue of rules and regulations lies in the limits they set down and not in the arc of spiritual progression that they define and point to. Secondly, such an approach fosters feelings of guilt and transgression and encourages a relationship with God based on fear of error and not confidence in divine acceptance. Yet the Texts say nothing of the kind, and the way the verses are arranged, as the third step in a progression, leads us to understand the meaning and the means of spiritual elevation.

Discipline is a vital consideration, which explains and justifies the imperative necessity of the five pillars of Islam, with their strict rules governing time, space, conditions to be respected and bodily movements to be made in a constant vertical relationship with God and in a horizontal relationship with humanity. Paradoxically, this same discipline guides believers onto the path of liberation, giving them the means to abandon their egos and to escape the prison of their ignorance and forgetfulness, in order to enter into the world of the heart, the spirit, the invisible, and the meaning of life itself. Rules and regulations are not an ultimate goal. They are a means and a condition by which humanity is uplifted and drawn closer to God. Ultimate sincerity and true excellence lie in feeling not like an accused in His presence, but as a being who has been called (has not God called all humankind to Him?) and who has been expected (did not the attestation of faith imply this ultimate destination?).

A prophetic tradition marvellously sums up this teaching:

> Whoever shows enmity to one of my beloved [friends], I shall be at war with him. My servant draws not near to Me with anything more loved by Me than the religious duties I have enjoined upon her/him, and My servant continues to draw near to me with supererogatory works so that I shall love him. When I love him I am his hearing with which he hears, his seeing with which he sees, his hand with which he strikes and his foot with which he walks. Were he to ask something of Me, I would surely give it to him, and were he to ask Me for refuge, I would surely grant him it.[17]

In a relationship of confidence and security with God, he who draws near is a 'friend of God' (*walī*). This is in turn one of the meanings of the word *imān*, most often translated as 'faith'. It begins with the ritual prescriptions, obligations and prohibitions, then is increased by the supererogatory acts that are not obligations but the conditions under which we can draw near to God. Only then does the believer enter into the love of God and, when God loves her/him, his eyes, her/his ears, her/his hands and her/his feet perform their functions through the spiritual mediation of His presence. Generosity then takes on an entirely new density; it becomes both the centre and the summit of the spiritual experience. Did not the Prophet often invoke God in these words: 'O God! I ask You for Your love and the love for her/him who loves You and the love for deeds that lead closer to Your love.'[18] Love is the ultimate hope, a love that has no reality except through sincere actions, and the love of good deeds.

SUFISM AND MYSTICISM

Early in the history of Islam, women and men sought out the ultimate goals of their religion by drawing nearer to God and His love [to love Him and to be loved by Him]. The scholar Hasan al-Basri (d. 728) speaks of removal from the world and from the sorrow of life; of hope for nearness to God. His search foreshadows that of the celebrated female mystic Rabi'a al-'Adawiyya (d. 793), who desires to act for the love of God alone, and not in the hope of paradise or the fear of hell.

The search for God through love does not give us from a dispensation respect for rituals and rules, but rather makes us see these as means and conditions. There is no place in their outlook for the formalism that sees rules alone as a justification for faith. A verse from the Qur'an points to this difference, addressing the tribes of the Arabian desert who had accepted Islam: 'The Bedouin say, "We have attained to faith." Say [unto them, O Muhammad]: "You have not (yet) attained to faith; you should (rather) say, 'We have submitted [outwardly]'– for [true] faith has not yet entered your hearts"' (49:14). For the ultimate goal is to live one's faith with the heart. Islam has designed a 'Way' – called *shari'ah* – and a set of practices – known as *minhāj* – to reach that goal and thus to become closer to God.

The beliefs and practices of the original mystics, known as *zuhhād*, who favoured asceticism to concentrate exclusively on the love of God, gradually became diversified and institutionalized, either as circles, called *ṭuruq* (sing. *ṭarīqah*), or other local structures (*ribāṭ, khanaqah, zawiyah*), which often developed national and even international branches. Each of these circles was to develop its own methodology of stages, levels and stations – *marātib, maqāmāt* – through which the *murīd*, the initiate, must pass in his effort to draw near to God and to experience the intense spiritual states (*aḥwāl*) that are the gifts of God.

Sufi teachings are diverse, but all of them share several features: the ultimate goal of faith in God is His love; ritual and action are necessary as ways of liberating the self but are not at all the ultimate goal. Raising oneself upwards towards God requires teaching, initiation and passage through a succession of stages – often presented as a journey, to symbolize the act of pilgrimage. Finally, faith must be visible through action, through good conduct and virtue, which outwardly demonstrate the spiritual evolution of the believer seeking initiation. Mystics in the Muslim tradition have placed the greatest emphasis on good conduct, morality and ethics, and on the following triangular relationship: respect for ritual and rules must lead to a change in conduct; reform of one's conduct must clarify the ultimate goal of ritual; and finally the two – ritual respected and conduct reformed – open the door to the fulfilment and the spiritual elevation of the believer, who draws near to God, sets free her/his ego and fulfils His love. Beyond the diversity of schools, sects and denominations, this is the message that lies at the heart of Islam.

There are innumerable mystical schools around the world. Some of them have remained faithful to tradition; others have become immoderate, either by trying so hard to distance themselves from obsessive legalism that they have come to neglect the rules entirely or by laying too much emphasis on elements that have led to divergence from the requirements of faith. Some mystical schools, ancient ones as well as some from the recent past, are both serious and rigorous, and preserve and perpetuate the original mystical teaching tradition. Others revere their guides or spiritual masters as near-infallible or near-perfect beings, blindly venerated as though they were gods or saints – though to revere any other being besides God is a deviation. The prescribed rituals of Islam are often neglected in favour of other practices (invoking the dead, sanctifying tombs, etc.) that could be considered, in the Islamic creed, as reprehensible innovations, known in Islamic legal terms as *bida'*. Like literalism or legalism, Sufism has been beset by excesses that have undermined it. Not surprisingly, certain schools have been politically exploited for purposes that are hardly mystical.

Four criteria define a mystical circle that respects Muslim

tradition: 1) the basic rituals and rules of Islam are respected while, consistent with prophetic tradition, other practices can be added but not subtracted; 2) the guide or master helps the initiate draw closer to God, and not to himself through the kind of veneration that would lend him a dangerously sacred aura; 3) the Sufi circle is not in the service of any regime or political power and clearly preserves its independence; and 4) the institution does not accept money from its members for non-transparent reasons (as when only the guide and his entourage profit, accumulating wealth and living a life of luxury while calling upon the faithful to turn their backs on worldly goods).

Such excesses do happen and can be seen in different Sufi groups around the world. But that fact alone is not enough to weaken, let alone destroy, the credibility of the ancient Sufi tradition, which has continued to remind all Muslims that rules cannot be applied unless they are understood, that fear of God and guilt provide no guarantee of spiritual elevation and, finally, that confident self-reform represents the path of salvation and happiness.

FAITH AND ETHICS

One of the earliest Islamic sciences was that known as *'ilm al ahklāq*, the science of ethics, which concerned itself primarily with moral values and good conduct. By its very nature, it impinged on all the other Islamic sciences; those to do with the creed, law, mysticism and so on. Ethics, however, were gradually downgraded and ended up present everywhere but visible nowhere. Nevertheless ethics came to play an essential role in establishing the essential linkages between studies of the creed, of law and jurisprudence and of mysticism. The human being, as we explained in the previous chapter, is characterized by primordial dignity. The model is Muhammad himself, he of 'the highest morality', who was sent to humanity 'to perfect good moral character'.

The rules of Islamic practice are designed to allow individuals to reform their conduct, to make it more noble and virtuous. To reform behaviour, through introspection and the conscious choice of the good – the touchstone of the mystical tradition – is to draw closer to God and to experience spiritual elevation. In sum, we can say that ethics – understood as proper conduct – is the ultimate *goal* of the rules and the *means* of spirituality in general, and mysticism in particular.

At once both ends and means, values and good conduct constantly oblige us to consider the ultimate meaning and superior goals of religious practice. This way we can avoid both legal formalism and the fragmentation of actions and sciences, which are in danger of forgetting their common purpose: to serve God and humanity.

Early scholars turned their attention to the ethical behaviour that flows from religious practice, for the Qur'an speaks of Muslims in terms of a combination of faith and action: 'those who believe and do good deeds' (95:6). Numerous treatises have been written on virtuous acts (and their classification) and on sins, both major and minor, in an attempt to categorize values and actions. With the passage of time, ethics came increasingly to be applied to other fields of knowledge and the sciences. For if these fields are to be of use to humanity, it is of crucial importance to define ethical behaviour for scholars and practitioners alike, be they scientists, physicians, economists, architects or artists. What are the ethical means and ends specific to each field? In the fields of medicine and bioethics, Muslim scholars and practitioners have extensively investigated such issues as abortion, euthanasia, cloning, genomics and the like. The same holds true for economics, finance, the environment, the human sciences and the arts; although in these fields, the research has been somewhat fragmented and remains in an embryonic state.

Our perspective, of course, broadens as we move from the strict rules of ritual practice to the higher objectives of human action and activity. Each stage in this process entails different approaches, means and conditions, but we must never lose sight of the coherent whole and must guard against the two dangers pointed to above: the formalism of ritual practice devoid of intelligence and virtue and the utilitarian fragmentation of knowledge and sciences 'without conscience', and thus bereft of responsibility.

ETHICS AND RECONCILIATION

No single Arabic term fully conveys the word 'spirituality'. Three notions are often combined to express the idea: *rūḥānī*, that which animates the breath, the spirit, or that which lies within; *rabbānī*, that which is ripe with God's presence; and finally *tazkiyah*, the purification of the self and the ego in order to draw closer to God. In light of what we have learned in this chapter, we can better understand the meaning of expressions such as 'bringing alive the breath within', 'causing the heart to overflow' or undertaking 'the purification of one's being' for the liberation of the self.

Ultimately, they direct us to 'be with God as though you

see Him', which is the definition of *al-iḥsān*, the qualities of sincerity and excellence. To apply these qualities in life, the human conscience must continually question itself about the meaning and the ultimate goals of its being and its acts. For spirituality does not mean withdrawing from the world in the search for meaning. Quite the contrary, it means preserving meaning and recognizing it everywhere in the world around us. The breath that animates us and the presence of God in the lives of every woman and man are given new life by the perpetual search for meaning, whether in solitude or in public, whether at prayer or at work, be one a scientist or an artist, a manual worker or an intellectual. But the ultimate goal must always be the good, service to humanity and respect for Creation – all of them ways in which we give thanks to God and honour our human dignity.

These are the questions – of values, of meaning, of virtuous conduct all linked directly to ethics – that can help bring together ritual with all its rules, action in all its forms, and knowledge in all its fields. They lend substance to spirituality and ensure that it will never become something ethereal, removed from the world, but will instead be intelligent, active, demanding and courageous. It must be intelligent, for its task is to grasp the intellectual and scientific challenges of the age; it must be active, in order to have a practical impact on both knowledge and respect for humanity and for Nature; it must be demanding, for a permanent awareness of God 'as if you see him' requires constant effort and commitment; finally, it must be courageous, for it dares to stand against inhumanity and excess, and dares to denounce the folly of humans and their powers.

In the Muslim tradition it is difficult to imagine spirituality without its religious underpinnings, for they form the very condition of its existence and the means through which it can be attained. The definition of full spirituality is this: to look for meaning in all things and to be permanently aware of higher objectives (*maqāsid*) at all time, everywhere and in all things. There can be no other way to protect religion – and all knowledge – from being exploited for political, economic, militaristic and expansionist ends.

Without a principle of reconciliation between faith in God, ritual, knowledge and human action, there can be no 'Way', no coherence, no centre, only a universe stripped bare of meaning, with fragmented, compartmentalized, utilitarian knowledge, where all truth has been deconstructed and relativized. Faith in God would no longer have any substance and, without a 'Way', all around us would be disarray and meaninglessness – literally and in every sense of the word.

The Way

The preceding chapters have reviewed the fundamental tenets, the pillars and the rules that govern Islam. Taken together, they set out a framework, comprising the underlying concepts (God, humankind and religion), the pillars and the meaning of faith, and practices (rituals, obligations and prohibitions). But Islam can also be understood as a path to be followed – a Way – with higher objectives. It is here, in fact, that all the teachings of Islam find their coherence.

The source and point of departure is the oneness of God, humanity and its link with the divine. Rules and laws lay down the limits of the path to be followed. The final destination, of which we must be acutely aware, imparts meaning to everything. In Islam, the notion of *sharī'ah* literally expresses the idea of the Way through which we make sense of life and death, the necessity of *jihād*, and give direction to education, to social relations, and to our relationship with Nature.

Sharia

Sharia is one of the commonest, but worst defined and most misunderstood terms used today, not only by Muslims themselves, but also by virtually everyone who enters into contact with it. In the mass media and in broader public perception, it is often conflated with the brutal and literalist application of a criminal code whose provisions include cutting off the hands of thieves, stoning men and women adulterers to death, imposing corporal punishments and liberally applying the death penalty.

Nothing, however, could be further from Islam's founding Texts. The word 'sharia' itself has been interpreted and defined in a wide variety of ways by scholars in different areas of specialization. For some of them, in the light of the Qur'an, sharia is exactly synonymous with Islam. For others, it refers specifically to the entire body of rules and regulations, while for others it is defined above all by its objectives and represents the philosophy of life drawn from the scriptural sources themselves.

IN THE TEXTS

The literal meaning of the word 'sharia' is 'the way that leads to a source of water' and, by extension, 'the path to be followed'. For the path that leads to water in a desert is the path of survival and salvation. The word appears three times in the Qur'an: once as *sharī'ah* and twice in related forms, *sha-ra-'a* and *shir'atan*. Read in the specific contexts of the *āyāt* in which they appear, we can understand why the term can be taken to mean several things. In the first instance, we read:

> And, finally, We have set you on a way (*sharī'ah*) by which the purpose [of faith] may be fulfilled: so follow this [way], and follow not the errant desires of those who do not know [the truth]. (45:18)

The verb *ittabi'*, which follows the term sharia, means 'to follow' (*ta-ba-'a*) and refers directly to a Way to be followed, which several scholars were to associate with Islam itself.

In another *āyah* we read:

> Judge, then, between the followers of earlier Revelation in accordance with what God has bestowed from on high, and do not follow their errant views, forsaking the truth that has come unto you. Unto every one of you We appointed a [different] Way and methodology [praxis]. And if God had so willed, He could surely have made you all a single community. (5:48)

Once again the word 'follow' appears with the notion of sharia; here, in the form *shir'atan*, the word can mean the Way, but could also refer to a theoretical frame of reference, as distinct from the method and the practice of ritual and good conduct. The third and final occurrence gives the root of the verb form:

> In matters of faith he has ordained (*shara'a*) for you that which he enjoined upon Noah and into which We gave you insight through Revelation – as well as that which we had enjoined upon Abraham, and Moses, and Jesus: Steadfastly uphold the [true] faith and do not break up your unity therein. (42:13)

Here, the Qur'an moves beyond the final Revelation, referring to the great guiding principles shared by the succession of monotheistic religions. The imperative was to follow that Way, and that Way alone, when establishing religion.

In reading these three verses, we understand why it is important to pay close attention to etymology, for in them the word 'sharia' clearly refers to the Way to be followed in order to aspire to salvation: the way of fidelity to the Source. A more holistic understanding, one that associates sharia with Islam itself or with its philosophy, referring as it does to the religions that preceded it, is equally justified. Finally, the legal aspect, which evokes a prescriptive framework and a set of rules, can in no way be discounted. What it is impossible to do, however, is to reduce sharia to a criminal code and to its literal application.

AMONG THE JURISTS

Scholars specializing in law and jurisprudence, as might be expected, defined sharia according to their own field of study. For them, the Way was first and foremost legal, with its eternal and immutable fundamental principles, the rules that govern the creed and ritual practice, likewise immutable, and, finally the prescriptive obligations and prohibitions that were to be followed and applied to different eras and cultures. In their reading, sharia could be presented as 'divine law' insofar as it comprised Islam's fundamental legal framework and principles. (A similar phenomenon can be observed in Judaism with regard to the *halakha*, which etymologically means 'way, path' and which came to mean 'Jewish law'.)

Extracted from the scriptural sources, these principles and rules represent the raw material of Revelation in matters of law. Rapidly, scholars were obliged to organize this raw material into a coherent system drawn from the Texts and faithful to their general thrust. So it was that sharia came to be seen as the framework – the organized Way – of the immutable principles and fundamental laws of Islam: in short, as its legal philosophy.

The jurists distinguished this fundamental reference from the practical work of applying rules and principles in daily life. The latter required law and jurisprudence, the translation – the descent (*tanzīl*) – of these overarching principles into the business of reality. Some prescriptions – particularly in relation to the creed, the rituals and certain obligations and prohibitions – were to be applied as they were transmitted, while others necessitated a process of interpretation of both the Texts and real-world circumstances. The role of human reflection and interpretation was substantial. Both were inevitably influenced by the socio-cultural context in which the legal scholars carried out their work. By virtue of its very nature, and because new situations continue to arise, the task of application is also one of perpetual renewal, in the light of ongoing evolution. This is where *ijtihād* (see p. 48) is necessary and makes full sense of the scriptural sources.

Historically, the narrow understanding of sharia as a body of law has led to three problems. The first, unavoidably, saw the Way, in all its breadth, reduced to 'the Law', with all its restrictions. By focusing on the organization of fundamental principles and rules and their concrete application in daily life, jurists on more than one occasion fell into the kind of legal formalism that no longer understands law as the means to a greater end. When sharia is treated as a body of 'divine laws' and therefore as an absolute, the role of humans in devising and organizing these laws is more often than not suppressed or obscured. It was only through the scholarly study, consultation and interpretation of the Texts that this version of sharia was derived, so it follows that there is a major human dimension to its emergence and in the articulation of its philosophy.

Historically, sharia and *fiqh*, or law and jurisprudence (see p. 128), have frequently been confused: almost overnight, the interpretative efforts of scholars of law and jurisprudence were elevated to the status of an absolute and sacred 'divine law'. Legal opinions became indisputable edicts; despite all the counsel of the earliest great scholars to maintain a critical and selective attitude as they developed a system of law and jurisprudence, some of their followers were not able to avoid temptation and began to treat certain opinions or interpretations as sacred. Immutable rules and principles (regarding the rituals of prohibitions such as interests or alcohol) are a part of Islamic law and jurisprudence, but the construction of a legal system, the application of the law and the exercise of jurisprudence are not 'divine law'. They are human constructs that must be assessed, criticized, viewed selectively and sometimes renewed.

AMONG THE SCHOLARS OF THE FUNDAMENTALS
The scholars of the fundamentals (*uṣūl al-fiqh*), also known as 'principalists'(*uṣūliyyūn*) took a keen interest in the question of sharia and, given their specialization, focused their attention on its sources and fundamentals. The earliest principalists were legal scholars themselves, who sought an orderly method for extracting rules from the Texts. For them, sharia was above all a matter of law. It was thus essential to devise a method of extracting laws from the Texts, to

prioritize their sources – the Qur'an, the hadith, reasoning by analogy, consensus, custom, etc. – and to list the principles that would make it possible to remain faithful to the Message as a whole, and to certain aspects of earlier Messages. So it was that the principalists adopted sharia in constructing both a legal structure and setting down general guidelines. Legal scholars were then able to carry out their work, research and interpretative efforts within established limits.

Though historically necessary, their work was to have disturbing, and even frankly negative, consequences. First, close scrutiny of the sources and setting up a structure often had the effect of restricting the breadth of the Qur'anic Message, which integrated law and justice into a much larger and all-encompassing worldview. Carried out by men at a particular historical moment, gradually and over time, their work laid down, once and for all, the criteria and the norms that were to become the point of reference or, more precisely, the prism through which the Texts were and are read. Some scholars pointed to the dangers inherent in an approach concerned only with the sources of sharia. One such scholar was al-Juwayni, who, in the eleventh century, along with his student al-Ghazzali, reversed the priority and refocused attention on the 'objectives of sharia'.

Though this approach drew on the same legal considerations, it placed them in a broader context. Law was clearly understood to be in the service of principles and superior values to be protected: religion, the person, the mind, family relations, goods and human dignity. In the fourteenth century, the Andalusian scholar al-Shatibi further refined the work begun a few centuries before. The meaning of the detailed rulings prescribed during the Medinan period, he argued, could only be grasped in the light of the general principles – *kuliyyāt* – revealed in Mecca. These are the principles that provide the outline – the legal philosophy, in other words – that make it possible to establish rules. How far we have come from the view of sharia as a body of never-changing Divine Law! In this new and broader perspective, the higher objectives (*maqāsid*) are to be attained by reasoning, interpretive effort and renewal. The aim is nothing less than to reconcile the Way and the law.

AMONG THE PHILOSOPHERS AND MYSTICS

The theologian-philosophers (*mutakallimūn*), the philosophers (*falāsifah*) inspired by ancient Greek culture and the mystics (*ṣūfī*), saw sharia as directly connected with the notion of the Way. For them it evoked a conception of life and death, of mankind and its ultimate aspirations on earth. As for the legal system, it was little more than a means to an end, or a component of a larger whole. What the theologian-philosophers and the philosophers underlined was not a body of laws and principles, but a value system drawn from the Texts, one that brought together in harmony three mutually reinforcing elements: a philosophy of life, a legal philosophy and a philosophy of being and of salvation.

So inclusive and holistic was their approach that sharia can almost be likened to Islam itself. In fact, it can be nothing else but the Way, in its detailed etymological meaning: the desert path that leads to a source of water. That path, and it alone, can lead those who seek truth to salvation. The theologian-philosophers, like the philosophers, naturally agreed on the rational effort that humankind must undertake to formulate the three philosophies of life, of law and of salvation. The Texts leave nothing unsaid in terms of general principles and directions; they point out the Way, but human reason, illuminated and guided by faith, must exercise its intelligence and determine priorities, categories and the order of ultimate goals.

To this quest for the Way the mystics add a reflection on the superior and spiritual objectives of the Message. Sharia must, first and foremost, be applied to the heart, and its ultimate goal – including its rules, obligations and prohibitions, and the Way to be followed – is the liberation of the self through introspection, self-purification and personal discipline. Their inward-looking view of sharia endows it with a magnitude that echoes the imperative of inclusiveness found among the principalists and in its focus on objectives, that of the theologian-philosophers and the philosophers. To reduce sharia to the Law, or to a body of rules and regulations, would amount to denaturing its spirit, and would open the door to formalism and literalism, neither of which are concerned with higher objectives. Sharia is indeed a way of being with God and with oneself; it is a way of acting, of respect for the rules and of promoting principles the better to attain the superior values of peace, justice, freedom and dignity.

APPLYING SHARIA

Sharia is – above all – a conception of life and of death that makes straight the Way for the relationship with God, with humanity and with Nature. It is a Way that has its sources (God and the Texts), its means (rationality and the human heart, Nature, culture) and its higher objectives (respect for faith, for being, for the mind, for human dignity). For Muslims, the path to be followed is that of fidelity, which, in spiritual terms, represents the Way to their salvation. Applying sharia calls for a constant effort of mediation between the Texts and context, between principles and their application, all in the light of the higher objectives that believers must seek out and strive to attain. By no means must they destroy or reject the world for the sake of immutable 'divine laws' to be blindly applied. They must, instead, struggle to reform and transform the real and existing world in the name of these very values, principles, rules and higher objectives.

The approach must be broad, inclusive and progressive. It must begin by respecting the fundamental rights and freedoms of individuals, by promoting education, by establishing social justice and by protecting and preserving the environment . . . to begin with. Everything that comes from other religious traditions or human inventiveness, all that is in accord with and does not oppose the values, the principles and the objectives of sharia naturally becomes an integral part of the Way in legal, intellectual, cultural, artistic, scientific, social, economic and political terms. The capacity to absorb and to make its own the heritage of humanity – of Greece, China, India, Africa and others – in all its diversity had long been the distinctive hallmark of Islamic civilization. It has incorporated the founding elements of earlier religions, different cultures and philosophies, scientific discoveries and artistic expressions and tastes. Its Golden Age was precisely that of its greatest openness and dynamism.

If sharia has long been understood only in its strictly legal aspect, that is the result of the work of legal scholars and the dominant authority wielded by law and jurisprudence over all other fields of knowledge. Over more than a century, however, the definition of sharia has shifted. Three particularly dangerous reductions have emerged.

First, the resistance to colonialism led political and religious leaders to transform it into an instrument of resistance. In response to the imposition of Western values, political regimes and legal systems exported by the forces of colonialism, sharia came to represent the only political order, legal reference and sometimes even cultural expression that could oppose foreign domination and occupation. In those specific historical circumstances, which gave birth to the Islamist movements, such a reaction was understandable – and was to have long-lasting political and legal consequences, with the rise of the notion of the 'Islamic state'.

The second is a consequence of the first, but developed independently. It saw sharia pared down to its most literalist and repressive aspect. From this perspective, to apply sharia has nothing to do with promoting education, freedom and justice in the name of the ultimate goals and values we have discussed, but instead imposes a full slate of rules and repressive measures to prove that sharia in its most demanding form is being fully applied. The point of departure is the application of a criminal code and its accompanying punishments. Today we witness organizations and groups that claim they are applying sharia as they abuse, torture and execute individuals in the most abhorrent fashion, in total contradiction with the principles of Islam and the meaning of the Way. Such practices are alive and well in the Gulf States, and in a much crueller version with Daesh (ISIS) in Iraq and Syria or Boko Haram in Nigeria. And whereas the Way has always set out to be inclusive in legal, cultural or scientific terms, integrating everything that comes from other religions, spiritual traditions and civilizations, it is today invoked in opposition to the West or to other civilizations.

Third, instead of being the Way along which universal values and principles are shared, sharia is reduced to a system of rules and practices whose objective is to underline the difference and the particularity of Islam and the Muslims. Some literalist currents, Islamist movements and extremist gangs, by their violent and spectacular actions, have perverted the meaning of the Way and depicted sharia, in the eyes of world public opinion, as a negative, repressive and dangerous force.

Jihad

We've all heard a great deal about jihad, in its approximate and often totally specious translations. In an echo of the Christian Crusades, jihad is presented as 'holy war' unleashed by the Muslims to 'convert the infidels' or to fulfil their 'expansionary mission'. The same notion is used to prove that violence is intrinsic to Islam and its teachings. Beginning with the second half of the life of Muhammad, and then with Islam's history of constant warfare down to the extremist violence of today, everything about the dominant image of jihad seems designed to prove that Islam is not a 'religion of peace'.

THE WAY AND JIHAD

The idea of jihad can only be properly understood as part of the Message of Islam as a whole. Its founding principles, rituals, obligations and prohibitions enable us to follow the Way – sharia – whose objectives, as we have seen, are the respect for religion, human integrity, intelligence, family relationships and worldly goods, alongside the promotion of the values of dignity, equality, justice and peace. The effort required for humankind to live and act in respect of these rules, and to promote these values, is what comprises jihad in each respective sphere, from the material to the spiritual.

Etymologically, *jihād*, from the Arabic root *ja-ha-da*, means an individual's 'effort' or 'expenditure of energy' to carry out an action or to defend a cause. The concept of *ijtihād*, as we have seen in these pages, derives from the same root and can best be interpreted as 'intellectual effort' whose aim is to remain faithful to the Message over the passage of time.

At the very heart of the Way, the effort is twofold: the commitment to promote the good means, in daily life, that we must resist evil and work to make things better. The two can only be taken together. The Way demands of us that we draw as close as possible to the ideals we espouse. It is not enough to avoid the worst; we must take a firm stand for the better. Jihad must then be seen as an 'effort of resistance and reform'. Contrary to contemporary perceptions, it has no connection whatsoever with the call to war, for the sake of war.

Some scholars, following al-Suyuti, have enumerated nearly eighty accepted forms or definitions of jihad, of which war (*qitāl*) is only one, and far from the most prominent. The term jihad appears in the Qur'an for the first time when the Prophet is called upon to wage a 'jihad of the mind': when he was confronted with the mockery and aggression of the Meccans, who rejected his Message and his mission, divine revelation enjoined him: 'do not defer to the desires of those who deny the truth, but strive hard against them, by means of this [the Qur'an], with utmost striving' (25:52). The life of the Way is a life of striving, of commitment and of resistance. It begins with the self and permeates every aspect of social, scientific, cultural, political, economic and even artistic life. In many ways, jihad is the visible countenance of the spiritual elevation not only of the individual but also of society as a whole when, in the search for good, people collectively decide to resist the worst.

SPIRITUAL JIHAD

The loftiest and most fulfilling form of jihad is the struggle that each and every one of us must wage within and against ourselves. All the meanings and all the objectives of jihad are clearly visible when the self encounters itself. For each and every individual harbours natural tensions, which the Qur'an mentions quite explicitly:

> By the human self, and how it is formed [in accordance with what it is meant to be], and how it is imbued with moral failings as well as with consciousness of God! To a happy state shall indeed attain he who causes this [self] to grow in purity, and truly lost is he who buries it [in darkness]. (91:7–10)

Spiritual jihad – called *jihād al-nafs* – is an individual's effort to master the dark side of her or his character (egoism, arrogance, evil, lying, violence, greed, etc.) and to reform it by choosing what will benefit it. The lonely struggle continues throughout life and ends only with death. Every conscience and every heart is called upon to resist, to strive, and work for the better. Call it universal intimacy; it is the individual endeavour that each of us know and must make, alone.

The idea of jihad as spiritual experience conveys three meanings. First, jihad is a commitment to peace and not a war cry. Our inner being is in a state of natural tension, torn between the attraction of evil and the call of good: jihad consists, then, of mastering the self, of controlling the evil that lies within us and torments us, in order to attain good. By managing our internal tensions and natural conflicts we can hope to achieve inward and intimate peace of the heart. The moral imperative that accompanies this commitment is to refuse to accept ourselves as we are and instead to make ourselves better. Such is the significance of *tazkiyyah*, a notion we encountered earlier: to purify oneself means to take charge of oneself, to recognize one's faults and the weaknesses of one's nature and personality – but never to submit or to succumb to them.

The objective is to lift oneself up in the quest for the most noble of human qualities by drawing close to the divine. Ultimately, along the Way, jihad is a means of liberation. To resist the ego, to overcome that ego through self-mastery and good deeds, leads to the freedom that is the sister of inner peace. The self is no longer in thrall to the blindness of the passions that corrode it and carry it away, but rises instead towards the freedom promised to hearts at peace. These are, then, the objectives of jihad: peace and freedom.

OTHER FORMS OF JIHAD

Whatever has been said thus far about the spiritual holds true for the individual as well as society. Depending upon whether we resist evil or promote the good, jihad will be 'for' right, of any kind, or 'against' wrong, in whatever form. The moral distinguishing mark of Muslims, wherever they may find themselves in the world, can be found in their commitment to goodness, to peace and to freedom:

> [the believers are] those who if We firmly establish them on earth, remain constant in prayer, and pay the purifying social tax (*zakāt*), and enjoin the doing of what is right and forbid the doing of what is wrong; and with God rests the final outcome of all events. (22:41)

But their status is directly connected with and conditioned by what they do: 'You are indeed the best community that has ever been brought forth for [the good of] mankind [insofar as]: you enjoin the doing of what is right and forbid the doing of what is wrong, and you believe in God' (3:110). The true motor of human activity lies in those basic ethical choices, every day renewed.

To confront possible intellectual or physical indolence, and as an extension to spiritual jihad, there is also a jihad to gain knowledge and science, and yet another for health and well-being. In social life and in the struggle for equality we must undertake jihad for education, for gender equality, for social justice and solidarity. We must persevere in the struggle against poverty, racism of every stripe, oppression, torture and demeaning treatment.

The double movement of resistance and reform is constant, no matter what form human action assumes. How remote we are from the unfortunate equating of jihad with war! Along the Way, we must make both our world and ourselves better by never abdicating our responsibilities as human beings. Spiritual, intellectual, social, scientific, cultural, political and economic striving – the true sense of jihad – all share two vital objectives: promoting peace by respecting all its conditions (dignity, education, justice, equality) and providing human beings with the freedom to be themselves and to choose their path in life free of injustice and alienation.

WAR AND THE ETHICS OF WAR

Jihad may also take the form of war (*qitāl*). The same principles that apply to all other forms of resistance and reform are fully applicable to war as well. The Prophet's life, as we have mentioned, can only be understood through his military activity in the Medinan period, in his resistance to the efforts of the Meccan aristocracy – the Quraysh – to eliminate him and destroy his community. As a general rule, war may be fought only in situations of resistance and must never be launched to acquire colonies, to occupy territory, to gain access to natural resources or impose religion by conversion. Against a conquering force, against colonizers and oppressors, the Texts reserve the possibility of legitimate defence in which the defending party can use the same arms as the aggressor. The aggressor imposes upon the oppressed the means of resistance: against armed aggression, armed resistance may be undertaken as a last resort, in the precise proportion established by aggression:

> if you have to respond to an attack, respond only to the extent of the attack levelled against you; but to bear yourselves with patience is indeed far better for [you, since God is with] those who are patient in adversity. (16:126)

Even for the victims of aggression, the first option must be that of patience and passive resistance. The conflict must end as soon as the aggression has ceased: 'But if they [the oppressors] incline to peace, incline thou to it as well, and place thy trust in God: verily, He alone is all-hearing, all-knowing!' (8:61).

War must be avoided. Even in the face of colonialism and repression, other avenues for the resolution of conflict must be sought. But on occasion, against dictators or against the inhuman folly of certain leaders or regimes, it becomes a necessary evil. The Message affirms: 'And if God had not enabled people to defend themselves against one another, corruption would surely overwhelm the earth' (2:251).

Such is the reality of the human condition. It requires a balance of forces against those who are tempted by exploitation and oppression. Such forces have always existed, but there must likewise be women and men who refuse to bend before their injustice. Absolute power in the hands of a regime, a nation or a civilization, without any balancing power, can only lead to corruption and destruction on earth, for nothing can then resist the boundless appetite of the powerful. All nations and all societies, on all continents and throughout human history, have commemorated their resistance fighters, their 'just' women and men, those who would not bend and who struggled – sometimes with legitimate violence as their last resort – against colonialism, fascism, tyranny and despotism. The teachings of Islam point in this direction. As a religion committed to the cause of peace, it demands that human temptations and combat situations be properly managed.

Shortly before his death, the Prophet dispatched an expedition led by a young Companion named Usamah to the north to repel an anticipated attack. The Prophet made several recommendations regarding the way Usamah should approach the attack, recommendations reconfirmed by Abu Bakr after the death of the Prophet. He ruled that the combatants were not to attack or harm women and children, nor men of religion; he insisted that they respect Nature and fruit-bearing trees. In times of war, the Caliph Abu Bakr's instructions to Usamah remain rich in teachings for us: only enemy soldiers can be attacked, civilians must be spared, the environment must be respected and, in the light of the Qur'an, combat must end when aggression has ceased. Nothing can justify 'collateral damage' or the use of bombs, of whatever kind, which by their very nature kill non-combatants and the innocent. To describe a nuclear weapon as an 'Islamic bomb', as in the case of Pakistan, is a glaring contradiction in terms.

Clear and noble as these principles are, it must be recognized that the Muslims, in their long history, have often been far from just and peace-loving. Islamic history is rife with war, with oppression, with exploitation and colonization. Idealization of the past is of no use in confronting the challenges of our era. Muslims have waged wars of expansion, have established colonial-type regimes, enforced religious conversion, upheld slavery, targeted civilians, manipulated religion and exploited their fellow human beings. Though they were clearly acting against the principles and prescriptions of their religion, some of them did so while claiming to be acting in the name of Islam.

We witness such a spectacle today, in which states and extremist groups betray the most elementary principles of Islam, the ethics of war, and yet justify their horrors by invoking Islam. Muslims cannot abstain from lucid criticism of the past and courageous commitment against the excesses and abuses of the present. The immense silent and peaceful majority of Muslims goes astray if it remains silent or attempts to justify unjust wars of the past or the present. Based on the very precise meaning of jihad, an intellectual and political (and sometimes armed) struggle must be deployed against those who have perverted jihad for the purposes of oppression and terror and who, in the name of Islam, torture, kill and destroy both Nature and the cultural and artistic heritage of humanity. This should start with a clear condemnation of dictatorial and corrupted states as well as organizations such as Boko Haram, Daesh (ISIS) and so on. We need a jihad against the 'jihadist' fraud.

Society

Sharia, the Way, as originated in the body of fundamental principles and higher objectives of Islam, gives direction not only to the lives of individuals, but also to the life of society.

Its general principles and objectives lend coherence and unity to both individual and collective action. But where the Texts are silent is in giving instruction about how these fundamental principles are to be applied. Neither do they provide a model that can be applied indiscriminately to changing times and in different cultures. While principles and objectives are universal and trans-historical, models and modes of implementation are historically and culturally bound and depend upon an awareness of technical and scientific progress and the shifting socio-cultural environment. Human beings must make the individual and collective rational effort of applying these laws and rules to the reality of the era in which they live, with constant respect for the objectives of the Way. Literalist interpretations, as well as those of the extremists, seek to impose the models of the past, as they trumpet that there is no other way to remain faithful to the Message of Islam. The confusion, the conflict between principles and models of application – between the 'what' and the 'how' – remains one of the greatest problems facing contemporary Islamic thought.

EDUCATION

From the first revealed chapter (*suwar*) of the Qur'an, the Message of Islam focuses upon the education of the human being. Human dignity depends upon the capacity to acquire knowledge; hence education is a fundamental human right, a right that consists of both the acquisition of knowledge by way of instruction and the development of proper conduct through education, with consideration of the rules and moral precepts laid down in the scriptural sources. Human beings can only become truly human through the education the family, and later society, can provide for them. A Muslim-majority society, or a community of faith, must distinguish itself by its investment in the education of its children as well as – through continuing education – that of its adult members. What begins as a fundamental human right then becomes an intellectual and moral obligation for every individual. Two authentic prophetic traditions underscore the point: 'The seeking of knowledge is obligatory for every Muslim [men and women]'[1] and 'If anyone travels on a road in search of knowledge, God will cause her/him to travel on one of the roads of Paradise'.[2] The obligation is therefore incumbent upon every individual, and its direct connection with salvation in the hereafter emphasizes the importance of collectively fostering education and knowledge.

Education cannot be restricted to religious or moral instruction. All knowledge that enables humanity to gain a better understanding of the world, to acquire the scientific knowledge of the day; all knowledge that offers each woman and man the opportunity to become an individual and free subject (the second characteristic of human dignity) is, by definition, the prerequisite of education. Islam's golden ages (in Mecca and Medina at its inception; between the eighth and the thirteenth centuries in Damascus, Baghdad and Andalusia; and in the Ottoman Empire under Suleiman the Magnificent in the sixteenth century) were all distinguished by a proliferation of the sciences, of philosophy and the arts in the very name of a profound understanding of the teachings of Islam. Two prophetic traditions are often cited: 'Seek knowledge as far as China' and 'Seek knowledge from the cradle to the grave'. Both are considered weak and perhaps even invented, but they nonetheless convey the spirit of the Message of Islam towards knowledge as a whole. For knowledge is to be taken irrespective of its origin and made to serve useful and ethical goals, for oneself and for humanity.

Islamic civilization in its golden ages never experienced tensions between science and religion similar to those that divided the Catholic Church and the scientific community, whose most eloquent examples were the cases of Giordano Bruno and Galileo, though there were many others. Inspired by Qur'anic injunctions, the Muslims sought scientific, human and experimental knowledge, not only in medicine, biology and physics, but also in the fields of sociology, urbanism, philosophy and the arts. The Qur'anic Message does not convey a series of dogmatic restrictions designed to control and restrict knowledge, but the moral obligation to give that knowledge an ethical orientation: it must remain in the service of humankind. Education, and with it knowledge, can only be conceived through their ultimate goals. Consistency with these goals must be continuously re-evaluated: the dangerous fragmentation of knowledge that is taking place today, along with the emergence of specialized sciences lacking a solid ethical foundation, are in direct contradiction with the principles and objectives of the Way.

Education impinges upon the entirety of human endeavour. Spiritual and religious initiation must be accompanied by a civic education that teaches individuals to become responsible subjects as part of the wider human collective. The exact and experimental sciences, and the humanities, form an essential component of human education, if we wish to remain consistent with the injunction of the Message, which calls upon humankind to live in harmony with its time, and to meet the scientific and ethical challenges of the day. Culture, languages and the arts must form an integral part of the curriculum: ways of life and methods of communication, alongside the expressions of the imagination and aesthetic sensitivity, all encourage and urge humankind to become autonomous and to expand its horizons. To be at one with God, argues the Muslim tradition, is to educate oneself, to struggle against intellectual sloth, to undertake a jihad for self-education and for the education of society. Many previous generations have lived in harmony with this Message. Yet we cannot escape the fact that today's Muslim-majority societies have gravely neglected basic education, coupled with the near-systematic elimination of disciplines considered as dangerous or superfluous. Islamic education, in their eyes, has no need of philosophy or the arts. But to so reduce education, to amputate it, illustrates the chasm that separates these contemporary educational systems from the higher objectives of the Way.

FREEDOM

Freedom defines the human being. In religious terms, the act of faith of an individual who attests that she or he believes in God is meaningless unless that person is free to believe or not. In like manner, human responsibility and the education that guides humans towards assuming responsibility is meaningless if humankind is not free. Thus sharia itself – the Way – presupposes the freedom of humans to accept it or not, to follow it or not. From a religious, philosophical, social and political stand-point, human freedom precedes sharia and stands as a pre-requisite to its recognition and eventual establishment. This means, in the final analysis, that education, and the religious, social and political spheres, must protect individual freedom and guarantee it as a fundamental human right.

The freedom of one's conscience is primary; every human being is free to choose whether or not to believe and must be respected for her or his final decision: 'Say, "The truth is from your Lord": Let him who will believe, and let him who will reject' (18:29). In terms of acts, the believer who has received a religious legal opinion on a given subject must be in a position to understand and to discuss it, as she or he is free to accept or reject it, for no religious legal opinion can have constraining force. The same holds true for conversion or changing one's religion, both of which conform to the pre-requisite of being able to choose. The collective freedom to practise a religion – a freedom that must ensure a faith com-munity the right to practise its rituals, its obligations and prohibitions – is of the same nature. Freedom of thought, like freedom of expression and movement, is an integral part of fundamental human freedom.

To form and express one's thoughts, to develop a critical mind and to be free to move about on the surface of the earth – and even more so if one is facing poverty, war and persecution – are all fundamental rights whose principles and general objectives sharia obliges us to respect. 'Was, then, God's earth not wide enough for you to forsake the domain of evil?' (4:97) the Qur'an reminds the persecuted and the downtrodden, thereby stipulating that migration, too, is a human right. Education must promote free, autonomous and critical judgement, just as the law and the social system must protect freedom of expression and engagement in collective action. Of course, there are limits to freedom of expression. Insults, racism and calumny must be restricted. All societies have established such restrictions. The imperative of public order may on occasion diminish the ways in which people express themselves, but it cannot call into question these fundamental and inalienable liberties.

Liberty is thus a prerequisite for sharia, one of the conditions that allows it to be carried out in fidelity to its objectives. What we see around us today contradicts this principle. Whether in religious, intellectual, social, political and artistic terms or in the mass media, basic liberties are suppressed, in the name – or so we are told – of the Islamic reference or of sharia itself. It is no exaggeration to say that the great majority of mainly Muslim societies limit the fundamental right to the exercise of freedom across the board. Repression is at its worst in the Arab world. There is no doubt that literalist, dogmatic and extremist interpretations of Islam are used to justify such treatment in the name of sharia.

According to this reductive and binary understanding, everything about sharia must be strict, harsh and restrictive in opposition to the 'permissive and decadent' West. But it would be a mistake to attribute the lack of freedom, the repression and the dictatorships that rule Muslim-majority societies to religious reference alone. Many dictators and regimes, past and present, have been secularist or non-religious without being any less repressive. A more exhaustive political analysis is needed, one that takes full account of the internal dynamics of a given country, and of course the role of outside powers – the United States, Europe, Russia, China – that may support such regimes. Equating 'Islam' with 'repression' or 'dictatorship', in simplistic fashion and without political and historical analysis, would be a dangerous mistake.

Still, some commentators have concluded that Muslims will never be able to attain democracy. Islam, they assert, has problems with freedom by its very nature. However, their position is not based on any analysis of the teachings of Islam. In fact, an abundance of indicators point to the existence of Muslim-majority societies that were historically open and protective of freedoms. Nor must we forget that, beyond the Arab world, numerous Muslim-majority societies in Asia and Africa protect individual and collective freedoms and Muslim citizens in Western societies are promoting the latter in the same way.

SOCIAL JUSTICE

Many eminent Muslim scholars and thinkers have affirmed, from the earliest days, that the supreme Islamic value is justice. A multitude of Qur'anic verses and prophetic traditions speak of justice (*al-'adl*) and equity (*al-qist*), while the same term, 'justice', is also one of the names of God. Justice must apply to all and can admit of no distinction or discrimination by religion, skin colour, gender or social status. As we read in the Qur'an:

> O you who have attained to faith! Be ever steadfast in
> upholding justice, bearing witness to the Truth for the sake

of God, even though it be against your own selves or your parents and kinsfolk. Whether the person concerned be rich or poor, God's claim takes precedence over [the claims of] either of them. (4:135)

Furthermore, *āyāt* 108 to 115 of *sūrah* 4, 'Women', were revealed when a Muslim, guilty of theft, tried to accuse a Jew in an attempt to profit from the conflict raging, at that very moment, between the Muslim community and a neighbouring Jewish tribe. Revelation absolved the Jew and exposed the guilty Muslim, warning: 'he who commits a fault or a sin and then throws the blame therefore on an innocent person, burdens himself with the guilt of calumny and [yet another] flagrant sin' (4:112).

At all times and in all circumstances and with all human beings, justice must be established and served: 'judge, then, between Men with justice, and do not follow vain desire, lest it lead you astray from the path of God' (38:26). Even in conflict situations, in the heat of the emotion and enmity we feel towards the aggressor, self-mastery and justice must prevail:

O you who have attained to faith! Be ever steadfast in your devotion to God, bearing witness to the Truth in all justice; and never let hatred of anyone lead you into the sin of deviating from justice. Be just: this is closest to being God-conscious. And remain conscious of God: verily, God is aware of all that you do. (5:8)

Justice thus ranks high among the principles and superior objectives of sharia. Its application begins with social justice.

As we have seen, the earliest Revelations insist on the relation between faith in God, on the one hand, and awareness and care for the poor on the other. *Zakāt*, the social purifying tax, establishes the primacy of the 'rights of the poor' on the accumulated wealth of their more fortunate neighbours and fellow citizens. In the same spirit, social justice demands respect for fundamental human rights, including education, housing, employment and equal opportunity. These rights must be guaranteed for all, and social reform must make them its objectives. Participation in civil society is the natural extension of these major requirements, for women and men alike, without the slightest discrimination. An extremely explicit *āyah* emphasizes that women and men, together, must be involved in public life and in the reform of society:

> And [as for] the believers, both men and women – they are close unto one another: they [all] enjoin the doing of what is right and forbid the doing of what is wrong, and are constant in prayer, and render the purifying social tax, and pay heed unto God and His Messenger. (9:71)

The verse begins with the equal social presence of men and women, which is confirmed by the identical ritual practices. The principle of social equality – and not merely that of 'complementarity' as repeated in literalist and traditionalist rhetoric – could not be spelled out more clearly.

It is a fact that numerous interpretations in Islamic literature throughout history and down to the present day have claimed that women should not work, that they should care for the household; all these claims are asserted from the vantage point of a patriarchal cultural outlook. But the

Qur'anic Text is clear in its formulation that wages must be paid for work: 'Men shall have a benefit from what they earn, and women shall have a benefit from what they earn' (4:32). Justice demands that remuneration for the same work, given identical competence, must be the same for a woman as for a man. Nothing can justify difference of treatment between man and woman.

Nor can religious and racial discrimination be justified. It is interesting to note that the original community of Companions around Muhammad was made up of persons of all origins, colours and social backgrounds. The underlying principle is that of equal treatment and justice, which must be accompanied with humility, according to two prophetic traditions: 'O people, your Lord is one Lord, and you all share the same father. All mankind is descended from Adam and Adam [comes] from dust.' There is no preference for Arabs over non-Arabs, or for non-Arabs over Arabs. Neither is there preference for white people over black people, nor for black people over white people. Preference is only through rever-ential consciousness of God.[3] 'Verily, the noblest of you in the sight of God is the one who is most deeply conscious of Him' (49:13). These were the last words of Muhammad in his farewell sermon, when he underlined the common origin of all mankind – this earth – and its insignificance on the spir-itual plane. In another tradition he adds: 'People are equal like the teeth of a comb.'[4]

Nothing can justify racism, discriminatory treatment based on national origin or skin colour. No form of racism, whether against blacks, Latinos, whites, Arabs, Asians or others, can ever be justified religiously, no more than it can be justified in human, social or political terms. Muhammad made the Jews and the Christians an integral part of the society of Medina by affirming that they were a part of the *ummah* – the community – and that they enjoyed the same rights and had the same duties as the Muslims. 'There shall be no compulsion in religion' (2:256); thus discrimination against Hindus, Buddhists, Jews, Christians and others is prohibited. Neither colour nor appearance distinguishes one person from another, only that person's heart and deeds: 'God does not look at your appearances or your status, but He looks at your hearts and your actions.'[5] Woman or man, rich or poor, black, Arab or white, the worth of human beings on earth depends on their capacity for justice and equality.

How far removed are today's Muslim-majority societies from those teachings. Not only do some scholars, as in the past, justify discriminatory treatment (up to and including slavery) towards blacks, women and the poor, but everyday reality also teems with contradictions, as discrimination against women, racism and abuse of the poor are endemic in these societies. The justification is not always religious, but the truth cannot be avoided: many Muslims are in a state of denial as they quote the Texts to demonstrate Islam's opposition to all forms of discrimination and racism. A yawning gulf lies between the Texts and the behaviour of some Muslims.

POWER

The question of power is central, especially in religious affairs. In their very essence, religions could not be clearer: supreme power is God's alone. The Islamic formula is well known: 'there is no power neither strength save with God' (18:39). But how is God's absolute power to be carried over into the administration of human affairs, which are anything but absolute? The most eloquent expression can be found in the example of Muhammad, who received Revelation directly from God while leading the Muslim community. From the very beginning, his Companions understood the difference between the authority that emanated from God through Revelation, which could not be questioned, and the human authority of Muhammad, which remained relative and could be debated and criticized.

The battle of Badr, in the second year of the Hijra (the Migration from Mecca to Medina), provides an excellent example. Upon arriving at what would soon be the site of battle, the Prophet set up camp close to the first sources of water that the Muslims happened upon. Noting this, Hubâb ibn al-Mundhir, one of his Companions, came to see him and asked: 'Has the place where we have stopped been revealed to you by God, in which case we must not leave it, either to retreat or to advance; or is it an opinion, a strategy designed to confuse our adversaries?'[6] When Muhammad confirmed that it was his personal opinion, Ibn al-Mundhir suggested as an alternative that they camp near one of the larger wells, the one nearest the road by which the enemy would approach, then block the other nearby wells to cut off their enemies' access to water. With this strategy, their enemies would experience greater difficulties. Muhammad listened attentively and immediately gave his assent: the Muslims broke camp, and Hubâb's plan was applied to the letter. Muhammad, who was 'nothing but a mortal' (26:154), was neither autocratic nor discretionary when it came to human affairs, always offering his Companions an essential role in consultation.

Revelation clearly enjoins Muslims to administer their collective affairs based on consultation and deliberation, a process known as *shūrā*: 'The Muslims are those whose rule [in all matters of common concern] is consultation among themselves' (42:38). The process begins in the intimacy of the couple, touching even on the weaning of the child when the couple has decided upon divorce: 'And if both [parents] decide, by mutual consent and counsel, upon separation [of mother and child], they will incur no sin' (2:233).

Consultation became the rule in the administration of social and political affairs. At the battle of Uhud, in the fourth year of the Hijra, the Prophet once more consulted his Companions about strategy. In his view, the best course would be to remain in Medina and wait for the enemy; the majority disagreed. Muhammad immediately accepted the majority opinion and prepared for combat. The Muslims marched out of the city towards Uhud, where the battle would take place. In the battle itself, the archers failed to follow orders and the defeat was decisive. Despite this defeat, the Qur'an rapidly confirmed the principle of consultation and deliberation that could not be challenged, whatever the outcome of a decision taken collectively:

> And it was by God's grace that you [O Messenger] did deal gently with thy followers: for if thou had been harsh and hard of heart, they would indeed have broken away from you. Pardon them, then, and pray that they be forgiven.

And take counsel with them in all matters of public
concern; then, when you have decided upon a course of
action, place your trust in God: for, verily, God loves
those who place their trust in Him. (3:159)

From the very beginning, a clear distinction was established
between the Prophet, when he received the Revelation (and
submitted to its rules and principles), and his authority as a
leader, which required discussion and deliberation, following which decisions were taken by majority vote. The clas-
sical studies long distinguished between the different roles
of the Prophet: as Messenger, as leader, as judge and as a
mortal man.

This way of understanding sharia casts light on a prime
principle of distinguishing and separating authorities.
Neither in its fundamentals, nor the manner in which it is
exercised, can religious authority be established or administered like political authority. The latter has a 'top-down'
structure and unilaterally imposes both principles and rules;
the former emerges from the 'bottom up', while fully respecting the nature of consultation and the clear principles of
deliberation, freedom of thought and expression and equality
of the participants.

Produced by fallible human beings, political authority is
always relative, debatable and circumstantial, both geograph-
ically and historically. Similar thinking, in the West, gave rise
to secularism: the powers of the clergy – the Catholic
Church – and those of the state should all be judged according to the same criteria. There are no clergy in Islam – not
even among the Shi'a – for their hierarchy is not identical

to that of the Church (as discussed on p. 17). But in the earliest days of Islam there was no confusion between orders: even though Muhammad was the political authority in Medina, he did not wield his power by 'divine right' or 'in the name of God'. His authority was never theocratic, but founded upon an open administrative process where decisions were taken in common, according to the principle of majority.

Religion does not provide political life and the exercise of public authority with a dogmatic template. It offers a corpus of values and ethical principles that any authority must do its utmost to respect. The hallmarks of a head of state or of a political leader are integrity, competence and accountability to those whom or she he administers. Power must be exercised transparently, with justice, equality and respect for the will of the majority, women or men, Muslims or not. In the first Muslim community, women as well as men swore allegiance to the Message: *bay'ah*. Even though they had not sworn the same allegiance, those who were not Muslims also belonged to the *ummah* (community) of Medina and enjoyed the same rights and duties as the Muslims by virtue of the charter drawn up under Muhammad's authority.

When, however, power is not exercised in a pluralistic manner and according to the requirements of democratic deliberation as understood by *shūrā* (consultation), it is incumbent upon humans to resist and to reform their society. Muhammad himself declared: 'The most virtuous jihad is a word of truth in front of a tyrannical ruler' and 'Fear the invocation of one who has suffered an injustice even though she/he is a *kāfir* (denier of Islam), for there is no veil (screen) between his invocation and God'.[7]

The history of Islam, however, shows that public affairs were not always administered according to the prophetic model. From early on, and down to the present day, its teachings have been muddled, distorted and betrayed. The literalist approach has often equated the two authorities and transformed political power into dogmatic religious power, making not the slightest distinction between the two. Failure to distinguish universal principles from the practices of the past have led some political groups to turn their back on social and political evolution and to seek to impose models that are obsolete and invalid.

Finally, the notion of 'the absolute power of God' has on occasion been translated, in political terms, into a denial of collective and individual human rationality, leading to the strict and literal application of principles and rules drawn directly from the Qur'an. The slightest variance with such an immutable application of principles is justification enough, in the eyes of literalist and extremist groups, for violence and the strict and cruel application of their version of the Islamic criminal code. Examples of such betrayals and tragic misconceptions abound and are currently unfolding in front of our very eyes, practised by constitutional dictatorships and literalist extremist movements in the Middle East and around the world.

FORGIVENESS

When talking about humankind, the teachings of sharia make continuous reference to forgiveness. Along the Way, between

first principles that must be respected and universal objectives that must be pursued, human beings will encounter
innumerable trials and tribulations. They must certainly persevere and reform by means of jihad, as has been explained;
but they must likewise learn compassion, gentleness and forgiveness: in Arabic, respectively, *raḥmāh*, *ifq* and *'afw*. It is a
learning process that must begin, of course, with themselves,
with confidence in God, no matter the obstacles to be overcome and the errors committed: 'Say: "O you servants of
Mine who have transgressed against your own selves! Despair
not of God's mercy: behold, God forgives all sins – for, verily,
He alone is much forgiving, a dispenser of grace"' (39:53).

The Way is an appeal for compassion, for generosity, for
self-protection and the protection of one's fellows. As a prophetic tradition reminds us: 'Whosoever covers [the sins of] a
Muslim, God covers [her/his sins] on the Day of Judgment.'[8]
Rules are not to be applied strictly, inconsiderately and
crudely. There must be no attempt to produce feelings of
guilt or to identify the guilty; quite the opposite. The teachings of Islam begin by celebrating the innocence of human
beings, before detailing their eventual accession to responsibility, which must be accompanied by gentleness and forgiveness. Human beings are not to cultivate a sense of guilt, nor
point the finger of guilt at one another. No; these teachings
lay powerful emphasis on God's mercy, His compassion, His
gentleness and His goodness. These are the sublime qualities
that should inspire humans in their own lives and in their
interaction with others. 'If someone shows no compassion to
people, God will show no compassion to her/him.'[9] On the
Way, the attitude of respect, self-mastery, protection and

forgiveness is one of the moral hallmarks of the believer, as made clear in the Qur'an: '[the God-conscious] are those who hold in check their anger, and pardon their fellow-men' (3:134). All, in the broadest sense, are called upon to accept, to forgive and never to make a definitive judgement, for that judgement belongs to God alone. As divine Revelation reminds the Prophet himself: 'your duty is [no more than] to deliver the Message; and the reckoning is Ours' (13:40).

As we travel the Way between principles and objectives, our humanity is illuminated by patience, protection, compassion and forgiveness. Forgiveness is a spiritual trait, a disposition of the heart that sheds a revealing light on the teachings of Islam. In our relations with everyone, we are called upon to reject mockery, denigration, backbiting, suspicion and spying:

> O you who believe! Avoid most guesswork (about one another) – for, behold, some of (such) guesswork is (in itself) a sin; and do not spy upon one another, and neither allow yourselves to speak ill of one another behind your backs. Would any of you like to eat the flesh of his dead brother? Nay, you would loathe it! And be conscious of God. Verily, God is an acceptor of repentance, a dispenser of grace! (49:12)

The image is striking! To spy, to backbite and to suspect is to eat the dead flesh of one's brother or sister in humanity.

The Way summons humankind to life, to good works, to forgiveness and to love. The *āyah* that follows is a call addressed to all humanity, reminding us that the distinction and the grandeur of human beings lies within them, of which God alone knows the secret:

O men! Behold, We have created you all out of a male and a female, and have made you into nations and tribes, so that you might come to know one another. Verily, the noblest of you in the sight of God is the one who is most deeply conscious of Him. Behold, God is all knowing, all-aware. (49:13)

Precisely because they do not know the secrets that lie in the hearts of others, human beings are expected to have a balanced attitude, to remain indulgent and filled with leniency when judging visible actions. For every heart has its secrets; and as we follow the Way, none of us can be judge and, even less, executioner.

Humanity and the Environment

The Message of Islam addresses both humankind and Creation. Its teachings demand equal respect for all human beings, who share a common origin and who will meet the same end. Likewise, relations between human beings and nations must be grounded in respect and reciprocal knowledge. It is no exaggeration to say that in Islam there exists a true and deep humanism, one that places humankind at the centre of Creation. But the same humanism expects of humans, as God's vice-regents (*khalīfah*), to administer their affairs in a way that is at once enlightened and respectful, spiritual and humane.

HUMANISM

The teachings of sharia are directed, above all, at the human beings who stand at the centre of Creation. They can be interpreted in five extremely explicit ways. First comes that of our common origin, for all women and all men have emerged from the self-same original being: 'O Mankind! Be conscious of your Lord, who has created you out of one living entity, and out of it created its mate, and out of the two spread abroad a multitude of men and women' (4:1). The Qur'anic Text makes no mention of woman being created from man, but speaks of the creation of both – woman and man – from the same unique entity.

Second, all women and all men possess the same original dignity, irrespective of their religion, their skin colour, their origin or their social status. 'Now, indeed, We have conferred dignity on the children of Adam' (17:70) and their weaknesses, their sins and even their most reprehensible acts cannot make us forget their fundamental dignity in the way we treat and even judge our fellow human beings.

Third, humanity is one, willed by God, with its diversity of nations and tribes that mirrors its diversity of languages and colours: 'And among His signs is the creation of the heavens and the earth, and the diversity of your tongues and colours' (30:22). Diversity in the heart of human unity requires respect for God's will and a commitment to know one another better, to gain greater knowledge of other religions, languages and cultures.

The function of the pluralism of nations and cultures is to maintain equilibrium between them, the better to avoid corruption on earth. But pluralism also – here lies the fourth point – invites humankind to engage in positive competition to accomplish good deeds:

> And if God had so willed, He could surely have made
> you all one single community: but [He willed it otherwise]
> in order to test you by means of what He has vouchsafed
> unto you. Vie, then, with one another in doing good
> works! (5:48)

A positive attitude towards others acts as a catalyst for the expression of good and reflects our common humanity. Tolerance alone is not enough. We cannot simply 'suffer' the presence of others, which would implicitly place them in an inferior category – for those who 'tolerate' always do so from a position of superior strength. We must respect their presence on the basis of true equality, recognize their richness and singularity through knowledge, and celebrate our mutual contribution through a healthy rivalry to perform good deeds.

Fifth and last, we must reserve judgement about peoples and nations:

> O you who have attained to faith! No people [community,
> men] shall deride [other] people [community, men]: it may
> well be that those [whom they deride] are better than
> themselves; and no women [shall deride other] women: it
> may well be that those [whom they deride] are better than
> themselves. (49:11).

Judgement belongs only to God, and as the Qur'an repeatedly declares: 'Unto God you all must return; and then He will make you truly understand all that on which you were wont to differ' (5:48). God, and only God, is the master of judgement. All humans, therefore, must endeavour to be individuals possessed of dignity, to be respectful of the equality of all women and men and attempt to perform good works in the best possible way. Certainly, a believer's conviction is that the last Revelation is the ultimate Truth emanating from the true God, *al-Ḥaq*. But it is precisely this belief that insists others be respected, that definitive judgements be avoided, and any distinction made must be an ethical one. In this sense, the universal Message of Islam instructs Muslims that diversity itself is universal.

Such is the wisdom that constitutes the keystone of Islamic humanism, embedded in the Texts and investing the Way and its fundamental teachings with full meaning.

NATURE

A large number of Qur'anic verses and prophetic traditions evoke Creation, Nature and all living creatures. God has indeed bestowed upon humankind a privileged status and role: 'Are you not aware that God has made subservient to you all that is in the heavens and all that is on earth?' (31:20) But the human being can never forget that each and every element of Creation sings the praises of the divine, that he is surrounded by the sacred and that he must respect God's gift:

> The seven heavens extol His limitless glory, and the earth, and all that they contain; and there is not a single thing but extols His limitless glory and praise: but you [O Men] fail to grasp the manner of their glorifying Him! Verily, He is forbearing, much-forgiving. (17:44)

With the eye of the heart we can see, moreover, that '[before Him] prostrate themselves the stars and the trees' (55:6).

Never is Creation empty of the signs of God, never is it 'disenchanted', for everything within it brings to mind and glorifies God. The spiritual and physical environment must therefore be respected, protected and administered with the greatest circumspection. In this perspective, the natural counterpart of Islam's inherent humanism can be found in its ecological teachings.

If Nature must be protected even in wartime (see pp 163, 164), Muhammad's prescription applies doubly in everyday life. In fact, it is a fundamental teaching of Islam that covers all animals and natural elements – water, fruit trees, etc. – without exception. One day, as he came upon his Companion Sa'd ibn Abi Waqqas, who was performing his ritual ablutions, the Prophet called out to him: 'What is this extravagance?' Sa'd asked: 'Is there extravagance with water even in ablutions?' The Prophet said: 'Yes, even though you were on the banks of a flowing river.'[10] Water, as a central element in Islamic teachings and practice, represents the purification of the body and of the heart, of the physical outer self and of the spiritual inner self. But here the Prophet counselled to Sa'd and his other Companions never to look upon water, or upon any other natural element, as a simple 'means' for their spiritual edification. Quite the contrary. Respect for the elements and care in their use was in itself an exercise in spiritual elevation, an 'ultimate goal' in the search for the Creator.

The fact that the Prophet would reject extravagance and waste 'even though you were on the banks of a flowing river' tells us what a lofty position he assigns to respect for Nature. It is among the first principles that must govern human conduct, irrespective of the situation and the consequences for human activity. What is being expressed is not at all an ecology born of foreboding, of the fear of human-induced catastrophe, but a kind of 'pre-existing' ecology that grounds humankind's relations with Nature in ethics, inextricably connected with the profoundest spiritual teachings of the Way. After he received the following *āyah* the Prophet wept for an entire night: 'Verily, in the creation of the heavens and the earth, and in the succession of night and day, there are indeed signs for all who are endowed with insight' (3:190).

The believer's connection with Nature can only be rooted in contemplation and respect. So powerful is the injunction that the Prophet one day declared: 'If the Hour starts to happen and in the hand of one of you is a palm shoot, then let her/him plant it.'[11] The believing conscience must, until the last moment, draw nourishment from humankind's intimate relationship with Nature, to such an extent that his final act recalls the renewal of life and its cycles.

The same example illuminates the Prophet's attitude to animals. The extreme situations of combat, during which the Prophet showed and reminded those around him that animals must be well treated, helped shape the teachings of sharia. Muhammad never ceased exhorting his Companions to be aware of the need to treat all animal species with respect. One day, he related this story to them:

> While a man was walking he felt thirsty and went down a well and drank water from it. On coming out of it, he saw a dog panting and eating mud because of excessive thirst. The man said, 'This [dog] is suffering from the same problem as that of mine.' So he [went down the well], filled

his shoe with water, caught hold of it with his teeth and climbed up and watered the dog. God thanked him for his [good] deed and forgave him.

The people asked, 'O God's Messenger! Is there a reward for us in serving [the] animals?' He replied, 'Yes, there is a reward for serving any animate creature.'[12] On another occasion, he related:

A woman was punished and was put in Hell because of a cat which she had kept locked till it died of hunger. God said [to the woman], 'You neither fed nor watered it when you locked it up, nor did you set it free to eat the insects of the earth.'[13]

Muhammad used examples such as these, as well as the example of his own behaviour, to remind those around him that respect for animals formed a crucial dimension of Islamic teachings, something he would never miss an opportunity to underscore. As mentioned in the discussion of halal meat above (see p. 113), Muhammad insisted that animals to be killed were properly treated. Seeing that an individual had tied down an animal and was sharpening his knife in front of it, the Prophet intervened: 'Do you intend inflicting death on the animal twice – once by sharpening the knife within its sight, and once by cutting its throat?'[14] He thus taught that the rights of the animal must be respected, and that proper treatment was non-negotiable. It was, in fact, one of the duties associated with being human and should be understood as one of the conditions of humankind's spiritual ascension as they follow the Way.

Historically, undue focus on the legal aspect of Islam's teachings has relegated to a subsidiary position or even obscured the humanism of the Message and the scope and power of its injunctions with regard to Creation, to Nature, to the environment and to living creatures. The community of humanity and respect for animal and vegetable life mirror one another. Thus does humankind, in full freedom, join in the concert of voices raised in praise by all Creation.

It is a sad fact that, in our day, many Muslims have come to neglect multiple teachings of sharia, the Way, whether in terms of spiritual edification and elevation, or respect for humanity and for the environment. The vice-like grip of formalism, coupled with a failure to seek out deeper meanings and ultimate goals and the refusal to accept the primacy of virtue and good conduct, have had a harmful impact on the practice of religion. Islamic renewal will come about only when Muslims come to reconcile themselves with the most profound Message of sharia, which is a conception of life, of humankind, of Creation and of death. The Way is one of education, and of perpetual re-education.

CHAPTER 5

Contemporary Challenges

As we have seen in the first four chapters, today's Muslims face serial challenges. The pillars of faith and of practice and the demands of the Way loom before them in the form of rules, objectives and principles that can be difficult to apply, even more difficult to attain, and often seem to be contradicted by the conduct of Muslims around the world. Faced with today's frequently negative perceptions, some seek refuge in the glories of the past, invent excuses or, graver still, lapse into denial. There can be little doubt that the greatest challenge is a psychological one, bound up with the temptation to idealize former glory, to discount the gravity of today's problems or, worse yet, to blame others. But Muslims have to face up to questions concerning their relationship with their founding Texts, the diversity of their interpretations, the confusion of religion and culture, and the deficit in intra-communal dialogue. The question of man and woman, their equality and their relations, remains a critical one. Several of these challenges are specific to Muslim-majority societies, while others touch upon Muslims as members of a religious minority. But in many cases – education, for example – these problems overlap.

Past and Present

Many words have been written and spoken about the notions of Islamic 'religion' and 'civilization'. But the contribution of the former and the definition of the latter are far from unanimously accepted. A vast majority of historians recognize periods of cultural flowering, the 'golden ages of Islam' under a succession of Muslim rulers. These are traditionally identified as the earliest years, in Mecca and Medina; Omayyed Damascus; Baghdad during the centuries of Abbasid rule; then the extraordinary contribution of Andalusia and the forty-six-year reign of Suleiman the Magnificent at the head of the Ottoman Empire. Perhaps the best reason for remembering and studying this illustrious past is to grasp the reasons for its success, just as it is no less crucial to understand the causes of its decline and decay and to draw lessons to better deal with the challenges of today.

THE GOLDEN AGES

Perhaps the expansion of Islam and of the Muslims and their influence across continents can best be explained by where they settled and by the nature of their relations with other civilizations, religions and cultures. Before Islam, Mecca was a nodal point of commerce and cultural exchange, with tribes from the surrounding hinterland congregating there and enriching one another culturally and economically. The extremely rapid expansion of Islam, the international gathering of the pilgrimage to Mecca and the settlements of Muslim traders along the caravan and sea routes linking

Saharan Africa, the entire Middle East, Asia as far as China and India, and along the shores of the Mediterranean to Europe, are among the objective circumstances that explain the dynamic nature of Islamic civilization.

Military conquests, though sweeping, cannot alone explain the success of Islamic civilization. Instead, it can be attributed above all to the merchants who migrated along the great trade routes, settled and everywhere adapted to local culture, from North Africa to Europe in the West, to India, China and Southeast Asia in the East, not to mention their success in the Middle East and in Central Asia, from Isfahan to Samarkand and beyond. Along with their faith, they carried their language, their commercial practices and their cultural diversity. The political and economic authorities of the successive Islamic empires kept pace with their movement, relying on a common language, instituting a currency and regulating trade while barely interfering in administration, which was left to local government. The double migratory movement from the periphery to the centre, by way of the pilgrimage, and from the centre towards the periphery, which brought with it a diffusion of faith, of language and cultures, made possible not only trade but also intellectual and cultural cross-fertilization and mutual enrichment.

The first golden age of Islam spanned the eighth to the thirteenth centuries, when Arabs, for the most part, wielded political and state power. During this period of some 500 years the spiritual, intellectual, commercial and military accomplishments of the successive Muslim empires were striking. In Iraq, shortly after the rise of Caliph al-Ma'mun (d. 833), the 'Baghdad Observatory' was established in 829, followed by the 'House of Wisdom' (*Bayt al-Hikmah*) three years later, then lesser centres of study, translation and research, open to all thinkers and experimental scientists. His father, Harun al-Rashid, had earlier designed similar facilities for the elite. 'Houses of Wisdom' multiplied rapidly and spread from Baghdad to Damascus, Cairo, Samarkand, Isfahan, Fez, Cordoba and beyond, where they came into contact with the civilizations of Persia, Rome, China and India and translated the scientific, philosophical and artistic masterworks of the age into Arabic, while Arab thinkers and scholars – Muslim but also Jewish and Christian – added their own contributions, creating connections between the world's systems of thought and science while drawing on their own faith and cultural heritage.

Astronomy, mathematics (algebra, arithmetic, geometry), medicine (the blood circulatory system, ophthalmology, surgery, anaesthesia, dissection and the establishment of the first hospitals), physics, chemistry, geography, botany, zoology and agriculture were only a few of the fields that were developed and enriched. The Indian numerical and decimal systems were adopted; new discoveries confirmed previously formulated hypotheses. The 'Houses of Wisdom' everywhere generated new and original scientific knowledge from both the diversity of their sources and the ways in which that knowledge was put to use. The same process was taking place in philosophy, with the Graeco-Roman heritage and Islamic theology-philosophy; in sociology, as in the work of Ibn Khaldun; in poetry; in architecture, with the adoption and perfection of the arch, the hypostyle, the cupola, the colonnade, among other features; and in the arts, with calligraphy, illumination, miniature painting, ceramics, wood inlay work, textiles and so on. From China, Islamic civilization adopted the use of paper from the eighth century onwards and spread it westward, accelerating as it did the expansion of knowledge and technology.

For five centuries the distinguishing feature of Muslim civilization was the pursuit and celebration of knowledge in all its forms: exact, experimental and human sciences. Faith, with its imperative for knowledge, education and movement, was a motivation, never an obstacle. The Mongol invasions of the thirteenth century may have been one of the reasons for the decline of Islamic civilization but, as we will see later, they were not the only one. Meanwhile, other centres, such as Andalusia, from the eighth century up to the fall of Granada in the fifteenth, flourished, drawing upon an intellectual ferment and religious diversity – Jewish, Christian and Muslim – similar to that which had transformed Baghdad into a centre of cultural effervescence.

Alongside its military successes, the reign of Suleiman the Magnificent (1520–66) during the Ottoman Empire was noteworthy for its reforms, both administrative and legal (which earned the sultan his soubriquet of 'the Lawgiver'), its monumental architectural projects (designed by the celebrated architect Sinan) and its artistic development by way of the artistic societies known as the 'Communities of the Talented', which flourished in Topkapı Palace in Istanbul. The imperial capital boasted more than forty such societies, each one numbering hundreds of members of all origins, where Turkish and European influences mingled with those brought by Muslim artists and artisans from across the empire.

Suleiman was at once a great military commander, a legislator and a poet: he recast criminal, tax and property law and showed a keen interest even in the rights of animals. Acts that incurred the death penalty were restricted, and tax legislation more favourable to Christians ('Code of the Raya') was enacted, with specific measures to protect the Jews (1553). He oversaw the development of free education and basic literacy, via the *mektebs* system. Courses in philosophy, astronomy, astrology and the arts were introduced in the middle schools (*medersas*) and universities. Diversity and respect for all religions, cultures and expressions of knowledge were everywhere proclaimed and everywhere visible (up to the present day) in Istanbul and in other Ottoman cities great and small.

These periods of cultural and civilizational flowering demonstrate clearly enough that Islam has never placed any limitations on knowledge, the arts and religious diversity, but that religion, properly understood, was the driving force at the international level for centuries. Great efforts have been made to downplay, and even to obscure, the Islamic contribution to Western civilization. Islam's detractors have claimed, in the face of powerful countervailing evidence, that the 'Arabs' and the 'Muslims' were little better than translators, 'bridges', humble transmitters of the Greek and Roman heritage to Europe. In brief, they accomplished nothing more than to restore to Europe what already belonged to it. They might have, at best, transmitted a handful of techniques that were never even theirs to begin with, imported from China (paper) and India (decimal calculation).

This is simply not true. The Muslim contribution was

infinitely more substantial and far-reaching in all the intellectual, scientific, social and artistic fields mentioned above, as serious studies have documented. European and Western culture has both Graeco-Roman and Judeo-Christian-Islamic roots. For centuries the denial of the existence of Islamic roots has gone hand in hand with an ideological construction that posits Islam as the 'religion of the other'. It is as though Europe has rejected this vital component of its inheritance to better construct itself as a self-made religious and cultural unit, by separating itself from Islam and by reducing it to a fraudulent caricature.

Denial of the facts of history has created, with the passage of time, a kind of self-confirming truism: that Islam has a problem with reason, the sciences, the arts, pluralism and the separation of religious and state authority. The most extreme accusations, alongside their diametrical opposites, have been fabricated, designed to depict Islam as the ultimate other. During the lengthy era of religious puritanism among Catholics and Protestants throughout the Middle Ages, Islam was scorned as a religion of permissiveness, where sensuality flourished in harems (and which, by the way, inspired courtly poetry). Today, in the era of sexual liberation, Islam has come to represent exactly the opposite: a world of prohibitions, restrictions, veils and frustrations.

In both instances Islam continues to be viewed as the 'other', as radically different. This ideological representation of Islam, which provided the driving force of Orientalism, has had a lasting impact and is still evident throughout Western society today. In negating and forgetting Islamic civilization's rich history, its religiously and culturally open and pluralistic societies, as well as its scientific, philosophical and artistic contributions, the dominant Western discourse rushes to simplistic and even dangerous conclusions about an imaginary Islam where rationality is absent, where faith is taken to excess, is expansionist and imposed, and where the sciences and the arts are proscribed. Historical and scientific investigation has long proved these claims false. It is high time that the curricula of Western educational institutions accept and integrate the great contributions of the Muslims to world civilizations – providing of course that they truly wish to bring knowledge in line with reality and reshape their perceptions as they do.

DECLINE AND ITS CAUSES

Most historians believe that the decline of Islamic civilization began in the thirteenth century with the Mongol invasions. It cannot be denied that upheavals on the borderlands of the Ottoman Empire, the weakness of the Islamic states and military defeats were determining factors. But internal factors were to prove even more influential in this decline and fall.

We cannot overlook, coming so soon after the death of Muhammad, the political tensions that led to the assassination of three of the first four Caliphs. These same tensions and the internal conflicts they engendered have been a constant in Islamic civilization and were amplified with the establishment of a hereditary dynastic succession in Damascus. The rapidity of expansion, the sheer extent of the territory to be governed and the diversity of the social and political cultures to be administered soon came to characterize the different Islamic empires.

Depending upon the vision, determination and strength of character of the Caliph, the Sultan or other leader, there were periods of great achievement, during which military power, political stability and cultural richness drove the expansion of Islamic civilization. However, there were also times when things went into reverse, and with the emergence of conquering foreign powers, energy and creativity suffered. The historian and philosopher Ibn Khaldun (d. 1406), who numbers among the earliest sociologists, analysed the cycles of civilization. He studied the reasons for their emergence, their expansion and their decline, and identified the internal and external factors that shaped this process of social evolution. Like all those that had come before it and those that would follow it, Islamic civilization passed through different phases.

Following the initial explosion of energy and all-conquering confidence, Islamic civilization suffered long periods of instability, doubt and fear of competing civilizations and empires. In the realm of knowledge, religious scholars concentrated upon the law as a protection against potential interference or colonization by an enemy (or someone seen as such). Determining the licit (*halāl*) and distinguishing it from the illicit (*harām*) created the impression of being better armed to resist the surrounding cultures and their influences. During its most confident phases, Islamic civilization had opened wide its arms to intellectual inquiry, to the sciences and the arts, but in time of crisis, it sought to protect itself through a natural but nonetheless questionable reflex, by favouring legislation and the imposition of limits. The pre-eminence accorded to law was to have, in the long term, a negative impact on Islamic thought. The relationship with God, human interactions and the structure of power were interpreted through rules and norms that conferred on them an Islamic character in opposition to what others might think or do. An intellectual attitude of this kind, which had already become perceptible as early as the eleventh century, led to political decline and invasion.

These were the two principal outcomes that caused grave prejudice to the further development of Muslim thought. Motivated by fear, some began to assert that the scholars of the past had said all there was to say, that there was nothing further to add. Some, among the Sunni – but not among the Shi'a – even dared to rule that the 'gates of *ijtihād*' (reason) were now closed and that it was no longer necessary, even less permitted, to carry the exercise of reason beyond the Texts, and the rules and norms established by the scholars of the past. With its focus on repetition and imitation (*taqlīd*), it was an attitude of manifest regression, an attitude that is alive and well today in certain Islamic ideological currents: contemporary literalists have little to offer aside from literal repetition of the models of the past, while the traditionalists can do little more than imitate the scholars of old.

The other main outcome was that Muslims came to view themselves as 'others' and to fear outside intellectual and cultural influences. Certain fields of knowledge were labelled as dangerous; an ever-increasing number of jurists (*fuqahā'*) openly opposed certain developments in the sciences, in philosophy and in mysticism. Fear of knowledge and dread of 'contamination' had been entirely absent in the early days, when the Muslims integrated, re-examined, adapted and made abundant use of knowledge in all its forms. The intellectual crisis of the Muslim world began as early as the twelfth and thirteenth centuries with this inversion, whereby the formalism of law overcame the meaning of ultimate ethical goals, imitation became the rule, stifling curiosity and intellectual production and, ultimately, an inward-turning mentality set rigid limits that excluded certain forms of knowledge. All this was in direct contradiction with the spirit of openness, of exchange and of commonality that characterizes the Message itself and that has made most flourishing periods of Islamic culture the civilizational beacons of the age.

Even today the consequences of this ancient intellectual crisis are visible everywhere, in Muslim-majority societies and among Muslim communities in the West. Fidelity to the Message can be located only within the space marked out by *ḥalāl* and *ḥarām*, in constant imitation-repetition and by the exclusion of any form of knowledge that is not 'purely Islamic'. The internal causes of Muslim decline form, in our day, the main obstacles to an intellectual, scientific and artistic renaissance.

IDEALIZING THE PAST

The greatest challenge of the modern era is at once intellectual and psychological. Throughout history, numerous Muslim scholars and intellectuals have idealized the past, and particularly the founding period. It is almost as though the Prophet's Companions were not mortal men living and acting within history but exceptional individuals who suffered little from human weakness. Their noblest pronouncements and bravest acts are recounted and invoked, and all the while serious historical analysis of the social dynamics and political tensions of the day, of the mismanagement of the Prophet's heritage and of the turmoil of the first post-prophetic generations are conspicuous by their absence. The upshot has been a particularly negative psychological attitude. With the past so idealized and often sanctified, critical analysis is interpreted as a lack of faith, or worse, as a malevolent attempt to destroy that heritage. Nostalgia – 'the malady of longing' – has transformed that past into an ideal of perfection. The psychological consequence has been to deprecate the potential and energy of living individuals, all of whom seem condemned to imperfection, ever unworthy of the original model.

The same affliction extends to the contemporary Muslim view of the 'great scholars' of the past. They, and no one else, are held to possess the true key to the interpretation of the Texts; they have said all that can be said and known all that can be known. The confusion between the preservation of a human heritage and being held prisoner to it can be observed in much of the intellectual production that has marked the history of Islamic thought up to the present day, from the law and its fundamentals to its philosophy and mysticism. One of the most adverse consequences of this backward-looking attitude has been to suggest that the scholars and thinkers of today are not equipped to produce anything of worth, anything reliable or appropriate that might help meet the challenges of the present.

So it is that the intellectual crisis of the Muslim world goes hand-in-hand with a deep psychological crisis: a glorious past has sucked the present dry of the confidence and intellectual strength it must have in order to renew itself. We contrive to hide the causes of these crises from ourselves and to repeat to the point of overkill that Islamic civilization itself is in crisis. As if to confirm the diagnosis, we hark back compulsively to the grandeur of yore, as if to demonstrate the 'genius of Islam' and of the Muslims, all the while pointing to the sharp contrast with the present day, characterized by the absence of a Muslim contribution. We have come full circle: a short-sighted analysis of the past, a negative assessment of the present and a defeatist – and sometimes fatalist – attitude towards the challenges facing us today.

To this must be added – another symptom of a crisis mentality – a keen sense of victimization. Far from taking account of the internal factors that led to this decline, the lack of historical studies and the critiques of Muslim thought from within, we blame others for the very evils that possess us. First the Crusades, then military and political colonization, and finally economic and cultural imperialism were and are the causes of all evils; the root of each and every one of our stinging defeats. The dominant West is said to have taken everything from Islam and from the Muslims the better to transform them into enemies, to exploit and divide them and to create conflict – as between Israel and Palestine – and to foment constant crisis.

While it is certainly true that we must analyse external factors, which are both real and numerous, with a critical mind, we cannot perpetuate the sense of victimization that has transformed Muslims into historical subjects who exist only as others perceive them, and not as autonomous actors. So pernicious is this process that it has obscured the very real contribution of Muslims to today's world. For numerous creative and energetic Muslim women and men are fully engaged and involved in the sciences and in intellectual, social, economic, cultural, environmental and artistic pursuits. They participate with full faith, with pride in their identity and their conception of life, death and the world. In Africa, Asia and the Middle East, as in the West, they have emerged as autonomous agents in their own history, doing critical work, grappling with the challenges of their times and contributing to the enrichment of the humanist inheritance of humanity. Not only does the all-powerful West not always recognize them, nor take them seriously, but their own societies and the world's Muslims also have difficulty in recognizing their value and seeing in them the signs of a renewal to come. For they are locked into the deep psychological crisis that has convinced them that they possess no agency, that they are nothing more than victims reacting to actions taken by others. The interaction of past and present has revealed a deep crisis of collective psychology – of this there can be no doubt.

Reading the Texts

As we have seen thus far, the role of its founding Texts is fundamental in Islam. One of the pillars of faith is the belief in the last Message as God's revealed word. The prophetic traditions are likewise essential for religious practice and must be treated with the utmost seriousness; at the same time the task of authentication and understanding must continue. For today's Muslims, the relationship with the scriptural sources remains a major challenge.

LITERALISM AND TRADITIONALISM

Textual interpretation is the key factor in distinguishing between the different trends and schools of thought within Islam. Today's Muslims are caught up in a fully fledged crisis of confidence that is the direct consequence of the intellectual and psychological crises outlined above. Some of these schools style themselves as the guardians of the Message and of the Islamic heritage, saying that the only true fidelity to the Message lies in its literal application, for example the *salafī* movements (also inadequately categorized as *wahhabī*) that have sprung up in many places. Some are apolitical and quietist, some are highly politicized, and some have chosen the path of violence. These movements set themselves apart from the traditionalists who adhere strictly to a particular school of law and jurisprudence and are content to repeat what scholars of the past have already enunciated. The only way to be faithful to the Message, for them, is to rely solely upon the past contributions of the great scholars, to whom no one today can be compared. The promise held out to Muslims by both *salafī* and traditionalists has an alluring simplicity, particularly in these troubled times. To succeed, they 'need only' apply literally the chapters and verses (*suwar* and *āyāt*) of the Qur'an and the prophetic traditions, scrupulously re-enacting whatever tradition has already laid down. No critical thought is needed; any attempt at reform, at rethinking existing interpretations, is seen as a pernicious attempt – now and forever – to 'destroy Islam from within'.

By insisting upon an intellectually ossified, dogmatic and sectarian reading of the sources, these same schools of thought have gravely diminished the Message and its teachings. Though the Qur'an remains their primary reference, the prophetic traditions are re-actualized to play a determining and often undifferentiated role; the core of the Message, now highly formalized, becomes the application of rules. Obsessively, they lay exclusive claim to 'true' and 'authentic' Islam, an Islam that has not been perverted like the other trends, which are often 'excommunicated'. These groups of individuals are not interested in the slightest in meeting the social, cultural and political challenges of the day, but in protecting themselves from them, even if, in the name of protection, they are obliged to overlook a multitude of contradictions or, worse yet, instances of outright hypocrisy.

The financial and logistical support of the Gulf States, or of powerful private individuals and institutions, enable these schools to train scholars and imams, to build mosques and to diffuse their literature throughout the world, often with the blessing of Western powers. And yet these literalist and traditionalist readings contain dogmatic and often dangerous interpretations that impact negatively upon people of other faiths, upon women, culture, democracy and diversity. They are opposed to the slightest idea of reform or renewal, one that would restore priority to the Qur'an and resume the work of authentication of hadith and of placing them in a proper perspective, of rethinking the models and the ways in which rules can and should be applied in the contemporary era. Put succinctly, in their eyes, for Muslims to reform their way of thinking is to betray the Texts.

CULTURAL HERITAGE

Distinguishing the cultural from the religious is a difficult task, yet it is vitally necessary. In interpreting the Texts, we need to understand and distinguish that which derives from Arab culture from that which is clearly an Islamic principle. This imperative applies not only to the scriptural sources, but also to the heritage bequeathed to us by generations of scholars. For all of them were influenced by the culture in which they lived. All of them read the Texts through the prism of their time and place.

Literalist and traditionalist readings added a 'cultural projection' to the Texts. Scholars who may have been open and even bold on certain issues were nonetheless powerfully influenced by their environment when it came to questions of political authority, of women or of slavery, to mention but a few. Several of their interpretations proved more typically Arab, Persian or Turkish than truly Islamic. Early on, many of them sought to reduce the culture of Islam to that of the Arabs. Against everything the Texts teach about pluralism, to become Muslim came to consist of becoming more Arab-like.

That bias still stalks the land. On the pretext of Arabic being the language of the Qur'an, Islam is generalized and essentialized as a religion whose culture must be exclusively Arabic too. Not surprisingly, four problems have arisen. The first is the confusion between culture and religion: that which has been interpreted on the basis of a given culture or as applied to a specific cultural environment is viewed as a religious principle. Secondly, an identical confusion can be traced back far earlier, to the scriptural sources themselves – particularly the hadith literature – and to the confusion between the Islamic principle and its cultural adornment, which is intimately bound up with a specific time and place. The third problem faced by Muslims is that of invoking religious principles to criticize cultural phenomena. No culture, be it Arab or any other, is free of defects, anomalies, discrimination or anachronistic customs, even if they are fully normalized. The principles, rules and objectives of Islam, which together constitute the Way, require that we evaluate cultures ethically and reject all that contradicts those principles, rules and objectives. Today, quite the opposite is taking place in front of our very eyes. Under the threat of dominant Western culture, only blind acceptance of Arab, African or Asian cultures is said to ensure fidelity to Islam. Nothing could be further from the truth. Each and every culture must be exhaustively re-evaluated and reformed, for among them unjust and discriminatory attitudes have become accepted and normalized. Such attitudes – this is the fourth point – encourage fear of any 'other culture' that might be 'un-Islamic'. In this view, there is no way one can be a 'good Muslim' and still be British, French, German, American or Canadian. As fearful as it is restrictive, a posture of this kind contradicts everything discussed in the preceding pages: nothing in any of these cultures could be described, in and of itself, as 'anti-Islamic'. We must apply to them the same critical effort of ethical evaluation and choose what is best in each. The universality of Islam has meaning only when it is built upon the unique bedrock of cultural diversity, that of all cultures, dominant or not, Western or not.

DIVERSITY AND INTRA-RELIGIOUS DIALOGUE

Anyone who travels through today's Muslim-majority societies or visits Muslim communities around the world cannot but be struck by the prevalence of division, discord and even internal conflict. The Muslims themselves are the first to complain about this state of affairs, from disputes over the beginning of the month of Ramadan to contradictory views on a whole range of sensitive subjects. The obsession with division has produced a collective psychology equally obsessed with unity, if not unification, which more often than not is mistaken for uniformity of thought. Muslims today have great difficulty in managing the diversity of interpretations, of schools of law and jurisprudence, of thought and, in a broader sense, of the trends reflected in them.

Islam has no clergy, no single or unified structure, a fact that would seem to point to the acceptance of diversity and the creation of mechanisms that would open up intra-religious dialogue.

Alas, such dialogue is today either non-existent or survives only in the most superficial or temporary form. Recent political upheavals – starting in Iran and Iraq and more recently in Iraq and Syria – have exacerbated tensions between Sunni and Shi'a to dangerous levels. The logic of conflict and unhealthy competition has elbowed dialogue aside. Between schools and movements, among Sunni as well as Shi'a, dialogue is all but absent, and divisions are amplified by political considerations, or by geostrategic and cultural imperatives. The diversity of interpretation of the Texts has nowhere to call home; nowhere can it be discussed, enriched or simply managed in an atmosphere of mutual respect. Many works have been written on the 'ethics of divergence' (*adab al-ikhtilāf*), but the overwhelming evidence shows that today's Muslims are loath to respect its principles and are even further from applying its teachings.

AUTHORITY

The question of authority is directly linked to that of the diversity of interpretations and trends. Though the Shi'a seem to be better organized and structured than the Sunni – which they are, in point of fact – conflicts of authority can be found among them just as they are among the Sunni.

Who, then, speaks for Muslims? How are authority, credibility and ultimately religious power generated? Of course, much is made, theoretically, of knowledge and competence. But we are obliged to conclude that authority today is not founded on any objective criteria. Between legitimacy based on the family, on the charisma of certain scholars, on the hearing offered to others or on ties with the powers-that-be, there can be no doubt that Muslims are experiencing a true crisis of religious authority. At the national as at the international level, the structures that organize religious representation are hotly contested, either because they represent or are exploited by the holders of political power, or because of the incompetence of their members, or, finally, because they represent no one but themselves.

In the midst of chaos, ordinary Muslims end up choosing their imam or their religious representative either because of geographical considerations or for their charisma, because he or she confirms what they consider to be just, or, finally, because of their countries of origin (when they live in exile) or, in the case of Saudi Arabia, because the literalists claim it to be the heartland – the one true source of knowledge, as the literalists claim. Some, frustrated by the plethora of contradictory opinions, take upon themselves the authority to interpret the Texts without necessarily possessing sufficient mastery of the language, of the hierarchy of Islam's prescriptions, or of the overall structure of the Message. Approaching the Texts in this way, for all its apparent democracy, creates more problems than it solves. For, given the absence of the requisite knowledge, it has generated radically diverse interpretations, ranging from the most liberal to the most extreme, by virtue of which some groups, in the name of a superficial reading, entirely devoid of context, of a handful of *āyāt*, can kill.

Councils have sprung up at the national and international level, bringing together scholars from various trends and schools of thought in an attempt to confer a semblance of order upon diversity and to restore direction and weight to religious authority. But these efforts have remained isolated and often ineffective. There is little probability that they will evolve unless, at the regional and national level, such structures can be established independently of the powers-that-be, and with the full support of rank-and-file Muslims and their local associations.

APPLIED ETHICS: SCIENCE, MEDICINE, BIOETHICS

The question of authority also arises with regard to more in-depth issues, in the applied and experimental sciences. While more than a few scholars of the past were able to combine a multiplicity of skills, to be at once legal scholars, philosophers and physicians, such a thing is no longer possible in our day. As knowledge has become more complex, and as the competences required in order to gain such knowledge become more sophisticated, no single individual can deal fully and adequately with the great scientific and technological issues of the times. In place of such individuals, councils of law and jurisprudence (*fiqh*) are convened to formulate legal opinions on issues ranging from medical ethics and technology to the economy. In consultation with specialists in each field, or drawing on reports, they put forward new and finely calibrated approaches.

Today, it is possible to read carefully researched literature on the situations in which abortion can be considered, most often on a case-by-case basis; where organ transplants are possible and recommended; and when (passive) euthanasia can be employed; or even on the very specific issues of bioethics, including genomics. The same is the case for economics and finance, including discussions of the definition, means and objectives of given economic measures, not to mention technology, media and the arts.

Legal opinions of high complexity and diversity have been produced in a variety of fields. However, many scholars, experts and specialists in these areas – the sciences, medicine, economics, finance, technology, the media – point to the very real disconnect between a given legal opinion on the one hand and prevailing practice in these disciplines on the other. The moral eminence of the legal scholars and their knowledge of the Texts are insufficient to give them the necessary authority and competence to offer direction to the sciences and to rule on their ultimate goals. To knowledge of the scriptural sources must be added a deep knowledge of the sciences themselves, and of their environmental, social and cultural contexts. But scholars in the exact, experimental and human sciences are more often than not the last to be consulted when a programme of applied Islamic ethics is being drawn up. Their authority is marginal, and yet they should be at the forefront of that demanding and highly detailed task; their abilities should be properly appreciated. Here, the Muslims are suffering the consequences of the absolute priority given in reference to the Texts while effectively neglecting the importance of context, and of the transposition and application of rules and norms into real life. It is at this level that the authority of the scholars and specialists of various disciplines is of fundamental importance, for their task is to provide properly adapted, well-thought-out and fully informed ethical responses. Such inclusion of technical expertise and delegation of authority remains a rare occurrence indeed.

The Woman – and the Man – Question

The flood tide of books and articles – worldwide – on the situation of women in Islam gives no sign of ebbing any time soon. Inequality, violence, the headscarf and polygamy are mustered either to demonstrate the inherently sexist character of Islam or to demonstrate how erroneous is the criticism. Few would deny that the question is fraught with complexity, with respect to both women and men. But paradoxically, it is the Muslim male who is passing through a historical crisis, as his status and his role are thrown into question, and into disarray.

BEING AND ROLE-PLAYING

Men have been responsible for the overwhelming bulk of contributions to law and jurisprudence, as to the Islamic sciences, while the contribution of thousands of female scholars has been neglected. This has had an impact on the literature that deals with the question of women and men. First, given the masculine prism through which the Texts were studied, in patriarchal societies for the most part, great interest has been shown in the role of women in society. Much has been written over the centuries about the status of the wife, the mother or the daughter, but not a single serious work exists that speaks of woman as a woman, as a fully realized being and a free and objective actor who lives her spiritual life and experiences her emancipation, and her inner growth and development, as a woman. It is as though the aspirations of the female were implicitly the same as those of men, and that the only thing that distinguished them was their respective roles and status.

This is a rather masculine way to approach the issue, it must be said. Furthermore, literalist readings of the Texts (reduction) and the influence of culture (projection), as discussed above, have weighed heavily in shaping the 'woman question' in Islam. Qur'anic verses and prophetic traditions are interpreted literally, taking no account of the Message in its totality. The cultural and patriarchal environment that enveloped the male scholars and jurists who studied and elaborated on the Texts could not but shape their understanding of those very Texts. As a result, the Islamic literature dealing with women is triply distorted: it concentrates almost exclusively on their role and not their being; it gives priority to parts (certain verses, *āyāt*, interpreted literally), in contradiction with the whole (the general and ultimate goals of the Message); it confounds cultural norms with religious principles.

The impact upon the interpretation of the Texts has been extremely serious. Even the greatest and most revered scholars have produced reductionist and dangerous commentaries that can be used to justify the most inappropriate behaviour. Who, from the twelfth century on, has ruled that the marriage contract was equivalent to the master–slave relationship? Who, down to the present day, has justified conjugal violence? Who has justified arranged marriages in which the woman – and sometimes even the man! – is not even consulted? All this while the Message, taken in its totality, says exactly the opposite. The Revelation brought the first Muslims, in succeeding stages, to experience equality and partnership within the couple, to consult the woman in her choice of a husband and finally to forbid all forms of conjugal violence following the example of the Prophet, who never struck a woman and who declared: 'Do not strike the servants of God [women].'[1] No one can deny that there have been extravagant interpretations and commentaries, nor that such unacceptable postulates and legal opinions have been put forward in the history of Islamic law and jurisprudence – even by some of the most acclaimed and respected (on other subjects, of course) scholars of the past.

EQUALITY AND THE CRISIS OF MASCULINITY

We have already discussed the literalist and traditionalist apologetics that describe women and men as equal before

God and complementary in their conjugal relationships and in society. The notion of 'complementarity' remains vague, however, and can even be used to justify, ultimately, the complementary relationship of master and slave, as indeed certain jurists insisted on doing for many centuries. The problem strikes much deeper and antedates the recognition of female and male beings in their equal aspiration for freedom, autonomy and individual, social and economic advancement. As a couple, as in social life, they are partners:

> And [as for] the believers, both men and women – they are close unto one another: they [all] enjoin the doing of what is right and forbid the doing of what is wrong, and are constant in prayer, and render the social purifying tax, and pay heed unto God and His Messenger. (9:71)

The claim to equality must arise from a detailed rereading of the Texts, by women as well as men. Scholars and intellectuals, both women and men, have identified the principles and objectives that must be employed to debunk reductive interpretation and cultural misreading. They have begun the work of reclaiming the rights of women, and some of them – women and men – define themselves as Muslim feminists. In no way should the relationship between men and women be considered in opposition to the Texts and principles of Islam, but as derived from them. Every effort must be made to criticize the three distortions mentioned above and their negative impact on daily life.

While much has been said and written of Islam's 'woman question', the modern-day crisis of the 'Muslim man' has been given short shrift. For centuries his status, the authority that flowed naturally from patriarchal society, and his prerogatives were protected, ensuring him a secure role in society. Modern-day cultural and lifestyle upheavals, the social problems that have accompanied the newfound female presence in the workplace and women's increasingly confident ascension have, taken together, touched off a psychological, cultural and social crisis in many men. The crisis – a genuine crisis of masculinity – must be taken seriously and analysed in depth, taking full account of the most widespread ills of the age: loss of bearings, a troubled sense of masculinity, the absent father syndrome, to name a few.

BACK TO FRONT: WHEN SECONDARY BECOMES PRIMARY

Reductive and culturally bound readings of the scriptural sources have had equally controversial effects in other fields, often with troubling results. Certain Muslim scholars – and ordinary Muslims – have come to adopt positions that are more closely aligned with Jewish or Christian prescriptions than with their own, Islamic references. In a problematic world, the claim is heard that the stricter the legal opinion, the more 'Islamic' it is: a conclusion that has no basis in fact. The Texts, after all, are explicit enough. The majority of scholars, both Sunni and Shi'a, have recognized that contraception is permissible, that abortion must be treated on a case-by-case basis, that women's economic autonomy must be protected, given that her fortune, her wages and her inheritance are her exclusive property. But these positions have been called into question by certain literalist and traditionalist movements who style themselves 'protectors of Islam', standing firm against the dangers of the modern world.

The same individuals are adamant in promoting the kind of legal opinions that justify unjustifiable behaviour. People in the West are shocked at the sight of men who refuse to shake women's hands, and vice versa, or women who refuse to be examined by a male physician. But opinions differ widely on these subjects. The Prophet most certainly declared that he, personally, would not shake a woman's hand, but there is no reason why his behaviour should be binding on all Muslims. The relatively numerous prophetic traditions that prohibit touching and physical proximity refer to contact involving sexual desire and not to ordinary, everyday contact.

The same holds true with regard to the gaze: there is nothing wrong with looking at a man or a woman in normal fashion during a conversation. In fact, the Qur'an is quite precise in its formulation: 'Tell the believing men to lower [a portion of] their gaze' (24:30), and in the *āyah* that follows, 'And tell the believing women to lower [a portion of] their gaze' (24:31). The 'portion' of their gaze here specified is that which corresponds to sexual desire and seduction. But today we have the spectacle of literalist and traditionalist movements forbidding a simple touch such as a handshake, or refusing to look their interlocutor of the opposite sex in the eye, as though they were major sins. In like manner they would forbid women from consulting a male physician when, in the view of most scholars, nothing should stand in the way of necessary medical treatment.

Why, we might ask, are their legal rulings less strict when it comes to men? We encounter the same double standard on the question of mixed bathing in public swimming pools.

With due concern for the elementary rules of modesty, many Muslim women avoid using mixed pools. Their reluctance is understandable, given the Islamic conception of a person's relation to the display of her or his body; every woman must be free not to exhibit her body if she sees fit. What is troubling is that such rulings apply only to women and not to men, who would appear not to be bound by the same rules, in what they show and in what they look at. Nothing, least of all a strictly masculine reading, can justify this tendentious interpretation.

MIXED AND INTERRELIGIOUS MARRIAGE

Mixed (intercultural) and interreligious marriage are frequently confused, but differ fundamentally. The Muslim tradition has always embraced and encouraged marriage between spouses of different cultures and nationalities, in the name of the Islamic brotherhood that transcends borders, skin colours and languages. Despite this tradition, it cannot be denied that Islam's inherent encouragement of culturally mixed marriage has not proven an obstacle, neither yesterday nor today, to intolerable racist attitudes among Arabs, Turks, blacks, Asians and even towards converts. Xenophobic nationalism combines arrogance and feelings of racial superiority to produce behaviours utterly foreign to the principles of Islam.

Furthermore, Sunni, Shi'a and Ibadi scholars agree that marriage between a Muslim man and a Jewish or Christian (monotheistic members of the 'People of the Book') woman is authorized. The general philosophy of the family – delineating the respective roles of the spouses, the patrilineal transmission of religion (according to tradition) which stresses the duty of maintaining the family – does not, however, offer the same possibility to Muslim women, who are required to marry Muslim men. Scholars have derived this stricture from the Qur'an (60:10: 'They are not lawful (wives) for the deniers of Islam [*kuffār*], nor are the deniers of Islam [*kuffār*] lawful (husbands) for them'). Interpretation of this verse, as well as several prophetic traditions, has led Muslim scholars (*'ulamā'*) to the near-unanimous conclusion that Muslim women are forbidden from marrying non-Muslim men.

Only a small number of scholars – a tiny minority – have suggested different interpretations, according to which Muslim women could wed believing Jews or Christians under strict conditions (that the husband respect the wife's religion, that the children receive a Muslim religious education, etc.). It should be noted that the situation is slightly different if the woman converts (or returns to religious practice) after marriage. Majority opinion has always held that, in such an event, the woman must seek a divorce. But in the scholarly tradition, for several centuries, numerous religious rulings have permitted the woman to remain with her non-Muslim husband as long as he respects her religious freedom and does not attempt to limit her practice (additional conditions have been laid down by various authorities, particularly with regard to the religious education of the couple's children).

Today the question of marriage has become a critical one, primarily due to the presence of millions of Muslims in the West. Here we can observe two converging phenomena. Numerous Muslim women have married, and continue to marry, men of other faiths (or even without religion), frequently because these women are non-practising (which can in turn lead to a crisis should they begin to practise or return to doing so), but in many cases in full knowledge and responsibility. Scholars may well reiterate the rules, but concrete realities within Muslim religious communities are changing. The majority of Muslim women continue to marry Muslim men, but the percentage of those who marry men of other faiths is constantly increasing.

Yet another fundamental problem has arisen. Large numbers of young women born into traditional families and not permitted to enjoy a social life outside the parental home have pursued academic careers. One to three generations later, these women have generally been successful in their academic aspirations. Highly qualified educationally, such women frequently enjoy an intellectual and social status superior to that of the average Muslim man. It is difficult to imagine that these women would – or will – find happiness with men in such a position, so flagrant does the imbalance appear between their impressive intellectual progress and the social and professional obstacles encountered by young Muslim men. This situation has now become a reality in the West, as well as in Asia, Africa and in the Arab world. The Muslim scholars seem all too content to repeat the near-unanimous opinion without making the necessary effort to understand realities on the ground. But these new realities should lead them to propound fresh and detailed approaches (often on a case-by-case basis) that would make it possible for women and men alike to approach marriage in a spirit of serenity as befits the search for personal, spiritual and religious fulfilment, and not as a formalistic structure that restricts and stifles.

POLYGAMY

Polygamy is a hotly debated subject, often invoked to demonstrate the intrinsically discriminatory attitude of Islam towards women. But a close analysis, based on Islam's underlying principles and objectives, can lay a number of these issues to rest and lead to a clearer understanding of the Texts. At the time of the Revelation, polygamy was widespread; there was no limit to the number of wives in the Arab tribes and clans. The Qur'an reduced the number to four, while adding stringent conditions. Monogamy is explicitly promoted, while polygamy is tolerated in situations where orphans are to be protected:

> And if you have reason to fear that you might not act equitably towards orphans, then marry from among [other] women such as are lawful to you – [even] two, or three, or four: but if you have reason to fear that you might not be able to treat them with equal fairness, then [only] one – or [from among] those whom you rightfully possess. (4:3)

Tolerance, here, goes hand in hand with the obligation of equal treatment of spouses, failing which monogamy prevails. Some scholars have added an additional condition: the agreement of the first spouse, who may register her opposition to polygamy in the marriage contract, which the husband, as a signatory, must respect.

In more than a few societies, Muslim men consider only the question of formal tolerance while failing to respect the conditions that govern it. In addition, above and beyond the consent of the first wife, the rights and property of the other spouse(s) must be given formal legal protection. Rarely is this the case today: women are forced to accept unjust and/or discriminatory contracts or living arrangements.

Polygamy is governed by strict conditions. Wherever the law forbids it – as it is nothing but a tolerance – polygamy can no longer be permitted, as a matter of principle (respect for the law) and for the protection of the second wife. The illegality of her status would mean that none of her rights would be protected. Just as in marriage, the woman's opinion is required and is in fact a necessary condition. All national legislation that sets an age limit for marriage should be hailed, for if a woman is to give her consent, she must necessarily be of age and be intellectually and psychologically independent.

HOMOSEXUALITY

The subject is a very sensitive one. The Muslim position ranges from absolute condemnation that justifies the death penalty to a re-examination of the Texts by some marginal thinkers, who are often homosexuals themselves and who affirm that Islam is not opposed to homosexuality. The Qur'an itself, and the prophetic traditions, leave very little room for reinterpretation – like the Jewish and Christian tradition, and many of the world's other spiritual traditions – meaning that homosexuality is considered a sin and forbidden in Islam. The consensus of religious scholars, Sunni as well as Shi'a, is near unanimous. A number of questions have nonetheless been raised, dealing with differentiating between homosexual persons and homosexual acts, passive and active homosexuality (the latter being forbidden), female homosexuality (which is less frequently encountered but also forbidden in the literature) or with the individual's right to a private sex life away from public view. Both Sunni and Shi'a scholars have devised severe penalties when masculine homosexuality is active and flagrant. Majority opinion confirms that homosexuality is not permitted and that it must not be publicly exposed in a Muslim-majority society.

Two questions have generated extensive debate over the last fifty years. Can a man or woman be a homosexual and also be considered a Muslim? Some legal scholars, more often than not belonging to the literalist and traditionalist school, claim that such a thing is impossible, and that an individual's homosexuality would make it impossible for him or her to be a Muslim. Such is not the view of the majority, which recognizes that a homosexual person can indeed be a Muslim, just as for any Muslim who may not act in conformity with established rules and principles. Doing evil or committing a sin has never been a cause for anyone to cease being a Muslim, and even though homosexuality is considered as a sin, no person has the right to excommunicate a homosexual.

What should the Islamic attitude to homosexuality be? It is important to differentiate between homosexual persons and homosexual acts, and stress the fact that our legal and ethical judgements are related to the acts. Moreover, the Qur'an reminds us: 'Indeed, We have conferred dignity on the children of Adam' (17:70); the act must be judged, not the person. In Muslim-majority societies and elsewhere, the guiding principle must be respect for the dignity of human beings even though we may disagree with their actions. Such must be the fundamental rule with respect to our fellow human beings, to their consciences and their conduct: thorough respect for all in their dignity, while remaining free to judge the act without condemning the person.

In Muslim-majority Societies

Terms like 'Muslim world' or 'Muslim countries' are often bandied about, but fail to do justice to the reality of the societies they claim to describe. A better, more accurate term, which I have been using for more than twenty-five years now, is 'Muslim-majority societies', which indicates that even if they are inhabited by a majority of Muslims, they are pluralist societies that cannot be defined by reference to Islam alone. From Africa to Asia by way of the Middle East, the challenges facing these societies are often similar and, insofar as they concern Islam, particularly numerous.

EDUCATION

While we have learned that, as we follow the Way, education must be our main objective, we observe that most Muslim-majority societies have neglected it, along with training, to an alarming extent. We begin with a general deficit in the educational level of the population, and school systems that are either totally obsolete or simply missing. State schools in Africa, in the Middle East and in Asia are often a guarantee of failure, and levels of training remain extremely low. The private sector produces better results but requires financial resources that only the elite can afford. The dysfunction of religious education is manifold.

What we tend to find is that rote learning is the rule: dates, rules and prescriptions are formally taught without any explanation of their meaning. There is justifiable rejoicing at the increasing number of young people who have memorized the Qur'an, but too little concern about real comprehension of the meaning of the Revelation, the prophetic traditions and prescriptions. Religious education of this kind, based on memorization, has two main consequences: young people either turn their back on religion, respect its principles for cultural and family reasons, or slip into formalism and develop, often dogmatically and through imitation, the most extreme and sectarian positions. The same phenomenon is visible in Muslim-minority communities.

The formalist education programme has all but banished the critical mind. Pupils are taught to revere the Texts, the traditions and the great scholars of the past, while questions are avoided, as though respect presupposes the absence of doubt and thought. While the Companions of the Prophet and the earliest legal scholars taught their students not to accept a legal opinion without questioning its source and interpretation, today's Muslims are expected, fifteen centuries later, to repeat without understanding and to follow without question.

Religious education of this kind is clearly deficient and makes it impossible to respond to the imperatives of meaning, direction and ethical concern that we have outlined earlier; not to mention that this form of religious education is often divorced from the contribution of the sciences. History – a non-idealized history – the sciences, culture, philosophy and the arts are pushed aside, if not left out entirely, in discussions of religious education. Beyond ritual, very little of what Islam requires in terms of respect for human beings, for social justice, for the rejection of racism, for protection of the environment or compassion for parents and the old is transmitted. Fragmented, formalized and superficial teaching cannot provide Muslims with what they need to meet today's challenges.

The process must begin with intellectual decolonization. Political colonization may now nominally belong to the past in most countries, but curricula, educational terminology and teaching programmes are often drawn up somewhere else. Paradoxically, the cultural impulse towards a natural relationship with the sacred – a latent individual and collective awareness – remains pregnant with the spiritual imperative. That impulse may well prove to be, as it has so often been in history, the germ of renewal, and the hope of rebirth.

MISSING: DEMOCRATIC FREEDOMS

The absence of freedom is also a common feature of most of the Muslim-majority societies of Africa, the Middle East and Asia. Dictatorship is almost everywhere the rule in Arab societies (Arabs make up no more than 30 per cent of the world's Muslims), while the regimes in most other Muslim-majority countries are anything but open in their administration of public liberties: a situation often attributed to Islam itself, which is said to have a problem with freedom. Close scrutiny of Islamic principles and of history proves the charge to be far from accurate: political, geostrategic, economic and historical factors more fully explain the prevailing state of affairs in the Muslim-majority countries.

Though it cannot be denied that the powers-that-be exploit religion in one way or another, it cannot be asserted that religion is the cause of the despotism or the dogmatism of any particular state. The absence of freedom of thought, expression and movement is bound to have an impact on the nature of the religious reference found among the population of a given country. It may be that institutions are fully regime-owned and controlled, as in Saudi Arabia or Egypt, or else that social initiatives in civil society spring up far removed from power, or, finally, organizations are set up that challenge the legitimacy of regimes and confront them either by legal means or by violence.

To the absence of democratic transparency must be added the endemic corruption that afflicts all Muslim-majority countries. Not only are political systems far from open, but financial and economic corruption is the norm, taking a different form in each country. Some apply the strictest of Islamic regulations when it comes to punishing the people, as in the Gulf States, where what is rightly public wealth has been usurped by corrupt and free-spending monarchies. Other regimes, or military establishments, control a substantial number of financial or economic sectors and rake in huge commissions by investing their money abroad rather than in social projects that might serve the public. The norms of Islamic ethics require service to the people. But Muslim regimes that have immense majorities operate in an atmosphere of absolute opacity, corruption and outright plunder. The contradiction is breathtaking. Contrary to the prevailing rhetoric on the responsibility of the West for the impoverishment and destruction of the societies of the Global South (which must not be minimized), the political leaders of the Muslim-majority countries must be held to account for the absence of freedom and the institutionalized corruption of the societies under their control.

POLITICAL ISLAM AND POLARIZATION

In the late nineteenth century, under British and French colonialism, there was a clamour of voices demanding the liberation of Arab and majority-Muslim countries from foreign domination. Born in Egypt and Syria, the movement known as Nahdah ('Renaissance') not only opposed political colonialism but focused its attention on the internal weaknesses of the Arab world, where, as the Algerian thinker Malek Bennabi would put it much later, 'We were colonized because we were colonizable.' Nahdah also emerged as a call for renewal of thought, and for reform in the Arab world in linguistic, literary, philosophical, political and religious terms.

As the Ottoman Empire was breaking up in the second half of the nineteenth century and the Arab countries sank into colonialism and political marginalization, Arab, Christian and Muslim thinkers brought their efforts to bear on organizing both resistance and renewal. Two dominant political trends were to emerge from Nahdah: the nationalist movements that sprang up throughout the Arab world and religiously inspired initiatives that were influenced by the ideas of Jamal al-Din al-Afghani (d. 1897) and Muhammad Abduh (d. 1905). Both called for reform of religious instruction and resistance to colonialism through the establishment of a united front of the 'Muslim nations' still under the British and French yoke. A return to the sources of the

Qur'an and to the prophetic traditions (newly interpreted), to Arabic (as well as Turkish and Persian) and to religious unity – pan-Islamism – would form the ideal path of political resistance. Their ideas were to have an immense impact on every organization that espoused 'political Islam' from the early twentieth century down to the present day.

In its founding principles, the Muslim Brotherhood (the first structured Islamic mass political organization), created in Egypt in 1928, was the heir to the ideas of al-Afghani and Abduh. It invoked Islam as its political and religious identity and made that identity the fulcrum of its struggle against colonialism. Hassan al-Banna (d. 1949) laid heavy emphasis on spirituality and legal norms and, even though his outlook was internationalist (like the pan-Islamism of his predecessors), he called for a transformation of Egypt that would begin with popular education leading, step by step, to the establishment of an 'Islamic state' (something the earlier reformers had never mentioned). Such a state would be Islamic in that it would reconcile the Muslims with their religion and their principles; it would also be an indigenous alternative to the nation-state models imported from Europe. In the beginning, the Muslim Brotherhood displayed the kind of political and theological accents that were later to appear in Latin American liberation theology. Violently suppressed by Nasser, the Brotherhood split into factions and currents, some within the organization, others as dissidents. Some would remain legalist and continue to preach popular education; others opted for armed resistance, while still others left the Brotherhood to found new violent radical organizations.

Political Islam, also called 'Islamism',[2] is made up of myriad trends and organizations with differing and often contradictory positions. If we are to use terms like 'political Islam' or 'Islamism', we must examine them more deeply and be clear what they mean. Properly speaking, political Islam formally emerged during the colonial era as a path of resistance among the collection of nation-states. Since then, it has taken on a variety of forms, ranging from those calling for an Islamic state proper that would apply sharia (with only a vague idea of what that would entail) and those who propose a secular state with an Islamic ethical basis (also ill defined), to those seeking the re-establishment of the Caliphate as it had existed under the Ottoman Empire, over and above individual states, in a reconstruction of the international Islamic *ummah*.

Political Islam can be found in all majority-Muslim countries: either as a ruling doctrine, as in Iran, as a force in government (as in Morocco and Turkey, where its doctrine has substantially evolved), or in opposition, where its members (in legal as well as armed movements) have been and are still being repressed. Today's greatest challenge turns on the nature of the political process in Muslim-majority societies, which have been paralysed for years by the debate between secularist organizations and 'Islamists'. The upshot is that they have proved unable to deal with such real-life issues as education, corruption and economic and cultural policy.[3] So virulent are both sides' slogans that it has become impossible to advocate an open and serious critical discussion of their respective theses: the secularists show scant concern for democratic representation, while the political, cultural and economic views of the Islamists are dangerously impoverished. Repression cannot offer a way out of the political impasse that now grips the Muslim-majority countries. Instead, there must be a genuine political and pluralist opening, one that would foster a critical exchange of views and, eventually, move beyond today's sterile and perilous polarization towards the emergence of new forces.

HUMAN RIGHTS; CITIZENS' RIGHTS

Hardly a day goes by without mention of women's rights in Muslim-majority societies. How easy it is to forget that, more often than not, the human rights of the entire population are being violated daily. For the poorer residents of those countries, the right to an education, to a dwelling, to basic necessities is rarely respected. In certain wealthy countries – and all the Gulf States – the poor, who are mostly migrant workers, endure conditions better compared to slavery. Maltreatment and torture are the rule in most of these countries, not to mention summary executions and prison rape. Political prisoners and innocent men and women may spend years behind bars without judgment, and certainly without consideration for their human dignity. We are far removed from Islam's ethical teachings. And yet, such is the prevalent situation in all but a handful of Muslim-majority countries. Respect for human rights, which most emphatically do not contradict Islamic principles, is trampled underfoot in most of these countries when it comes to the poor, native residents, immigrants, people with opposing views and, very often, women.

Nor can respect for the rights of all citizens be ignored. The formula 'Muslim-majority countries' implies the existence of a minority of citizens who are not Muslims and who must be treated equally and equitably. Many Muslims attempt to sidestep the issue, noting that in the past Jews and Christians were well received by the Muslims, and that never was there an attempt to exterminate people on the basis of their religion, as happened with the Jews of Europe. While it is true that Muslims in Africa, the Middle East and Asia have frequently contrived to live on good terms with their Buddhist, Jewish or Christian fellow citizens, it cannot be denied that discrimination exists and endures. Minorities are forbidden from establishing houses of worship and from practising their faith (as in the Gulf States), discrimination in housing and employment is a fact (in the Middle East and in Asia), and even minorities holding citizenship are suspected of loyalty to other countries. Equality among citizens is a right and a condition; it continues to be one of the greatest challenges facing Muslim-majority societies.

VIOLENCE

Violence is today ever-present in the Middle East and in many Asian and African countries. At first glance, there even appears to be a correlation between Islam and violence. Some sweep aside the criticism, arguing that violence has nothing to do with Islam, and that those who engage in violence 'are not Muslims' but simple criminals. Others affirm the exact opposite, that 'Islam is violent' by its very nature. Both positions are wrong, but closer analysis is needed to understand why.

We must use two analytical methods, the historical-political and the religious, to understand the climate of violence that prevails today. Violence can be explained by history, by a succession of events – colonialism, international relations, geostrategic and economic interests – that must be placed in proper perspective, as historical, political and economic considerations that must be taken into account. At the same time, instead of reducing Islam to violence, it is essential to analyse the way Islam is exploited by the leaders of violent extremist movements.

The claim that 'violence has nothing to do with Islam' is neither true nor relevant. After all, the leaders of today's violent movements invoke it and cite Qur'anic verses and prophetic traditions to justify their acts of terror. A closely reasoned critique of the exploitation of religion by extremist movements has yet to be developed. But such a critique would be pointless unless it were accompanied by an equally detailed political analysis of the prevailing geopolitical context. Though we abhor violence, we cannot place armed resistance to oppression, struggles for national liberation and terrorist acts on the same footing. No serious, self-respecting historian or political analyst would tolerate such a confusion of terms, and yet we frequently find a total lack of nuance and caution in analyses produced in the West.

Armed resistance to colonial occupation, such as in today's Palestine, has nothing whatsoever in common with the violent and extremist action of Daesh (ISIS) in Syria and Iraq, which impose a repressive regime, oppress the people and kill whoever resists them. It is imperative to distinguish the nature of violence when the colonialist or the oppressor wields it. However, as a matter of principle, it is imperative at all times to condemn the murder of civilians and innocents: the Palestinian resistance is legitimate, yet some of the means they have used, such as targeting civilians, are never justifiable.

Muslims must provide answers to these questions; they must undertake the task of criticizing certain interpretations of the Texts. Some extremist groups, for example, have fabricated justifications for the idea of martyrdom in Islam. True, in defence of justice, of one's faith, one's dignity, one's homeland and one's property, it may be understandable to go so far as to sacrifice one's life in resisting the oppressor and the colonialists. But under no circumstances is it right to invert the order of priorities and, like some extremist groups, celebrate death the better to justify all imaginable forms of horror. Life is sacred in Islam; the rhetoric of death is totally devoid of legitimacy. The violent extremist and terrorist actions we have been witnessing around the world, in New York, Madrid, Bali, London, Amman, Casablanca, Beirut, Baghdad, Damascus, Paris and so on must be condemned as they betray the essence of the Islamic teachings. Muslims have the responsibility not only to condemn terrorist attacks but to deal with the causes (religious, social, political, etc.) leading to such deviations.

Some have called for the democratization of textual interpretation. But an uninformed reading is not necessarily the guarantee of a liberal and open mind. Ordinary, untrained Muslims lacking knowledge of the Message, its chronology and its context, may well take literally an *āyah* that speaks of war, of 'killing the enemy', and conclude that Revelation has issued them a 'licence to kill'. The risk is not only a real one; it has been confirmed by events. The challenge is serious. Unfortunately, it will continue to plague us for many years to come.

In a Minority

Several of the challenges I have outlined are of immediate concern to all the world's Muslims: education, formalism and the lack of a critical mindset. But several issues relate specifically to the situation of Muslims residing in countries where they are a minority (as a religious community). An impressive amount of legal theory has been developed over the last few centuries and has continued, with even greater energy, in recent generations. Scholars and jurists, either individually or working in duly constituted councils, have examined the situation and evaluated its potential impact on a wide range of juridical issues. From Asia to Africa by way of North America, Europe or Australia, great efforts have been expended to adapt the legal approach; some scholars have even spoken of 'minority law and jurisprudence' (*fiqh al-aqaliyyāt*).

CHANGED CIRCUMSTANCES?

The lively exchanges of opinion that have accompanied the new presence of Muslims in the West have caused certain scholars and commentators to conclude that this is an entirely novel situation and that, historically, Muslims have never been in a position of being a 'religious minority'. But the claim does not match the reality, for from Islam's earliest days Muslims have repeatedly found themselves in the minority. The fact of belonging to a minority has been well known for centuries: from the presence of Muslims in Abyssinia in the prophetic era to the African countries, to India, China, and several other nations of Asia and even the

Middle East. Jurists have issued numerous legal rulings on the subject from as early as the ninth century. The situation is not a new one, and the doctrinal literature on questions dealing with the administration of Muslim affairs when they are in a numerical minority is ancient and abundant.

What is new, with the arrival of Muslims in North America (the United States and Canada), in Europe (mainly in Western Europe, for Muslims have been living in Eastern Europe for centuries), in Australia and now even in Japan, derives from two principal demographic shifts. The first of these was the mass migration of Muslims between the two world wars, and primarily in the 1950s. Their strong presence, which has expanded exponentially, has made the Muslims unexpectedly visible, which has come as a surprise and indeed a shock to some. In addition, all the societies into which they have migrated have, without exception, become secularized and have created, to varying degrees, a secularist legal structure that has eliminated religion from public life. Muslims who found themselves a minority in Africa, the Middle East and Asia still lived in societies where religious and spiritual references were a part of daily public life. In the West, as in China where atheism was imposed as a state doctrine, a double effort was necessary to respond to the needs of Muslims: to envisage the form the Islamic reference must take in secular societies and to promulgate a legal framework adapted to the presence of millions of Muslims.

Over the last fifty years the production and evolution of law and jurisprudence has been more than substantial. Paradoxically, when Muslim scholars in the past dealt with minorities and identified individuals by the religion they belonged to, they never spoke of a 'minority *fiqh*', minority law and jurisprudence, but formulated their legal approach based on the established general methodology (used for the Muslim-majority countries). The concept of 'minority *fiqh*' arose recently to deal with these questions in societies that, in the name of secularism, stipulated equal citizenship for all. These were and are societies in which religion does not impinge on the status, the duties and the rights of citizens. The concept itself is problematic because it confuses the religious and the civil status of the individual. Some have criticized it for not taking enough into account the legal status of Western citizens of Muslim faith, for there exists no such thing as 'minority citizenship'.

WHAT IS 'ISLAMIC' AND WHAT IS NOT

The rapid influx of Muslims from the 1950s onwards was not immediately visible, as most of them settled in the inner cities (such as in Great Britain and North America), or on the periphery, in isolated neighbourhoods or suburbs (such as in France Belgium and Germany). The new arrivals – like the countries that had accepted them – believed that they would only be staying long enough to accumulate sufficient money to return to their countries of origin. Family reunification, the creation of new families, the birth of children and the process of acculturation combined to nullify their best-laid plans of return. What had been temporary became permanent. Immigrants became residents, and residents became citizens. For many years, Islamic jurists counselled Muslims not to adopt the citizenship of countries that 'were not theirs', and to prepare to 'return home' eventually. But the historical experience of the arrival and settlement of Muslims in the West soon convinced these same jurists to reconsider their judgement and, after a generation had passed, to issue legal opinions that directly contradicted the original: it was now preferable to adopt the nationality of the country to protect one's rights and to play a positive role in society.

The second, third and fourth generations, in countries like England, France, the United States or Canada, were born in the West and now possess full citizenship. Over time they have moved out of the inner cities, the isolated districts and suburbs where their parents lived in relative isolation, and had thus remained invisible. The new visibility of Islam, due primarily to large numbers of young people – because of their national origin, skin colour and dress – enrolling in the schools and universities and all the professions and trades, created the impression of a massive, intrusive and dangerous presence, where that of their parents – who had been 'invisible' – harked back to one or two generations before.

In point of fact, the presence of large families indicated that 'integrating religion' had not been a problem at all. Instead, it had been a historic success, a process of uneventful normalization. And yet, the historic conjunction of the surprising visibility of the new Muslim citizens on the one hand, and the social problems arising from living conditions in the inner cities and suburbs where most young people still lived, on the other, engendered some confused analysis. There was an unseemly rush to explain the social marginalization, delinquency and rebelliousness by the Muslim identity of the young people who were suffering from those very social ills.

'Islam' and the 'non-integration of the Muslims' were now

purported to explain, in the United States and Canada, and in Europe and Australia, the persistence of academic failure, anti-social behaviour and delinquency. But serious research in the respective countries has shown that these questions have no direct connection with Islam. Instead, the real issue is public policy and 'integration through socialization'. The Islamic reference is secondary and often used as a pretext to conceal the incompetence of national governments and local authorities. Many Muslim jurists and representatives have fallen into the trap. They have attempted to transform social problems into 'Islamic' or 'ethnic' issues and, in so doing, only exacerbate the general confusion. Emphasis must be placed on equality of opportunity, access to education, housing and employment, the fight against racism (both informal and structural) and social justice.

IDENTITY AND SPACE

None of the above should be taken to imply that Islam, both as a religion and as a structure of reference, presents no problems where its adherents reside in societies in which the majority of citizens belong to other denominations or profess no religion, and where the legal system is a secular one. The first question that arises is that of identity. It is only natural that people feel impelled by their social environment to declare who they are. In the eyes of their fellow citizens, these new arrivals, seen yesterday as Pakistanis, Africans, Turks or Arabs, have now become almost exclusively 'Muslims', of whom it is quite legitimate to ask, now that they have settled in the West, if they are British, French or Americans first, or Muslims first.

Many, out of pride or in frustration, have responded by affirming that they are first and foremost Muslims, boasting of their difference – or that they are Americans or Europeans, often for fear of being stigmatized or singled out for racial discrimination. The 'assigned identity' foisted on Muslims is a recurring motif in political debate in the West, which in turn has been distorted by the binary manner in which issues are formulated. They reveal a mindset that has already cast Muslims as 'others', while at the same time the prevailing political and social climate has induced many Muslims to adopt a sense of 'otherness' for themselves.

No one, however, has a single identity. Every single individual has multiple identities (woman, man, black, white, Jew, Christian, Muslim, Canadian, Belgian, Indian etc.) that may predominate depending on the context. In the voting booth, an individual is German or Swiss; at the hour of death, that same individual may be an atheist or a person of faith. Identities complement and harmonize one another depending on time and place; they do not necessarily contradict one another. Muslims who find themselves in a situation of religious minority must find ways of overcoming the crisis of confidence that causes them, often under stress, to doubt their ability and their right to claim a multitude of identities.

The same holds true for defining one's place of residence. For centuries Muslim scholars divided the world into a 'house – or space– of Islam' (*dār al-Islām*) and a 'house – or space – of war' (*dār al-ḥarb*). These notions are not Qur'anic, but they made it possible to distinguish between societies where Muslims were in a secure place or in power, and those where their survival was at risk. But these notions no longer apply; numerous scholars have demonstrated that they no longer reflect contemporary reality: Muslims are often more secure in their freedom of conscience and of expression as residents of Western societies than they would be in Muslim-majority ones.

What are we to call such societies? The global world has shattered the old categories, and the world has become for all nations a global area of attestation (*dār al-shahādah*). The old binary perception belongs to the past. It is for every Muslim woman and man, wherever they might live, to attest to their faith and ethical principles by becoming a committed citizen aware of their rights and obligations, accepting of the culture in which they find themselves and seeking out and actively promoting the good.

Islam is a Western religion, and Western cultures are now cultures of Islam. Western Muslims now attest to their principles, as do Jews, Christians or atheists (to their philosophy of life) – with their multiple identities, nurtured by the cultures that are now theirs. The challenge now facing them consists of remaining faithful to these principles without excluding themselves from the social, political and media environment, even though that environment may in the short term be hostile. Such is the historical experiment in which Western Muslims now find themselves participating.

We must never forget, as they do not forget, that Eastern Europeans have been both Europeans and Muslims for centuries; that they have all accepted the heritage of European cultures with their multiple influences, and without a doubt their Muslim antecedents as well. The wealth of European

Islam in the Balkans is often forgotten, just as is the richness of Andalusian Islam. Closer to home, Islam as practised by African-Americans and the conversion of tens of thousands in the West oblige us to rethink the binary schema that would set Western culture against the principles of Islam. To fully realize the multiplicity of identities in the unique and yet shared space of attestation will need study, confidence, and participation. The challenge for the present generation and for the generations to come will be to move beyond integration, now outmoded, to making a contribution.

COMMUNITY, SELF-ISOLATION, 'INFIDELS'

Muslims make much of the idea of 'community' (*ummah*) and often convey the impression that they define themselves only by and within that community. Some literalist and traditionalist movements understand and experience the idea in exactly this manner: Muslims, they assert, are part of a specific and singular community and must absolutely distinguish and set themselves apart from 'those who are not Muslims'. And yet, the notion of *ummah* has never had such a restrictive connotation. The idea can be understood on two levels: on the plane of faith, the *ummah* is a spiritual community, whose believers share a common religion, rites and aspiration towards the Transcendent. This spiritual *ummah* vibrates with the shared sense of dynamism and communion experienced during the month of Ramadan or the greater pilgrimage. All religions and spiritual traditions recognize the dimension of spiritual communion that inspires each of their believers with contagious energy.

But the idea of *ummah* is also that of a community of

shared principles, which may well be greater than the Muslims alone and may even turn against them should they betray it. It was in this light that Muhammad considered the Jews of Medina as members of the *ummah* he founded, fulfilling the same duties and enjoying the same rights as the Muslims. Likewise, the Revelation obliges the Muslims, in the name of their higher principles, to struggle against Muslims who are oppressors:

> Hence, if two groups of believers [Muslims] fall to fighting, make peace between them; but then, if one of the two [groups] goes on acting wrongfully towards the other, fight against the one that acts wrongfully until it reverts to God's commandment; and if they revert, make peace between them with justice, and deal equitably [with them]: for verily, God loves those who act equitably! (49:9)

In the same spirit, Muhammad asserted: 'Help your brother whether he is an oppressor or he is being oppressed.' A Companion hastened to ask how to help a brother who is an oppressor, to which the Prophet responded: 'By staying his hand.'[4] It is unacceptable to assert special privileges or to claim: 'My community right or wrong.'

A community founded on principle must stand against the temptation of splendid isolation, against sectarian remoteness and against special treatment or privilege for its members. On the contrary, its members must display a critical and open attitude, one that embodies full justice for members of other faiths (or with no faith), and chastises injustice when it is the work of one's co-religionists. The community of faith opens out onto the community of principles and as such forbids self-isolation. Participation in a human collectivity, whether national or cultural, must be governed by shared principles and laws in the name of the faith that has always laid strong emphasis on the imperative of respect for those very principles.

The notion of *kāfir* (pl. *kuffār*) must then be understood in an entirely different light. The word is often erroneously translated as 'infidel', a term some Muslims use to deprecate their fellow citizens of other religious traditions or those with no faith, and even to insult them. But this notion has a strict normative sense; it defines those who, with knowledge aforethought, deny God and/or the truth of the last Revelation and the mission of Muhammad. It cannot be used to stigmatize or to insult and must be employed with the greatest caution, as it is impossible to determine if a person who denies the existence of God has sufficient knowledge to assert as much, or if that person's denial is the result of ignorance, in which case it is not conscious negation. In addition, Revelation points to the relationship to be maintained with those who negate religion, and who reject it in full knowledge. The formula is clear: 'Unto you, your religion, and unto me, mine!' (109:6). The principle of freedom of conscience is inextricably linked to the basic requirement of justice for all, without distinction based on religious belief, skin colour or social status. Nor can it be an option to retreat behind the walls of one's own community.

THE LEGAL FRAMEWORK – AND THE COMMON NARRATIVE

Over the last thirty years, legal scholars have laid a solid groundwork for relations between Muslims and their new-found Western societies. They have often drawn on the experience of religious pluralism in Eastern European societies, in Africa or Asia, where harmonious coexistence has been the rule for centuries. A succession of legal opinions has contributed to a renewal of Muslim awareness of secularism, identity, nationality, citizenship, equality before the law and patriotic loyalty. With the exception of the literalist and traditionalist mindset, which has retained its minority stance on these issues, a strong majority of legal scholars and ordinary Western Muslims have been able to develop an open-minded and serene approach, concluding that nothing stood in the way of Muslims living their lives in a secular environment, of being loyal citizens of the countries they called home and of identifying culturally with their fellow citizens.

Despite the efforts of politicians and the mass media to stir up controversy, to propagate negative perceptions and encourage narrow self-identification, the expanded awareness of Western Muslims is now beyond doubt, and generally positive. The presence of Muslim citizens in every sphere of society, in academic institutions, in all the trades and professions, in the media and political parties, in culture and sports, is now a firmly established fact. Confronted with crises and provocations, from Danish cartoons to the Islamophobic commentaries of a handful of self-styled intellectuals, politicians and journalists, their reaction has been overwhelmingly calm, critical and self-possessed, with the exception – once again – of a handful of marginal groups whose violent and excessive behaviour only underlines the commitment of the vast majority to reasoned and responsible debate. In so doing, they are in full accord with the ideals of the pluralist societies in which they live, societies that require a loyalty that is both responsible and critical.

But we must move beyond simple respect of the legal structure and strive to apply the prerequisites of the 'Four Ls': knowledge of the country's Language, respect for its Laws, Loyalty to its society and Liberty for the citizens. Today, in an atmosphere increasingly hostile to Islam, the rhetoric of Muslim otherness and the normalization of anti-Muslim racism – Islamophobia – have had a negative impact on the principle of equal citizenship for Muslims. It is as though a new category has been created to fit the same people who yesterday enjoyed full citizens' rights: that of 'foreign citizens' who may well possess the nationality but are too Muslim, and too 'foreign', to be true citizens. It is difficult, to say the least, in such circumstances to feel truly at home in the West, to develop a genuine sense of belonging, not merely out of respect for the laws of the land, but as part of the common narrative of the country, and the nation.

Therein lies one of the sternest challenges to Western Muslims: how are they to overcome all obstacles and become value-added participants in the societies in which they live and work, and as they were able to become in Africa and Asia, in spite of their religious minority status? The time has come not only to integrate – most Muslims have reached and even moved beyond this stage – but to contribute actively to the organization and reform of their societies for the well-being of all. This means, paradoxically, that Muslims should speak less of Islam, that they should leave behind them and put aside their obsession with defining their religious identity, in order to take a direct interest in the dignity and public welfare of their fellow citizens and of their fellow human beings – irrespective of belief – in education and social justice, in women's rights, in the fight against racism, in immigration, in the environment, culture and the arts.

More than an intellectual revolution, it would be first and foremost a psychological transformation born of the confidence that an action, an effort or a value is truthful to Islam not because it is labelled 'Islamic' (or because its instigator is Muslim), but by virtue of the principles, the ethical standards and the ultimate goals that it brings forth. It would be a revolution of confidence that opens the believing conscience to the world and to humanity in the spirit of resolutely universal ethics, rooted in a profound sense of inner peace.

Conclusion

We have arrived at the end of our journey into the heart of Islam. You will – I hope! – by now have gained a greater appreciation of a world religion and of a world civilization. My primary objective has been to sketch out the principles and rituals that unite all Muslims, be they Sunni, Shi'a or Ibadi, while at the same time pointing to the diversity of interpretations, of schools of law and jurisprudence and thought, not to mention the wide variety of practices that can be found in Islam.

As a civilization, Islam has experienced several golden ages and suffered several periods of darkness, years of intellectual and cultural flowering and years of crisis. In this short introduction I have not sidestepped a single question, no matter how challenging. Nor have I attempted to deny the contradiction – occasionally flagrant – between the nobility of the religion's guiding principles and the far less dignified conduct of Muslims themselves.

The Islamic referential universe, as we have discovered, comprises a specific terminology, and with it a set of notions that can be properly learned and understood only in the context of a coherent value system. The act of translation from one language to another – as from the Arabic of the Qur'an and the prophetic traditions into vernacular tongues – is not enough; we must also grasp how these basic notions shed light on and interact with one another. The pillars of faith and of practice, alongside the body of obligations and prohibitions, lead into the strictly religious framework of faith that has been a source of inspiration to jurists, philosophers and mystics, as well as to architects and artists. Their work has given form and beauty to, and has found inspiration in, the principles and ultimate goals of the Message. The same work has nurtured intellectual and scientific inquiry, culture and the arts. Through it we have gained a deeper understanding of the meaning of the Way – sharia – that is, as we have seen, far more open to human intelligence and creativity than the literalist, traditionalist or dogmatic interpretations of Islam would have us believe.

Deeper knowledge of the history of Islam, of its different phases, of the contributions of its legal scholars, thinkers, philosophers and artists, should have by now shaken the complacent assertions of those thinkers and commentators who insist that Islam, by its very nature, is unable to promote rationalism, pluralism, science and philosophy. Nothing, however, can be simplistically reduced to a handful of propositions: not for the better, through uncritical praise for the great principles and values of religion; nor for the worse, by demonizing Islam, as do the Islamophobes, far from any nuance and remote from any real-world context.

This short work has attempted, one page at a time, to return readers to the basic principles of Islam. It has made it a point of honour to identify the diversity of opinion and even the failures and the contradictions – historic and current – in Islamic education, and in the application of its rules and teachings. For Buddhist, Hindu, Jewish and Christian readers, as well as for those with no religious belief, these pages represent a humble attempt to stimulate the curiosity of seekers of understanding, in simple but not simplistic terms.

Muslim readers have been invited to search for a deeper, more self-critical understanding of their religion. Have not the Muslims themselves often been guilty of neglect, of forgetting and even of betraying the genius of Islam? Lack of self-confidence, a deficit of energy and creative intelligence; the prevalence of literalism and traditionalism, the vice-like grip of imitation and repetition and even intellectual colonization; idealization of the past, present-day lassitude and hope for a better future: these are undoubtedly the main reasons why Muslims are experiencing a triple crisis of confidence, of intelligence and of authority.

Rediscovery of the Way, in a holistic manner, points to nothing less than an intellectual and psychological revolution – one that must begin with a process of reconciling understanding of the Texts and their higher objectives, by restoring the meaning of ritual practice and rules to the central position it once held, and by accepting and welcoming all that the human heritage has produced for the common good. Islam expects nothing less of the Muslims than that they rediscover, with all their faith and their intelligence, the meaning of the Message, its spiritual power, its defence of liberty, its invitation to knowledge and its appeal to attest before humankind and to serve all humanity.

In these few pages we have addressed a multitude of

complex and sensitive issues. I have not attempted to justify the unjustifiable or to defend the indefensible. My responsibility has been to respond, to the best of my ability, to the most frequently asked questions about Islam and the Muslims. Answers to these questions have been deliberately integrated into the general presentation, placed in proper perspective and assigned to their rightful place at the heart of the Islamic value system. Though it has been impossible to deal with each question exhaustively, this introduction to Islam has one overriding aspiration: to provide the basic keys to comprehension for those readers who would like to expand and deepen their understanding of a religion, a belief system and a civilization.

I suggest that those who wish to expand their knowledge consult more specialized works on each of the subjects taken up in these pages. When dealing with complex questions that must always be examined within a definite historical, juridical and theological-philosophical context, it is not always easy to keep things short and simple.

My aim has been to make this book accessible to the largest possible number of readers. Every person who has read these pages and then closes this book with greater understanding – even with the certainty of not having understood everything – will have given me the humble satisfaction of a job well done.

Ten Things You Thought You Knew about Islam

There is no lack of received opinion about Islam. Over time, and under the influence of historical events and media-generated controversy, a number of particularly stubborn prejudices and stereotypes have taken hold, even among Muslims. I have dealt with many of them in these pages and attempted to set the record straight. But some people who claim to know and understand Islam continue to repeat these 'truths' as if they had suddenly become acquainted with the subject. Could you be one of them without knowing it? Don't laugh! The question could not be more pertinent: what do you know, and what do you think you know?

Sharia

In a host of introductory texts about Islam, and in the media, sharia has become a negative notion, and even a frightening one. It is presented as the application of Islamic legislation, defined as 'God's Law' and reduced to the equivalent of a criminal code with its catalogue of inhuman penalties: cutting off the hand of thieves, corporal punishments and the stoning of adulterers (men and women, even though it is falsely asserted that stoning is reserved for women, following the biblical precedent).

Few would deny that many Muslim states and violent extremist groups claim to apply sharia, in the form of an arsenal of laws and repressive punishments that must be condemned. But the notion of sharia, which has widely varying definitions depending on the field of study, literally means 'the path that leads to the source'. It represents the Way that must be followed in order to remain faithful to the principles and ultimate goals of the Islamic Message. It begins with the believer's intellectual and emotional connection with God, with self-reform, with a proper understanding of creed and ritual practice and, on an individual and collective level, with the promotion of education, the responsible exercise of freedom and the equality of all humanity; with social justice and the quest for inner, social and international peace.

Jihad

There is seemingly no end to the books that present jihad as an Islamic 'holy war', the Muslim version of the Catholic crusades. But jihad means – literally – 'effort', and applies to everything human beings can do to resist temptation, the negative impulses within themselves or in the society around them on the one hand, and on the other to promote the good and to attempt to reform themselves and their surroundings. The effort is twofold: one of resistance and one of reform. A person can wage a spiritual jihad against egoism and arrogance, against poverty, racism or corruption, just as that person can wage jihad for education, social justice, equality and peace.

Of the some eighty accepted definitions of the term, only one applies to war (*qitāl*) and involves strict conditions: war is legitimate only in self-defence against aggression or colonization. The weapons used must correspond to those used by the aggressor, and the conflict must end as soon as the aggression ceases. War can never be justified to exploit or to colonize, to seize territory or natural resources, and even less to force conversion upon anyone. The Qur'anic verse could not be clearer: 'Had your Lord so willed, all those who live on earth would surely have believed, all of them: do you, then, think that you could compel people to believe?' (10:99) Furthermore, the ethics of war as legitimate defence are strict: women, children, religious people and non-combatants cannot be attacked. The concept of collateral damage does not apply in any circumstances, and nature – animals, trees and plants – must be safeguarded.

Messengers

The devotion shown by Muslims to the Prophet Muhammad is clear to all. The bitter controversy surrounding the caricatures published in Danish and French publications have had a powerful impact on Muslim perceptions. Violent demonstrations have taken place in Muslim-majority countries, as well as attempted (and sometimes successful) assassinations, and public threats against those who had dared to belittle the Prophet of Islam.

Indeed, Muslims are expected to respect and to love the last of the Messengers. But at the same time they should avoid making his person sacrosanct, an object of emotionally charged adoration. Upon the Prophet's death his faithful friend Abu Bakr warned the mourning Muslims: 'O People! If anyone among you worshipped Muhammad, let him know that Muhammad is dead. But those who worshipped God, let them know that He lives and will never die.'[1] In fact, Muslims respect all the Prophets and Messengers, and the majority position holds that they should not be represented, either by drawing or sculpture, the better to avoid the temptation of idol worship that would ultimately transform the last Messenger into an object of adoration in the place of the only God. Islam recognizes and teaches the equal respect of all the prophets, from Noah, Abraham, Moses and Jesus to Muhammad, as well as all those mentioned or not in the scriptural sources. Respect cannot, however, be used to justify the extreme and, on occasion, hysterical or violent reactions of some Muslims to crude caricatures and/or disrespectful words. Intellectual critical distance is the best response. Combined with calm and confidence, it avoids blind emotionality; with wisdom, it will not react to provocation.

Religion and Culture

In eighteenth-century Europe, 'Allah' was identified as the 'God of the Arabs', making Islam the 'Arab religion'. It was not known that Christian Arabs prayed to God, whom they also called 'Allah'. Everything that touched upon Islam was represented through the prism of the Orient, its distance and its exoticism. It cannot be denied that many cultural elements taken from the societies of what we today call the Global South were integrated into the way of life of many, if not most, Muslim-majority lands.

Two distinct phenomena sprang up: first, confusion was rife among Muslims themselves about what was derived from the Islamic religious prescriptions, themselves extracted from the Texts and the cultural forms that emerged from the way the first societies understood and applied the Islamic religious prescriptions; the second derived from the conviction that fidelity to Islam consisted of remaining or becoming even more oriental.

But the principles, rites and objectives of Islam are compatible with all cultures, which lends the Message its universal vocation. To be an American, African, Arab, Asian or Western Muslim is in no way contradictory, but rather the result of the encounter between a unique body of principles and rituals on the one hand and the diversity of cultures on the other. Western Islam is an Islam faithful to the Texts in terms of creed, ritual practices and prescriptions, while asserting Western culture as its own. The process is not a new one; Islam has already produced its Indian, African and Arab variants. There is, in fact, one sole Islam as expressed through cultural diversity. The Muslims, in their respective cultures, must distinguish what is compatible or not with their faith and their principles from within, through careful selection and evaluation, rather than through rejection, demonization and condemnation.

Islam and 'Western Values'

Stereotypes of Islam are many, and Europe has done much to present it as the 'Other'. During the Middle Ages the Catholic Church, with its puritanical views on sexual morality, abhorred Islam for its alleged permissiveness and sensuality. True, Islam was accepted as a source of knowledge in the sciences, philosophy and the arts, but at the same time it was claimed that Arab and Muslim scholars had been little more than vulgar translators, transmitters who merely helped to restore the Graeco-Roman heritage that was Europe's alone. Even today, the same voices assert that Islam is notable for its lack of a religious updating, its tortured relationship with reason, the sciences, liberty and sexual morality. Quite the opposite of the arguments heard during the medieval era and the early Renaissance, contemporary Islam is said to be distinguished by closed-mindedness, rigidity and prohibition of every kind. Perceptions have indeed changed, but what has not changed is the effort to maintain the otherness of Islam.

To hear many intellectuals, politicians and journalists claim that Islam today has a difficulty with reason, with liberty and progress, all seen as 'Western values', is hardly surprising. But even a cursory glance at the history of the eighth to thirteenth centuries, and until the fifteenth in Andalusia and the sixteenth in the Ottoman Empire under Suleiman the Magnificent, should be enough to challenge the stereotyped view of Islam. Such a glance would show instead that Islam was a dynamic participant in the evolution of world knowledge, that rationality has always been honoured, and that humanity owes much of its scientific and technological progress to Islamic civilization. The values that the West would later claim for itself are not its exclusive property. They are shared by a number of other civilizations, including, of course, the Islamic. Lastly, it would be a grave error to ignore the intellectual contributions of today's Muslims to the sciences, to medicine, economics, sociology, anthropology and more.

Fatalism (*in shā'Allah*)

The most conclusive proof that all Muslims are fatalists can be found, some say, in the well-known formula '*in shā'Allah*' – 'God willing'. When they utter these words they see themselves not as autonomous participants in their own lives, but as persons entirely dependent on divine will, victims of a crippling historical determinism that the thinkers of the Enlightenment in France, Italy, Germany and England had already identified, analysed and criticized. Their conclusions only confirmed that the Muslims, as a result of their religion, were already encountering problems with the idea of the autonomous individual who reasons, searches and emancipates her- or himself by way of discovery and knowledge.

But the meaning of *in shā'Allah* is quite definitely not a call to fatalism and passivity. The Message of Islam as a whole, both in the Qur'an and the prophetic traditions, calls upon Muslims to acknowledge that they are alone and responsible before God, free agents of their actions, obliged by their religious belief to set out in search of knowledge and to act positively in the world. *In shā'Allah* can best be seen as a formula for spiritual humility on the part of the believer who is active both in her or his life and in history. Such persons know that they must give of themselves, make all necessary effort and gain the knowledge they require to carry out projects or practise a trade or profession. They also know that, despite the responsibility and power they have assumed, the ultimate result is never in their hands. Thus the expression *in shā'Allah* can never be used to justify a passive fatalism; instead, it well expresses the necessary spiritual humility of the autonomous actor who is aware that she/he must commit himself to the full extent of her/his capacity, to acquire the knowledge to reform her- or himself and to reshape the surrounding world.

Polygamy

Polygamy has long been a subject of controversy and disagreement, and the presence of such a notion among the Muslims is itself – so goes the claim – proof that gender equality is foreign to Islam, that it has a problem with the rights of women. When the Qur'an was revealed, the Arabs practised polygamy; there was no limitation on the number of spouses a man could have. We know now that certain prohibitions, recommendations or obligations – such as those regarding alcohol, interest and the like – were broached in successive episodes of Revelation, as a kind of divine pedagogy that guided the Muslims in a certain direction. The Revelations touching on men, women, married couples and polygamy belong to this category.

Polygamy was, at first, restricted to four spouses, and to very specific situations such as providing a family for orphans. In this sense it must be seen as a tolerance and not the rule, which is clearly monogamy. In those cases where polygamy may be contemplated, strict rules of transparency, equal treatment and legal protection must be respected (as in numerous countries), and if they are not, a man may take only one spouse, in conformity with the Qur'anic injunction. In addition, according to certain legal scholars, the first wife may stipulate in her marriage contract that she rejects polygamy, thus forbidding it to her husband who has accepted the terms of said contract. Tolerance for polygamy has been regulated, and the evolution of the Revelation points clearly to the establishment and protection of monogamy.

Dress Codes

The notion of modesty is central in Islam and applies to men as well as to women. Modesty is not merely a physical trait but reflects a certain conception of the relationship between the self and life: intellectual and emotional modesty mirrors how physical modesty should be manifested in men and women alike. Intellectually, emotionally and physically, both sexes are called upon to avoid superficial visibility, indecent exposure, arrogance, ostentation and egocentrism.

Four criteria can thus be applied to the public conduct of believers who desire to apply the principles of Islam to the question of dress: in public, (a) transparent and (b) tight-fitting clothing must be avoided; dress must be (c) discreet without neglecting personal aesthetics or (d) a pleasing appearance. For women, the prescription extends to the wearing of the headscarf, of which much is made in the West. It must also be noted that the majority of scholars do not recognize covering the face (*niqāb*) as an obligation in Islam. The headscarf, however, is an Islamic prescription. But it is not an essential one. It should be understood as an act of faith and as such must remain a matter of free choice for a woman in her spiritual journey as a practising Muslim. The principle must be clear in both cases: it is unjust, in Islam, to force women to cover their heads (as happens in certain countries, communities or families), and it is contrary to human rights to force them to remove their headscarves against the dictates of their conscience.

Ritual Slaughter

Numerous animal rights organizations in the West have levelled criticism of the Jewish and Muslim methods of ritual slaughter, pointing to what they describe as the cruel treatment of cows, sheep and poultry and to the method used to slaughter them. But it would be difficult to deny that industrial meat production is equally if not more shocking in its confinement of animals, their treatment in slaughterhouses – which includes stun guns that frequently fail to stun, electrocution tanks and, at every step of the process, no apparent regard for the suffering of the animals.

Muslim ritual slaughter, on the other hand, must be carried out in a specific manner that lays great emphasis on the treatment of animals during their lifetime. The Prophet Muhammad made it clear that animals must be respected and well fed, that the knife used for slaughter not be sharpened in front of them, and that no animal should be sacrificed in the presence of another. To spare them suffering is a moral obligation. Nothing, in fact, can justify inflicting it on animals: neither the significance of the ritual, strictly speaking, nor the need to respond to a demand that is calculated in the millions.

The forms of ritual slaughter are strictly regulated by the invocation 'In the name of God, God [is] the Greatest!', which transforms the act into one of adoration of God, Who has permitted humankind to consume the meat of animals. The only justification for ritual slaughter is the intention to consume the meat of the animal being killed; there can be no other circumstances. The act of slaughter must be skilfully performed using techniques that bring instant death without suffering. By no means can a handful of formalist rituals added to industrial livestock breeding and killing excuse practices that all defenders of animal rights correctly describe as cruel and scandalous.

Meat can only be considered halal – licit for human consumption – when all criteria are satisfied, including the dignified treatment of animals, from breeding to slaughter. Far too many Muslims are satisfied with a purely formalist approach as they clothe industrial methods of slaughter in 'Muslim dress' that is more cosmetic than anything else: a few verbal formulas and ritual techniques are not enough to make such meat halal. Some Muslim organizations are committed to developing methods of breeding and slaughter that are more respectful of religious norms. They encourage Muslims to prefer organic breeding and slaughtering, which fully correspond with the criteria of Islamic ethics, and at the same time suggest that Muslims consume less meat, which would be a welcome step forward. Permission, after all, does not sanction excess.

Who Is a Muslim?

The four traditional schools of law and jurisprudence do not agree on an answer. They do agree that once a woman or a man has uttered the attestation of faith – 'I attest that there is no god but God and that Muhammad is the Messenger of God' – in full knowledge of its meaning and with a sincere heart, she or he becomes a Muslim. The majority of religious scholars require that the attestation be pronounced before two witnesses and be followed by the major ritual ablutions, which consist of a shower and the normal Muslim ablution procedure. Following these simple acts, the individual becomes a Muslim, and her or his past is totally erased and therefore pardoned. For those born Muslim, the attestation pronounced at the age of reason confirms, as an act of conscience, the primary and natural fact of their belonging to Islam. Some insist that to be truly considered Muslims, individuals must practise their religion – five daily prayers, *zakāt*, fasting during Ramadan, etc. – or avoid the major sins.

Still others, found in extremist movements, hold that any support for usurpers or despots (or simple passive complicity) automatically 'excommunicates' such individuals, or entire groups, from Islam. These positions are baseless; they derive from literalist readings of the sources and reflect ideological and political considerations. By definition, any person who has pronounced the attestation of faith with her or his whole mind and heart, and who feels Muslim, must be considered as such, whatever her or his practice, conduct, sins, errors or contradictions. No authority, institution or Muslim legal scholar has the authority to 'excommunicate' (*takfīr*) a person from Islam. It is certainly possible to judge speech, behaviour or actions and to deduce their compatibility or not with the prescriptions of Islam. But it is not possible to deny an individual's status as a Muslim if she or he asserts it. For the ultimate judgement, the judgement of beings and of hearts, belongs to God alone.

The Months of the Islamic Calendar

The Islamic calendar consists of 12 lunar months in a year of 354 or 355 days. As a lunar year lags behind a solar year by around ten to eleven days, the months of the Islamic calendar correspond with different parts of the Gregorian calendar each year.

The first year of the calendar began in 622 CE with the Prophet Muhammad's migration from Mecca to Medina. This migration was known as the Hijrah, which is why many Muslims call their calendar the Hijrah calendar.

The Islamic calendar is used by Muslims globally to plan numerous religious events, including when to observe the annual month of fasting (Ramadan), when to make the obligatory pilgrimage to Mecca (the Ḥajj), and when to celebrate the festivals of ʿīd al-aḍḥā and ʿīd al-fiṭr.

The number of months in the calendar is ordained by God in the Qur'an, and it is therefore a sacred duty for all Muslims to observe it.

1	*Muḥarram*	SACRED MONTH
2	*Safar*	
3	*Rabī' al-awal*	
4	*Rabī' al-thānī*	
5	*Jumādāh al-ūlā*	
6	*Jumādāh al-thāniyyah*	
7	*Rajab*	SACRED MONTH
8	*Cha'bān*	
9	*Ramaḍān*	
10	*Chawwal*	
11	*Dhū al-qi'dah*	SACRED MONTH
12	*Dhū al-ḥijjah*	SACRED MONTH

Glossary

abwāb (sing. *bāb*) : gates of entry (mystical)

adāb (sing. *adab*) : letter, literature, good conduct

'adl : justice

'afw : forgiveness, grace, pardon

aḥkām (sing. *ḥukm*) : rules, prescriptions

aḥkām taklīfiyyah : rules setting the legal and moral responsibility of an action

ahl al-bayt : members of the Messenger's family

ahl al-ḥadīth : those who refer to the strict narration of the sources

ahl al-'ilm : people (guardians) of knowledge

ahl al-kitāb : people of the Book (mainly Jews and Christians)

ahl al-ra'y : those who place opinion above literality

aḥwāl (sing. *ḥāl*) : states and divine gifts (mystical)

akhlāq (sing. **khuluq**) : ethics, virtuous conduct

akhlāqiyyāt : ethics (as applied to codes of ethics)

a'māl (sing. *'amal*) : action

amān : security

amānah : trust

'āmmah (pl. *a'wām*) : general, ordinary people

amr : commandment, order

amwāl (sing. *māl*) : goods, possessions

anṣār : auxiliaries/the first Muslims of Medina

'aqīdah : creed, principles of faith

'āqil : endowed with reason

'aql : reason

'ārifūn (sing. *'ārif*) : initiates, the knowledgeable (mystics)

arkān (sing. *rukn*) : pillars, fundamentals

asbāb an-nuzūl : causes of revelation

ash'arī : follower of the *ash'ariyyah* school of thought

ash'ariyyah : school for which Texts determine morality

asmā' (al-) wa ṣifāt (al-) : names and attributes of God

'aṣr : the third daily prayer

'aṭash : thirst (mystical)

awdiya : valleys (stage of mystical initiation)

awliyyā' (sing. *walī*) : friends of God (mystical)

āyah (pl. *āyāt*) : signs, verses

barzakh : residence of the soul after death and before Judgment

baṣīrah : discernment

basṭ : effulgence, effusion

bāṭin : hidden, esoteric, interior (mystical)

bay'ah : allegiance

bida' (sing. *bid'ah*) : innovations

bidayāt : premises

birr : piety, kindness, affection

ḍābiṭ (pl. *ḍawābiṭ*) : norm, regulation

ḍamīr : conscience

dar' : closing, prevention

dār al-ḥarb : space, house of war

dār al-Islām : space, house of Islam

dar al-shahādah : space, house of testimony

ḍarūriyyāt : essential or imperative prescriptions, higher objectives

dhawq : taste

dhikr : remembrance, memory

ḍhuhr : first afternoon prayer

dīn : religion, conception of life and death

du'ā' : free invocations, supplications

faḍā'il (sing. *faḍīlah*) : virtues

fajr : first daily prayer

falāḥ : success, achievement, well-being, joy

falāsifah (sing. *falyasūf*) : philosophers

falsafah : philosophy

fanā' : extinction (mystics)

faqīh (pl. *fuqahā'*) : legal scholar, jurist

faqr : poverty

farḍ : obligation

farḍī : obligatory

fardī : individual

farīḍah : obligation

fasād : corruption, perversion

fātiḥah : opening (first *sūrah* of the Qur'an)

fatwa (pl. *fatāwā*) : legal opinion

fiqh : law, jurisprudence

fisq : perversion

fitnah : trouble, crisis, division, civil strife

fiṭrah : natural disposition towards the Transcendent; the search
    for meaning; inherent nature

fujūr : immorality, licence, libertinage

ghayb : invisible, hidden, unseen

ḥadīth (pl. *aḥādīth*) : prophetic tradition; what the Messenger
    said, did or approved

ḥājiyyāt : secondary prescriptions linked to needs

Hajj : annual pilgrimage

ḥakīm : wise

ḥalāl : licit

Ḥanafī : follower (or following) of the school of law and
    jurisprudence founded by Abu Hanifa

Ḥanbalī : follower (or following) of the school of law and
    jurisprudence founded by Ibn Hanbal

ḥanīf (pl. *ḥunafā'*) : monotheist in the Abrahamic tradition
    without being either Jewish or Christian; literally: pure,
    purified

ḥaq : Truth (one of the names of God)

ḥaqā'iq (sing. *ḥaq*, *ḥaqīqah*) : truths, revealed truths; sing.: Truth, God (mystical)

ḥarām : illicit

ḥassan : good, handsome, beautified

ḥassīb : the One who keeps account (name of God)

ḥayā' : modesty

ḥifẓ: protection

hijrah : the Hegira, exile, migration

ḥikmah : wisdom

Ḥilf al-fuḍūl : the Pact of the Virtuous

ḥiyal : trickery (legal)

ḥub : love

ḥudūd : limits, criminal code (juridical)

ḥuriyyah : liberty

ḥusn : good, beneficial

ḥuzn : sadness

'ibādāt (sing. *'ibādah*) : rituals of worship

'ibārah (pl. *'ibārāt*) : expression, verbal formula

'īd al-aḍḥā : feast of sacrifice that marks the end of the pilgrimage

'īd al-fiṭr : Ramadan fast-breaking feast

'iffah : temperance, mastery, abstinence

iḥrām : state of ritual sanctity

iḥsān : sincerity, excellence

ijmā' : consensus

ijtihād : autonomous and original reasoning, ethically directed, in the light of the Message

ikhlāṣ : sincerity

ilhām : inspiration (by conscious thought or dream)

'illah (pl. *'ilal*) : cause, *raison d'être, ratio legis*

'ilm : knowledge

'ilm al-kalām : theology-philosophy

imān : faith

'imārat al-arḍ : power, installation and management of the earth

infiṣāl : separation

insān : human being

insān kāmil : man in full, reaching plenitude (mystical)

iqāmah : call marking the beginning of prayer

irādah : will

'irḍ : honour, dignity

'ishā' : the fifth daily prayer

ishārah (pl. *ishārāt*) : indication, allusion

'ishq : exclusive spiritual love (mystical)

iṣlāḥ : reform, renewal

isnād : chain of transmission

istinbāṭ : extraction of rules and principles from the sources

istiqāmah : the true path, righteousness, fidelity

istislām : the complete gift of the self (mystical)

istiṭā'ah : capacity

i'tidāl : justice, righteousness

i'tikāf : retreat in the mosque during the last ten days of Ramadan

ittifāq : accord, conciliation

ittiḥād : union

ittiḥādiyyah : consummated union (mystical)

ittiṣāl : connection, connected (mystical)

jabriyyah : determinist school of thought

jahmiyyah : determinist school of thought

jalb : contribution, acquisition, integration

jamā'ah : congregational prayer

jamā'ī : collective

jinn : benevolent or malevolent spirits

jum'ah : Friday; the Friday congregational prayer

juz'iyyāt : details, parts

kabā'ir : cardinal sins

kāfir (pl. *kuffār*) : he who negates God (or a part of revealed truth)

kāmil : complete, fully realized (mystical)

karāmah : dignity

kasb : acquired (by effort)

kashf : unveiling (mystical)

kawn : Creation, the Universe

kawniyyah : related to the order of Creation

khalīfah : vice-regent, leader

khāliq : the Creator

khalq : Creation, that which is created

khanaqah : Ṣūfī circle

khāṣṣah : specific, special, particular

Khawārij : extremist religious movement in early Islam

khawāṣ : the singular, the elite (mystical)

khawāṣ al-khawāṣ : the elite of the elite, the initiates, friends of God (mystical)

khayr : good, positive, beneficent

khilāfah : vice-regency on the Earth

khimār : cloth covering the hair and breast

khushūʿ : awe, reverential love of God

kitābah : writing

kufr : negation of God (truth); etymological: veiled, covered, sealed

kullī (pl. *kulliyāt*) : total, complete, global, universal

laṭāʾif : secrets, subtle beauties and truths (mystical)

Laylah al-Qadr : the Night of Merits, Destiny, Power

luṭf : goodness, kindness, gentleness

madhhab (pl. *madhāhib*) : school of jurisprudence

mafsadah (pl. *mafāsid*) : corruption, corrupt, corrupting

maghrib : fourth daily prayer, the West

maḥabbah : love

maḥjūb : veil (mystical)

maḥẓūr : divined, partially revealed (mystical)

majālis fiqhiyya : Islamic legal councils

makārim : the most noble, virtuous

makāsib : recompense (for effort)

makrūh : detestable, not recommended

Mālikī : person or ruling that follows the Maliki school of law and jurisprudence

manāṭ : *raison d'être*, *ratio legis* (sometimes synonymous with *'illah*)

manāzil (sing. *manzilah*) : stage, station (mystical)

mandūb : recommended, permitted

manzilah bayn manzilatayn : position between two positions (**mu'tazilah**)

maqāmāt (sing. *maqām*) : stations, stages (mystical)

maqāṣid (sing. *maqṣid*) : ultimate goals, higher objectives

maqāṣidyyūn : partisans of the school of ultimate goals

marātib (sing. *martabah*) : levels, degrees, stages of mystical elevation

ma'rifah : knowledge (of Truth, God, among mystics)

marja' : source of interpretation, authoritative (human, texture) reference (often referring to Shi'a scholar)

ma'rūf : known, good, positive, licit

maṣādir (sing. *maṣdar*) : textual sources of reference

maṣīr : the path, the way (mystical)

maṣlaḥah (pl. *masāliḥ*) : individual or collective ethical interest or concern

mas'ūliyyah : responsibility

matn : the textual corpus of a religious tradition (juridical)

matūrīdī : partisans of the school that associates revelation and reason

mawāhib : contributions, gifts (mystical)

mawlā : master, guide, scholar

millah : community, religion, spiritual community

minhāj : methodology, praxis

mū'ākhāh : the pact of brotherhood settled in Medina

mu'allim : teacher

mu'āmalāt (sing. *mu'āmalah*) : interpersonal relations, actions and transactions

mubāḥ : permitted

mufassirūn (sing. *mufassir*) : exegetes of the Qur'an

muḥaddithūn : specialists of hadith

muhājirūn : Muslims who left Mecca for Medina (in exile)

muḥarram (pl. *muḥarramāt*) : forbidden

muḥāsabah : self-evaluation

mujāhadah : effort

mukallaf (pl. *mukallafūn*) : age of reason, responsible for one's acts

mukhtār : chosen

muktasab : acquired (by effort)

mumārasah : experimentation, practice

mu'min : believer, who holds belief

munkar : bad, rejected, illicit

murabbī : educator

murāqabah : self-control

murīd (pl. *murīdūn*) : aspirant, initiate

murji'ūn : current in Islam that defends an individual's belief despite her/his major sins

mursalah : situation where there is no specific Text and in which ethical orientation must be considered (legal)

murshid : guide

murū'ah : facility, suppleness

musawāh : equality

Muslim (pl. *muslimūn*) : Muslim (those who have faith and devote their being to the search for God's peace)

muṣṭafā : purified (one of the names of the Messenger)

mustaḥab : preferred, recommended

mu'tazilah : partisan of the rationalist school

mutaghayyirāt : legal situations and applications subject to change

mutakallimūn : theologian-philosophers; jurist-philosophers

mutaṣawwifūn : Sufis, mystics

nabī (pl. *anbiyā'*) : Prophet

nāfi' : useful, profitable

nafs : being, the soul that inhabits the body

nafs ammārah : the soul-being that inflicts and suffers evil

nafs lawāmmah : the soul-being torn between good and evil

nahy : forbidden

naql : the Texts (Qur'an and prophetic traditions)

naqshbandī : Sufi school of thought and order

nasl : lineage, extended family

naṣ (pl. *nuṣūṣ*) : the Text, the scriptural sources

nāss : people, mankind, humanity

nihāyāt : the ultimate effulgence and fusion (mystical)

nissāb : amount upon which *zakāt* must be calculated

nūr : light

qabḍ : contraction (mystical)

qabīḥ : ugly, bad, evil

qadā' : God's will (predestination)

qadar : divine determining (predestination)

qadariyyāh : school favouring free will

qādiriyyah : Sufi school of thought and order

qalb (pl. *qulūb*) : heart

qalb salīm : sound heart (faithful to its original state)

qanūnī : Lawgiver (Turkish and Arab title given to Suleiman the Magnificent)

qaṭ'ī : definitive, without interpretational leeway (legal)

qaṭ'iyyah (pl. *qaṭ'iyyāt*) : clear principles and rules as to source and meaning

qawā'id : rules, principles

qiblah : direction of Mecca for ritual prayer

qisṭ : justice, equity

qiyam (sing. *qīmah*) : values

qiyās : reasoning by analogy

qudrah : power, capacity

qudsī : tradition inspired by God, expressed in the Messenger's words

qulūb (pl. *qalb*) : hearts

Qur'ān : revealed book; the final Revelation for Muslims

quraysh : inhabitants of Mecca

rabbānī : filled to overflowing with God's presence

raḥīl : departure, exodus

Raḥīm : the Most Compassionate (one of the names of God)

raḥmāh : mercy

Raḥmān : the Most Merciful (one of the names of God)

rak'ah : the ritual prayer cycle

rasūl (pl. *rusul*) : Messenger(s), envoy(s)

ribā : interest, usury, speculation

riddah : apostasy

rūḥ : spirit

rūḥānī : that which sustains breath, the spirit, the innermost

sa'ādah : felicity, happiness

ṣabr : patience, perseverance, endurance

ṣadaqah : non-prescribed gift or charity

ṣadāqah : friendship, confidence

ṣafā' : purity

Safā (al-) wa al-Marwa : two stations between which pilgrims hasten to commemorate Hajar's search for water

sakīnah : peace, inner tranquillity

salaf : the first three generations of Muslims

salafī : those who follow the teachings of the first three generations; today, literalists (sometimes reformists)

ṣalāḥ : good, positive, straightforward

salām : peace

ṣalāt : ritual prayers

ṣāliḥ : good, virtuous, wholesome

sālikūn (sing. *sālik*) : aspirants searching for God (mystical)

samāḥah : pardon, graciousness

sha'ā'ir : legal prescriptions

Shāfi'ī : follower (or following) of the school of law and jurisprudence founded by al-Shafi'i

shahādah : attestation of faith

shāhid : witness

shahīd : martyr

shāmil : complete, whole, full

sharaf : honour, nobility

sharī'ah : the Way towards faithfulness, laws (legal)

sharr : evil, negative, malfeasant

sharṭ (pl. *shurūṭ*) : condition

shawq : spiritual desire

shir'ah (*shara'a*) : see **sharī'ah**

shirk : associating someone or something with the adoration
of God

shuhūd : witness, lived experience (mystical)

shukr : gratitude

shūrā : consultations, deliberation

shuyūkh (sing. *shaykh*) : scholar, guide, reference (literary: aged, old)

ṣidq : sincerity, veracity

ṣifāt (sing. *ṣifah*) : divine attributes

sīrah : biography (of the Prophet in Islamic studies)

sirr : secret

ṣubḥ : beginning of the day, first morning prayer

ṣūf : wool, the mystic's way of dressing

ṣūfī : a mystic, a Sufi

ṣuḥuf (sing. *ṣaḥīfah*) : ancient scrolls (Revelations)

sukr : spiritual intoxication (mystical)

sullam al-qiyām : scale of values

sulūk : behaviour, practice, aptitude

sunan (sing. *sunnah*) : traditions, customs, prophetic traditions
(legal)

sūrah (pl. *suwar*) : chapter of the Qur'an (114 in total)

surūr : joy

ṭabīb : physician

tābi'ūn : the generation following the Companions of the Prophet

ṭā'ifah : group, tribe, sect

tafakkur : meditation

tafsīr : Qur'anic commentary

tafwīḍ : self-renunciation in God (mystical)

tahajjud : night prayer

ṭahārah : ritual purity

tahdhīb : discipline, refinement, sublimation

taḥsiniyyāt : third-class prescription related to beautification

tajallī : epiphany (mystical)

takfīr : excommunicate, expel someone from Islam

taklīf : ritual and legal responsibility

tanzīl : application of a rule in actual circumstances (legal)

taqārub : nearness, proximity (mystical)

taqdīrī : appreciation, imagination of new situations

taqlīd : imitation, emulation (Shī'a)

taqwā : awareness and reverential love of God, piety

tarawīḥ : night prayers during Ramadan

ṭard al-hamm : rejection of care, trouble

ṭarīq : the path

taṣawwuf : Sufism, mysticism

taṭbīq : practical application

tawāḍu' : humility

tawbah : repentance

tawḥīd : Oneness of God

tawḥīd al-rubūbiyyah : Oneness of God as His Being, in and of Himself

tawḥīd al-ulūhiyyah : Oneness of God as the human search for this exclusive adoration

ṭayyib : good, positive, generous

tazkiyah : purification, self-reform (mystical)

thawābit (sing. *thābit*) : immutable, universal principles

thiqqah : confidence

turāth : scientific or cultural heritage, tradition

ṭuruq (sing. *ṭarīqah*) : Sufi, mystical orders

'ubbād : 'enslaved' to God's will (mystical)

'ubūdiyyah : adoration, disposition to serve God

'ulamā (sing. *'alim*) : scholars

ulū al-'azm : the five principal Messengers who demonstrated patience and firmness: Noah, Abraham, Moses, Jesus and Muḥammad

'ulūm al-ḥadīth : sciences devoted to the study of prophetic traditions

'ulūm al-Qur'ān : sciences devoted to the study of the Qur'an

ummah : spiritual and religious community; community of faith and principle

'umrah : minor pilgrimage (at any time during the year)

uṣūl (sing. *aṣl*) : the fundamentals

uṣūliyyūn : scholars specializing in the legal fundamentals, principologists

wa'd : promise

wa'īd : warning, threat

waḥdat al-shuhūd : unity of the experience of presence (mystical)

waḥdat al-wujūd : unity of being and presence (mystical)

wājib (pl. *wājibāt*) : obligation

wāqi' : reality, environment

wilāyāt : nearness of the initiated friend (mystical)

wujūd : presence

yaqaẓah : awakening (mystical)

yaqīn : certainty

Yathrib : former name of the city of Medina

ẓāhir : the apparent, the exoteric (mystical)

ẓāhirī : partisans of the literalist school of Ibn Hazm

zakāt : purifying social tax (third pillar of Islam)

zakāt al-fiṭr : purifying social tax at the end of Ramadan to be distributed to the poor

ẓannī : conjectural, open to interpretation

zawiyah : Sufi centre or circle

zuhd : asceticism, removal from worldly goods

zuhhād : the ascetics (mystical)

ẓuhr : second daily prayer

ẓulm : injustice

Notes

CHAPTER 1: HISTORY

1   Ibn Hisham, vol. 6, pp. 75–6.
2   Ibn Hisham.
3   'Twelver' Shi'as believe that there were twelve infallible Imams, while the Ismailis hold that there were seven; they agree on the lineage up until the sixth Imam, Ja'afar al-Sadiq.
4   See Tariq Ramadan, *The Quest for Meaning: Developing a Philosophy of Pluralism* (London: Penguin, 2010), Chapter 13.

CHAPTER 2: FUNDAMENTAL TENETS

1   This could also mean 'we ask You to be loved by the poor'.
2   Reliable (*hassan*) Hadith reported by al-Daraqutni.
3   Hadith reported by Bukhari.
4   Hadith reported by Tirmidhi and Abu Dawud.
5   Some Muslim scholars assert that other religious and spiritual traditions can be considered as 'religions of the Book'.
6   'Gospel' always appears in the singular in the Qur'an; Muslim tradition holds that Jesus received a Revelation that was later modified and added to by humans, producing 'the Gospels' – canonical or apocryphal – that are not always faithful to the Revelation contained in the original Gospel.
7   The Prophet (*nabī*) receives the Message, but his mission is not one of transmission to humankind, while the Messenger (*rasūl*) is charged with spreading the Message. A Messenger is necessarily a Prophet, but a Prophet need not always be a Messenger.

8   See Tariq Ramadan, 'The Word and Its Signs', *Introduction to the Qur'an*, Malaysian edition (Kuala Lumpur: Islamic Museum, 2014).

9   There are substantial differences in classification according to the accepted readings of the Qur'an; some versions contain 6,213 verses.

10   During the last Ramadan before his death, the Archangel Gabriel caused him to recite twice over the totality of the Qur'an (in the order that we know it today), which would indicate that his mission was approaching its end, and the Text resolving into its definitive form.

11   Based on the compilation in the possession of Hafsa, daughter of the second Caliph 'Umar (ruled 634–44), during the reign of the first Caliph, Abu Bakr (ruled 632–4), immediately after the death of Muhammad.

12   Hadith reported by Bukhari.

13   Hadith reported by Tirmidhi and Abu Dawud. Considered by a majority of the 'ulamā' as weak, whose substance remains true in the light of the Islamic teaching.

14   Beings of flame or spirit in the Muslim tradition.

15   Hadith reported by Ahmad and Ibn Hibban. Of doubtful authenticity; rejected by numerous scholars.

16   The Arab term *ta'ārafū* (mutual recognition, knowledge of one another) expresses the perfect equality of the movement from one to another.

17   Hadith reported by Bukhari and Muslim.

18   Hadith reported by Bukhari.

19   Authentic hadith reported by Bukhari and Ahmad.

20   Pierre-Joseph Proudhon, *Qu'est-ce que la propriété?* (Paris, Livre de Poche, 2009), Chapter 2.

CHAPTER 3: FAITH AND PRACTICE

1   Hadith reported by Muslim.

2   Hadith reported by Abu Dawud.

3   Hadith reported by Muslim.

4   Hence some people who accept Islam assert that they are not 'converts' but 'reverts', and that they have simply returned to their primordial state as a Muslim.

5   As well as performing the major ablution, i.e. a full shower, with the intention of ritual purification.

6   *Jum'ah* means literally 'day of reunion, gathering'.

7   Qur'an, *sūrah* 37, verses 12–109.

8   The call to prayer is not an obligatory, but a recommended act.

9   Bearing in mind the postures associated with the prayer, women pray behind the men, with the exception of Mecca, where they pray side by side. In the Prophet's day, women and men shared the same space; since then, separate places have been set aside for women.

10 Hadith reported by al-Tirmidhi.

11 Hadith reported by Ibn Majah, Ahmad and several others.

12 Polygamy has always been tolerated in Islam, and as a conditional permission and not an obligation. It is discussed at greater length in the appendix 'Ten Things You Thought You Knew about Islam'.

13 Hadiths reported by Bukhari.

14 The literalists (*salafī*) reject Sufism, which they consider to be a dangerous foreign influence.

15 See Tariq Ramadan, *Radical Reform: Islamic Ethics and Liberation* (Oxford: Oxford University Press, 2009).

16 Hadith reported by Muslim.

17 Hadith reported by Bukhari.

18 Hadith reported by al-Tirmidhi.

CHAPTER 4: THE WAY

1   Hadith reported by Ibn Majah.

2   Hadith reported by Muslim.

3   From Muhammad's 'Farewell Sermon', authenticated by al-Albani.

4   Hadith reported by Bukhari.

5   Hadith reported by Muslim.

6   Ibn Hisham, op. cit., vol. 3, p. 167.

7   Hadiths reported by Ahmad.

8   Hadith reported by Muslim.

9   Hadith reported by Bukhari and Muslim.

10 Hadith reported by Ahmad and Ibn Majah.

11 Hadith reported by Ahmad.

12 Hadith reported by Bukhari and Muslim.

13 Hadith reported by Bukhari and Muslim.

14 Hadith reported by Bukhari.

CHAPTER 5: CONTEMPORARY CHALLENGES

1   Hadith reported by Abu Dawud.
2   The term 'Islamism' is today used amid widespread confusion. It is often impossible to understand who and what is being spoken of. Those organizations styled as 'Islamist' are not at all in agreement and are often in radical disagreement on the means and ends of political commitment. Labelling all of them as 'Islamist' without further qualification will be of no help in understanding contemporary political actors and issues.
3   See also Tariq Ramadan, *Islam and the Arab Awakening* (Oxford: Oxford University Press, 2012).
4   Hadith reported by Bukhari.

TEN THINGS YOU THOUGHT YOU KNEW ABOUT ISLAM

1   Ibn Hisham, op. cit., vol. 6, pp. 75–6.

Further Reading

- Abou Fadl, Khaled, *Reasoning with God: Reclaiming Shari'ah in the Modern Age*. Maryland: Rowman & Littlefield, 2014.
- Armstrong, Karen, *Islam: A Short History*. London: Weidenfeld & Nicolson; new edition, 2011.
- Brown, Jonathan A. C., *Misquoting Muhammad: The Challenge and Choices of Interpreting the Prophet's Legacy*. London: Oneworld, 2014.
- Esposito, John L., *The Future of Islam*. New York: Oxford University Press, 2010.
- Esposito, John L., (ed.) *The Oxford Encyclopaedia of the Islamic World*. Oxford: Oxford University Press, 2009.
- Hamid, Abdul Wahid, *Islam The Natural Way*. Northfleet: MELS, 2nd edition, 2004.
- Le Gai Eaton, Charles, *Islam and The Destiny of Man*. Cambridge: The Islamic Texts Society; new edition, 1994.
- Ramadan, Tariq, *The Messenger: The Meaning of the Life of Muhammad*. London: Penguin, 2008.

Index

N ———————————

O ———————————

Economics:
The User's Guide
Ha-Joon Chang

What is economics?

What can – and can't – it explain about the world?

Why does it matter?

Ha-Joon Chang teaches economics at Cambridge University and writes a column for the *Guardian*. The *Observer* called his book *23 Things They Don't Tell You About Capitalism*, which was a no.1 best-seller, 'a witty and timely debunking of some of the biggest myths surrounding the global economy'. He won the Wassily Leontief Prize for advancing the frontiers of economic thought and is a vocal critic of the failures of our current economic system.

A PELICAN
INTRODUCTION

Greek and Roman Political Ideas
Melissa Lane

Where do our ideas about politics come from?

What can we learn from the Greeks and Romans?

How should we exercise power?

Melissa Lane teaches politics at Princeton University, and previously taught for fifteen years at Cambridge University, where she also studied as a Marshall and Truman scholar. The historian Richard Tuck called her book *Eco-Republic* 'a virtuoso performance by one of our best scholars of ancient philosophy'.

A PELICAN
INTRODUCTION

How to See the World
Nicholas Mirzoeff

What is visual culture?

How should we explore the huge quantity of visual images available to us today?

How can visual media help us change the world?

Nicholas Mirzoeff is Professor of Media, Culture and Communication at New York University. His book *Watching Babylon*, about the Iraq war as seen on TV and in film, was described by art historian Terry Smith as 'a tour de force by perhaps the most inventive – certainly the most wide-ranging – practitioner of visual culture analysis in the world today.'

A PELICAN
INTRODUCTION

Human Evolution
Robin Dunbar

What makes us human?

How did we develop language, thought and culture?

Why did we survive, and other human species fail?

Robin Dunbar is an evolutionary anthropologist and Director of the Institute of Cognitive and Evolutionary Anthropology at Oxford University. His acclaimed books include *How Many Friends Does One Person Need?* and *Grooming, Gossip and the Evolution of Language*, described by Malcolm Gladwell as 'a marvellous work of popular science'.

A PELICAN
INTRODUCTION

Revolutionary Russia, 1891–1991
Orlando Figes

What caused the Russian Revolution?

Did it succeed or fail?

Do we still live with its consequences?

Orlando Figes teaches history at Birkbeck, University of London and is the author of many acclaimed books on Russian history, including *A People's Tragedy*, which *The Times Literary Supplement* named as one of the '100 most influential books since the war', *Natasha's Dance*, *The Whisperers*, *Crimea* and *Just Send Me Word*. The *Financial Times* called him 'the greatest storyteller of modern Russian historians'.

A PELICAN
INTRODUCTION

The Domesticated Brain
Bruce Hood

Why do we care what others think?

What keeps us bound together?

How does the brain shape our behaviour?

Bruce Hood is an award-winning psychologist who has taught and researched at Cambridge and Harvard universities and is currently Director of the Cognitive Development Centre at the University of Bristol. He delivered the Royal Institution's Christmas Lectures in 2011 and is the author of *The Self Illusion* and *Supersense*, described by *New Scientist* as 'important, crystal clear and utterly engaging'.

A PELICAN
INTRODUCTION

The Meaning of Science
Tim Lewens

What is science?

Where are its limits?

Can it tell us everything that is worth knowing?

Tim Lewens is a Professor of Philosophy of Science at Cambridge University, and a fellow of Clare College. He has written for the *London Review of Books* and *The Times Literary Supplement*, and has won prizes for both his teaching and his publications.

A PELICAN
INTRODUCTION

Who Governs Britain?
Anthony King

104120

Where does power lie in Britain today?

Why has British politics changed so dramatically in recent decades?

Is our system of government still fit for purpose?

Anthony King is Millennium Professor of British Government at the University of Essex. A Canadian by birth, he broadcasts frequently on politics and government and is the author of many books on American as well as British politics. He is co-author of the bestselling *The Blunders of Our Governments*, which David Dimbleby described as 'enthralling' and Andrew Marr called 'an astonishing achievement'.

A PELICAN
INTRODUCTION